# GUY FIERI Food

MORE THAN 150 OFF-THE-HOOK RECIPES

food network

with Ann Volkwein

Guy!

wm
WILLIAM MORROW

An Imprint of HarperCollins Publishers

# Also by Guy Fieri

*Diners, Drive-ins and Dives*
*More Diners, Drive-ins and Dives*

Illustrations by Joe Leonard
Food photography by Ben Fink
Lifestyle, food preparation, and ingredient photography by John Lee
*Guy's Big Bite* set photography by David Clancy
Guy Fieri Road Show photography by Alan M. Poulin
Ferndale Meat Company photograph courtesy of BriggsArt.com
All other photographs courtesy of Guy Fieri

HarperCollins books may be purchased for educational, business, or sales promotional use. For information please write: Special Markets Department, HarperCollins Publishers, 10 East 53rd Street, New York, NY 10022.

FIRST EDITION

*Designed by Kris Tobiassen*

Library of Congress Cataloging-in-Publication Data
Fieri, Guy.
    Guy Fieri food / Guy Fieri with Ann Volkwein.
        p. cm.
    Includes bibliographical references and index.
    ISBN 978-0-06-189455-8
    1. Cooking, American.   I. Volkwein, Ann.   II. Title.

TX715.F453 2011
641.5973—dc22

                                                    2010054059

11  12  13  14  15  [QG]  10  9  8  7  6  5  4  3  2  1

*To my sister,*

## *Morgan*

*Thank you for the love and energy you bring to our family.*

*You are an amazing teacher, and your message is in our lives every day.*

*We miss you and love you.*

*Namaste.*

# CONTENTS

I can't play the guitar, but I can rock the pizza peel!

# INTRODUCTION

In 1970, when I was two and a half, my mom walked into the kitchen to find her friend Gary leaning down toward me growling, "Rah rah muck!" and then I'd scream, "Rah rah muck!" back to him, and he'd say it back to me, and I'd scream it again, back and forth.

MOM: Gary what are you doing?

GARY: I don't know! Your kid comes in here and screams, "Rah rah muck!"

MOM: He'd like some rah rah (crackers) and muck (milk).

My first words were always about food, and I seriously considered titling this book *Rah Rah Muck*.

This book tells my story—the best way I know how—through photos and stories of my family, my great friends and mentors, and of course, the awesome food along the way.

I grew up in Northern California—camping, riding horses, raising pigs, and cooking (and performing) at family reunions. I had my own pretzel cart business as a kid and carted myself off to France (and a year of great food) in high school. At every step and stage, there have been key dishes that keep the memories alive, like the Cherries Jubilee and Caesar Salad I mastered while working as a teen flambé captain or the Tequila Turkey Fettuccine Alfredo that was my ace-in-the-hole on *The Next Food Network Star*.

These dishes and many more tell the story of my life, but I challenge you to make them your own; I want you to! The other day a valet told me he'd added bacon to my recipe for jalapeno muffins, and I said, "Yes, that's it, dude! Go for it!"

People often ask me, "How did this happen for you?" And beyond the path I'll tell you about in this book, in the end I know it's not luck. All along the way, from opening restaurants to hosting *Triple D* and *Guy's Big Bite*, one of the most important things I've had going for me was the support and belief of my family. If we're measured by our families, then I am a giant. But I've also had great business partners and team members and producers—the list goes on and on.

My first manager, Jack Levar, once taught me an important lesson: Surround yourself with good people—successful people—who merit honor and respect. It comes down to whether you want to plant a seed in the sand or in fertile soil. So, I've felt like a quarterback with a great front line. Yes, I've had energy and enthusiasm for the things I've done, but quite honestly, just as Superman had Lois Lane and the Karate Kid had Mr. Miyagi, it's the people who have believed in me that have been my biggest blessing.

Now let's get cookin'!

# OPENING JOHNNY GARLIC'S

In May 1996, my business partner, Steve Gruber, and I moved to Santa Rosa, California, and began one of the most intense periods of my career. I'd gotten to know Steve in Southern California when we were both working for Louise's Trattoria. Pretty soon we'd divided and conquered, and we each managed half the restaurants in that region, growing a small chain of seven to seventeen locations. Steve describes the next stage like this:

"One day after many, many monthly manager

Cutting the ribbon at Johnny Garlic's in Santa Rosa. The small boy on the left is Steve's son, Jonathan (Johnny), and the baby on the right is my son Hunter.

meetings in our very corporate restaurant world, Guy and I were sitting in his old monster Chevy, and he asked if I ever wanted to open a restaurant on my own. So I patted Guy down to see if he was wearing a wire, then we drove up into the hills over Los Angeles and started working on concepts. One day I called Guy and told him I was going in and giving my notice that day. I don't know if he believed I was ever really going to leave, but that was the first step. So I gathered my wife and newborn and moved to Lake Tahoe to scout it out."

After Steve had checked out Tahoe and decided that the slow season was just way too slow, he moved his family to Santa Rosa, where my wife, Lori, and I were living. When I was a kid, Santa Rosa was the first "big" city you came to when driving south four hours from my tiny Northern California town of Ferndale. There was a big mall where we'd all go school shopping. (If you'd been to the mall at Coddingtown, you'd seen it all; this was the big-time!) It was also where people would come after graduating from high school to get jobs. By this time, Lori was pregnant and I cooked, waited tables, and bartended in order to network and get to know the community.

For everything we did, we were low on money and long on planning. We'd do our recipe testing in our garage for the menu every night—and if we were testing garlic soup (which we perfected), then that's what our wives were eating that night for dinner. We already knew that my Cajun Chicken al Fredo (see page 178) was going to be the first thing on the menu, and we had very strong ideas about how we were going to break out of the norm with a made-from-scratch focus to all our food.

In looking for a place to open, we came across a man named Big John Pavelka, who owned the building that used to be the Big John's Chicken and currently was a failing Italian restaurant. Here we were, two twenty-five-year-old guys, and here comes Big John, pulling up in his big blue Cadillac and checking us out. In the end, he decided he'd give us a shot and carry part of the purchase price of the business. It was a big risk, but he had the swagger of John Wayne and the heart of a lion. The funny thing was, I'd been turned down for a job in that very restaurant when I'd gotten into town, because the manager wanted to date a girl who was also applying! That was a funny conversation after I became the leader . . .

Thanks to Gruber's mom and my parents (who, to my surprise, mortgaged their house to help), we had just enough scraped together to open Johnny Garlic's. Steve had come up with Johnny because ever since his kid had been born I'd insisted on calling him Johnny instead of Jonathan. And we added the Garlic's because our bold, flavorful, eclectic food gave a lot of love to the bodacious garlic bulb, which is used the world over. By October, six months after arriving in town, we were about to open with about twenty-five thousand bucks in operating capital.

We'd done all these models about how we'd stay open if we didn't get any traffic. Well, that didn't happen. We had a three-hour wait the first night and every night for the first three years. It was one of the loudest restaurants people had ever visited,

**With my sister, Morgan, on the opening night of the first Johnny Garlic's.**

with an open-theater kitchen and great music, and it was packed like a subway station. Everyone left jacked up on fun. The Sizzler next door had to send guards out to keep people from parking in their driveway. People were tailgating outside while they waited for a table, on lawn chairs, playing music and drinking beers!

That first night we were just getting hammered with orders in the kitchen. Steve remembers, "I called over to Guy, 'Come here!' and I pulled the tickets off the printer—they were lined up the rail and touching the floor. I held six feet of it in the air, and said, 'Hey Guy, how about you wait tables and I'll cook?' And that moment was like *Rocky* music started in the background, and all of a sudden we started commanding the kitchen and the dining room. Having been outsiders in the beginning, we became leaders in the town."

For Thursday Night Market on Main Street Santa Rosa, my dad helped us build a metal shack out of corrugated siding. From there we served Cajun

Chicken al Fredo and fresh-fried potato chips. The day we started there was a line down the street. We would kill it doing four thousand dollars in a three-hour period and couldn't make the food fast enough. We were flying by the seat of our pants, with a lot of support from the local radio stations. One strategy I'd had was to take food to all the stations and get to know the DJs. There was Q105, KZST, Brent Farris, Jeff Blazy, Rob and Pat in the Morning, and Big John Snyder, and I'd met a guy named Jack Levar who had his own advertising agency and had formerly been at KSRO. They gave relentless support and Jack became an important mentor, business adviser, and even my manager after I won *The Next Food Network Star*, before passing away in 2007.

We went on to open a Johnny Garlic's in Windsor and eventually opened a third location along with catering in Petaluma. And then one night I got a late call from the restaurant manager, Dawn Baldwin, that the Santa Rosa restaurant was on fire. I drive up and it's three-alarm; this baby is *en fuego*, but nobody was hurt. I felt as if my world was collapsing.

---

### Stocking Johnny G's

We have a rule. Dry storage in our restaurants should take only a few shelves. It's one of the first things I judge a restaurant by for **DD&D**, because it's a direct indicator about how much is made by hand. At Johnny Garlic's we have sugar, pasta, paper goods, tomato sauce, apricot preserves, lemon juice—and that's about it. Inside the walk-in freezer you'll find ice cream, frozen bread, and some desserts. But we use all fresh meats, and make all our soups and dressings. We try to make it all from scratch and keep it fresh.

Steve came into play, negotiating with the insurance company, getting business interruption insurance—he really was born to be an attorney or negotiator. The building was made of cinder blocks, and the fire department had done a great job protecting the equipment, so between Steve, my dad, and me it took two years to rebuild. We displaced the staff to Windsor and Petaluma, and customers headed there for their Caesar Salad and Cajun Chicken al Fredo fixes.

We had some time to develop a new concept while we rebuilt, and Tex Wasabi's was the phoenix that came out of the fire (see page 276). And after a brief stint trying out a chophouse concept there, we reinstated Johnny Garlic's in its original location.

As we grew, Steve took on more of the administrative and business role, while I ran operations. The major motto we've had is: If two people always agree, then one of them isn't necessary. The yin and yang have really been a major component of the partnership. But my final words of advice on opening a restaurant come from my mentor Jack Levar: Stick to your word, and always over-deliver.

Fire at Santa Rosa Johnny Garlic's.

# GUY'S DAD: JIM

My dad, Jim, has always been Obi-Wan Kenobi to my Luke Skywalker. A lot of my fundamental ideas about respect and work ethic and the importance of imagination and having an open mind stem from Jim. He's everybody's big brother, and he almost *always* has the answer. Here's a little riff from the big guy, sharing some of his wisdom and philosophies.

## Jim on Imagination

*We're all born with imagination—that's the first thing we have going for us. Kids are fantastic to watch—they don't speak for the first two years because they're so busy learning! For that reason I've always felt it's important not to rush them from the imagining stage to the memory stage of their growth, such as learning to speak or teaching them the alphabet. There's a connection between imagining and doing, and I'd argue that it's just as important throughout adulthood as it is in childhood.*

*For the most part, if you can't imagine doing something, there's a good likelihood you can't actually do it, and vice versa. I can't imagine walking on a tightrope between two high-rise buildings, but I know it can be done. Some people have no problem taking a long pole and going for it—but that wouldn't be me! On the other hand, there are people*

*who are unemployed for three years who can't imagine ever getting a job again. But without the ability to imagine it, how can it ever happen?*

*We must be very careful not to destroy children's imagination, because we don't have a good framework for getting it back. How do we get people to start imagining again?*

## Jim on Starting a Business

*It may seem amazing, but sometimes people go into a business without really knowing anything about it. No matter what, it's going to take a lot of hard work to start a business. So before you begin you should have some idea of how much money will make you happy and how many hours a day you want to work. Asking those questions in the context of whether your chosen business can support your expectations will save you a lot of frustration and discouragement in the long—and short—run!*

*Before you begin, ask yourself these questions:*

• *Do I know anything about the business I am about to start?*

• *How much money do I want to have in the bank, after taxes and debts, each year? (This number should* represent a 10 percent net profit, which is about average for a small business.)

• How much gross revenue must I make to support #2? (To bank $60,000 a year, you must gross $600,000.)

• How many days a year do I want to work?

• Divide #3 by #4. If you work 245 days a year, you'd need to gross almost $2,450 a day to make $600,000. Can that equation of time to money actually be attained by your business?

If you can answer those questions to your own satisfaction, you've got my blessing.

## Jim on Managing a Project

**1.** You have to have a clear idea of what you want the finished project to look like. If you can imagine that, then you can do it; if you can't, then there's no point in starting.

**2.** Hire people who share your vision to help you enhance the end product. It's important that you trust their input and that you resist micromanaging their work.

Micromanagement is a common mistake (particularly for type A creative personalities). But why would you want the people you hire to simply regurgitate what you've described as your original vision? The creativity they bring to the project could take your idea up the next two or three levels. Paying good money for professional, talented people without giving them the opportunity to do what they can for you is just shooting yourself in the foot.

## Jim on Ducks

Keeping all our ducks in a row is simply not a model to strive for. That cliché is mistakenly taken as a goal when it's actually pointing out a trap or a dangerous diversion. Time changes everything, water flows downstream, and you can never get back to that one single point. We're wasting our time if we're obsessed with getting everything neatly lined up. The ducks are life, life is to be enjoyed, and life is change. Don't be afraid.

# PENNY'S PERSPECTIVE

When I was young, I wanted ten kids, and then Guy was born and that was the end of that. We got our ten kids—it's just that they were all rolled up into one! Guy was a bundle of energy from the time he woke up in the morning until he crashed at naptime. He'd actually say to his friends, "I have to go take my nap now." He knew his limitations then, but he outgrew that phase and now there's no stopping him.

My super redhead—Penelope Ann.

Guy was not an easy kid, by any means, just because he liked to take naps. He was simply recharging for his next adventure! Guy was two and a half when we moved from Los Angeles to Humboldt County, California, in 1970. We were attracted by the energy of the redwoods and the natural beauty of Humboldt, and thought that after the experience of raising a kid in L.A. we'd try a town of 1,500 residents called Ferndale, the Victorian Village. We weren't exactly hippies, but if you drove a van, you were hippies to most of the folks there. To further confirm their fears, we

Downtown Ferndale then . . . if these streets could talk . . .

Downtown Ferndale today.

did leatherwork as a hobby and opened a leather shop called Abraxas. Since I couldn't get a real teaching job, being a hippie and all, I did some substitute teaching, and my husband, Jim, drove the school bus while he worked on his degree from Humboldt State University. We lived above our store for a year and a half while we decided if we did indeed want to raise Guy in a small town that had more cows than people. We decided we did, so we bought a house on the edge of town and had another child when Guy was four and a half—a darling redheaded girl named Morgan.

Later we moved to the edge of the town on two acres, and when we closed the store for the night and went home, Guy would be out in the barn doing his projects while Jim and I made dinner. We experimented with being vegetarians for about nine months [note from Guy: "It seemed like a lifetime"], and Guy didn't really seem to mind, or at least we didn't think he did, until one day he said to a friend of ours, "When I grow up, I'm gonna eat meat, have a motorboat, and listen to rock and roll!" Yep, we liked classical music and had a sailboat!

Guy loved being out in the country, and over the years we had almost every animal known to man. He loved horses from an early age, and a neighbor girl would let him ride her horse, Rebel. Rebel looked like one of

At a 1987 family reunion, Morehead City, North Carolina—a lean mean cooking machine.

## Don't Feed Me, Please!

**Guy was raised on the streets of Ferndale and immediately established himself as the youngest entrepreneur in town. When there were a lot of tourists, he'd bring down the toys that he was tired of and sell them on the sidewalk outside our store, or he'd take paper bags from underneath the counter and some colored pens and sell his one-of-a-kind scribbled drawings, which he'd pin up on the barnwood fence next to the store. The tourists went nuts for this darling blond-headed kid (his hair was natural then) and would actually buy his stuff. Then they'd bring the toys in to us and give them back. So with all the money that Guy earned, he'd trot on down to the nearby Laundromat and feed the vending machine, which would spit out all sorts of candy. He was the face of innocence when one of us would peek out the door of our shop to check on him. Not only did tourists give him money, they bought him treats, so we had no recourse but to make a sign and pin it on his shirt that said, DON'T FEED ME, PLEASE. That was the absolute wrong thing to do because the tourists thought it was so funny that they took more pictures of him and gave him more money!**

those Budweiser draft horses, but oh how Guy loved him. When he was about eight, Rebel was Guy's Christmas present, and I don't think he's ever had a present to match it. (The day his Lamborghini arrived was pretty close.) So now Guy had transportation, and he and Rebel could be seen riding down to the Blue Room, across town in Arlynda Corners, for breakfast on Saturday mornings. He couldn't quite get on Rebel by himself, but there were always fences or car bumpers to help him. Guy developed a lot of independence in Ferndale. It was the kind of town where we didn't have to worry about where he was—someone would always call and say where they'd seen him recently.

Guy was the entertainer of the family. Since we'd moved 3,000 miles away from our families, we had a family reunion almost every year, and that's where Guy's career in show business got its start. His antics had all of us in hysterics and, even funnier, he got all of us involved in various skits that he'd make up. I'll never forget when he had twenty or more of us walking like the Church Lady from Saturday Night Live. Everyone had to participate! Then there was the funky chicken, which to this day he's famous for in the family. No matter what was going on, Guy was in the middle of it, involving his cousins and making us all laugh. Gosh, I remember when he was barely two and we were at a concert at Whittier College, and all of a sudden we lost track of Guy. But there he was, up on stage rocking out to the band. I don't think they appreciated his stealing attention away from them, but the audience loved it.

People always ask me where Guy gets all his energy, and sometimes I wonder myself. All I know is, when Guy does something that's his idea, he loves it and gives it all he's got. When he was in fifth grade, Guy wanted to be at the Humboldt County Fair all the time, and we couldn't just let him hang out down there unattended, so we told him no, as any good parent would. So he asked us if he could get a job at the fair, to which we said yes, never thinking that he'd get one. Wrong. The first day of "job hunting" got him a job mucking stalls for the racehorse owners. Talk about work! Well, that wasn't exactly what Guy had in mind, as he wanted to be where the action was, so he talked this man who had a booth selling trinkets and balloons into giving him a job. The old guy liked Guy and gave him a shot, telling him that when he made a sale, he was to bring the item and the money over to him and he'd give Guy the change to give the customer. So Guy would take the item over to the man, tell him how much it was, and tell him how much change to give the customer. He could figure it out in his head faster than the man could, so after a day, the man just gave Guy the money belt and went back to his trailer and took a nap. Guy knew how to charm the public; he'd been doing it all his life—and now he was getting paid for it. Sweet! Next was Guy's Awesome Pretzel Cart venture (see page 342 for that story).

At that time, we were also super busy at our Western store. Eventually all four of us got horses and used to pack into the mountains with another family with kids, and Guy started to learn how to cook over an open fire with somewhat limited provisions. He always loved horses, but sports became really big in his life at an early age, too. He loved Earl Campbell and the Houston Oilers so much that when we got our first motorboat, we had to name it Love Ya Blue. Jim and I were definitely not into football or any other professional sports teams,

At Abraxas. Where did this photo come from? My clothes were never this clean!

Cookin' and campin'—two of my favorite things to do. Ruth Lake, 1980.

but we supported our kids in whatever they were doing.

It was actually Guy's love of football that showed us what a great cook and entertainer he was. So here's the story . . . Guy broke his foot playing football when he was about fourteen and stayed home the next day. As we were leaving for work, Guy said we should invite some friends over for dinner that night and gave us a grocery list. We dropped off the groceries at lunch and loaded up our horses to go riding at the beach, as we had been instructed to do by Guy. We walked into the house after a few hours of riding, and I started to panic, as nothing had been done and we had people coming over in an hour for dinner. I figured that Guy had fallen asleep, so I opened the fridge to see what I could put together in a hurry, and to my surprise and relief, everything was prepped and ready to go! Thank God for small miracles! We walked into the family room and saw that he'd set the large round tabletop on props on the floor and had laid pillows around it for us to sit on. After an incredible Asian dinner, Guy and Morgan put on their karate uniforms and did a martial arts demonstration for us all. I knew right

**Nothing like burning it in the backyard—here I'm cooking for my mom's fiftieth birthday. (1994)**

**The original member of the clean plate club.**

then that he was going to be not only a successful restaurateur but also an entertainer.

Guy's collection of friends has always been eclectic to say the least. He never tried to up his social status in any situation by hanging out with the jocks or the so-called popular kids. He liked who he liked and that was it—no ulterior motives. His friends loved being around Guy, just like his krew today, as it was never ever boring. He could make painting the house a party, and they were lined up to help him. Whenever we were at a place like Marine World and there was some situation where a volunteer was needed, Guy was always picked. He's a people magnet and it's served him well in his career, but his generosity with his time and resources has also been a big part of his success in life. When he and his partner, Steve, opened up their first Johnny Garlic's in Santa Rosa, it was an immediate hit, and I think one big reason is that they exceeded their customers' expectations. Guy became involved with various culinary programs in the county, was involved with many charity fund-raisers, and mentored scores of youngsters.

One of the things I'm most proud of Guy for is his big heart. People often ask me if I'm blown away by Guy's success, and I usually say yes, but we've always known he was destined to do something big in life. What I'm most happy about is that he's still the wonderful human being he's always been. He's still that energetic, funny, caring, determined kid. He adores his wife and two boys, Hunter and Ryder, and knows what's most important in life—the love of his family.

# FOOD NETWORK FUSE

About two years before I appeared on *The Next Food Network Star*, I was in a barbecue competition called the American Royale with my barbecue team, the Motley Que. The promoters of the event approached us with two guys who wanted to highlight us in a show they hoped to produce called Barbecue King. Long story short, after shooting our antics for a while they asked if I'd be interested in hosting the pilot for the show. So a few weeks later we all met up in Tennessee for the Jack Daniel's invitational. I'd never done anything but commercials for my restaurants, but I had a great time. The guys went back to L.A. to edit and create the show, but six months later, nothing had come of it. I was pretty wowed by the whole TV thing, but after that experience I thought I'd just go back to what I do best—cooking and running my restaurants.

Fast-forward two years, and my buddy tells me there's this show starting on the Food Network called *The Next Food Network Star*. He thought maybe I should put a tape together and try out. I said, "No way, I've gone down that road before and it didn't turn into anything. It is what it is."

The next year rolled around, and I was sitting at the computer with my friend Mustard (Matt Sprouls). Mustard says, "*Hey,* weren't you going to film that three-minute application video for *The Next Food Network Star?*"

I brushed him off—"Yeah, yeah, I don't know, not my cup of tea."

But he said, "Listen, I saw it last year, and you can totally win this."

"Yeah, yeah, yeah."

We continued to argue about it until Mustard said, "Well, I'm going to Tex Wasabi's for a red dragon roll." (They're his favorite; he can eat fifteen at a visit to Cali.)

So we go down to TW's. Of course, when we get there another buddy, Rob, is waiting with his camera. I was like, "All right, to get you guys off my back. Let's do this!" I did a walk-through of what I was going to do, keeping it simple, making a sushi roll. I said, "Friends call me Guido," then gave the peace sign, and out. We did two takes, and then I forgot all about it and didn't turn in the DVD. A few weeks later Mustard noticed that they'd extended the deadline. He asked, "Did you mail the DVD?" I told him no. But he continued to ride me about it, so I popped the DVD in the mail on the last day and thought, *That's the end of that.*

That was on a Tuesday. Two days later, at ten o'clock at night, I got a phone call at home. No one calls us on the home phone because we use our cell numbers, so we let it keep ringing and ringing. My wife, Lori, got up to look at the caller ID and saw that

WHO WILL BE
THE
NEXT food network STAR
EMOTIONS
SIMMERING
NIGHTLY
SUNDAY NIGHTS 9|8c
food network
nighttime
WAY MORE
THAN COOKING
SCRIPPS NETWORKS
©2006 Television Food Network, G.P. All rights reserved.

it was a Manhattan number. It rang again and she answered it. I can still hear her saying, "No, I don't know where he is. I'm not sure. Can I tell him what this is regarding?"

All of a sudden she handed me the phone, whispering, "It's the Food Network," and I was sure it was one of my buddies playing a prank. "Yeah, sure, this is Guy Fieri, what do you need? . . . Yeah, yeah, you saw my DVD. It was a masterpiece. You know what I think? I like to watch the Discovery Channel." The poor woman on the phone (the casting director) was trying to convince me that she'd gotten my DVD for *The Next Food Network Star* and they loved it and wanted to know if I'd be interested in being on the show. And I wasn't buying it. They'd already FedExed a contract, and it'd get to me by the next morning.

So there it was, November 15, and I was supposed to report to New York for four weeks for the taping of the show. Meanwhile, I was about to open Tex Wasabi's in Sacramento and Lori was eight months pregnant with Ryder, with a New Year's due date. I told the producer that if my wife went into labor I was out of there, breach of contract or not. Mom, Dad, and Lori were there to see me off to New York, and Dad said, "Hey, the number one thing is to stay true to yourself." (I still get choked up on that one.)

I arrived in New York wearing a leather jacket, shorts, flip-flops, and stepped out of the cab into six inches of snow. I was the last one to get to the set—all the contestants were sitting in the common room, and they started running tape. Everybody had been to culinary school, and I said, "I own three restaurants and didn't go to culinary school. I learned in restaurants. I don't bake—I'm just Guy." I thought for sure I was dead.

The first day we went into competition, and it was out of control. One contest was to make a dish using your favorite ingredient. Other contestants chose red wine, shrimp, and bacon, but I asked for onion and demo'd onion rings. I talked too much and didn't finish making the onion rings on time—and that was just the beginning of the crazy challenges. Long story short, we shot until December 15, and I ended up in the final two—just Reggie Southerland and me—and I couldn't tell anyone. The new restaurant was going nuts, and Ryder was born on New Year's Eve.

When my partner, Steve Gruber, finally knew I'd won, he asked what I was going to do. And Jack Levar, who was like an uncle to me and would become my manager, said, "This is going to blow up!"

I was like, "Yeah, right, I'm going to go shoot my six shows of *Guy's Big Bite* and come back to run the restaurants. Food Network thinks I'm too crazy, and hey, they've already got Bobby Flay."

But Jack insisted, "It's not going to happen that way." He was right—this was when the rocket was launched, and my feet haven't touched the ground since. . . . This all happened thanks to my great family, crazy friends, business partner, great team members, and especially, and most important, the best fans a "Guy" could have. Thank you all so much.

A great gift from Dwight Maddox of MDX Guitars, who works with the band Cowboy Mouth.

Matthew, is my drumming putting you to sleep?

# BEHIND THE SCENES OF GUY'S BIG BITE

The captain at his helm—ha ha.

That's Mark Dissin, my VP. We call him the Big Dunkee! How much is that Dunkee in the window?

A Ricky Bobby moment—"I don't know what to do with my hands!"

My brother Santos, with me from the days of *The Next Food Network Star*.

Great minds at work! (I think . . . )

Dirty P on set, stealing Matthew's last bite, and he's not happy—ha ha.

It's the battle we've all been waiting for—lobster versus lobster—an all-out grudge match.

# GUY'S BIG BITE KREW

Some of these people are wanted by the authorities . . .

**Mark "Big Dunkee" Dissin— Executive Producer and VP of Production**

**Geoff Campbell—Producer**

**Ashley "Triple A" Archer—Senior Culinary Producer**

**Danielle de la Rosa— Culinary Producer**

**Mike Schear—Director**

**Suzanne Flood— Production Manager**

**Jenna Zimmerman— Associate Culinary Producer**

**Santos Loo— Senior Food Stylist**

Claus "Hans" Stuhlweissenburg— Steadicam Operator

Charles Granquist— Culinary Manager

David Mechlowicz— Purchasing Manager

Matt Michaels—Best Boy Electric

Rick Young—Key Grip

Michael Gonzales—Grip

Frank Arant— Best Boy Grip

Deboriah Dupree— Assistant Art Director

Louise De Teliga— Wardrobe Stylist

Kathleen Brown— Makeup

David Clancy— Production Assistant Coordinator

Ben Weston—Talent Production Assistant

Josh Chavez—Set Production Assistant

Kyle Baker—Set Production Assistant

Steve Doskey—IT and Set Production Assistant

Matt Webb—Set Production Assistant

Sal Eliazo— Graphics Designer

Toby Woods— Production Coordinator

Chris Dono—Head Carpenter

Steve Morden— Production Assistant

# GUY'S BIG BITE KREW

Al Ligouri—
Camera Operator

Athen Fleming—Steward

Charlie Trapani—
Tape Operator

Desmond Neal—Utility

Sandra Tripicchio—
Cook

Tracy Carter—Cook

Steve Blum—Assistant
Director

Jacob Shiffman—
Purchasing Coordinator

Chelsey Bawot—Cook

Megan Mitchell—Cook

Curt Lachowin—Audio

Jamie Tulchin—
Prop Coordinator

Joe Lazo – Food Stylist

Ali Clarke—Cook

Jeff Christian—
Director of Photography

Jen Messina—
Floor Manager

Katie Proctor—
Purchaser

Morgan Hass—
Food Stylist

Mark Mardoyan—
TV/Video Engineer

Frederic Menou—
Camera PED

**Jon Minard—
Lighting Designer**

**Mark Putnam—
Camera Dolly**

**Steve Benlien—
Tape Operator**

**Tony Gotta—Gaffer**

**Jon Piereth—
Studio Supervisor**

**Dave Eastwood—
Camera, JIB**

**Mike Schmehl—Utility**

**Shaun Regan—Utility**

**Kevin O'Connor—
Video Engineer**

**Ian Benham—
Assistant Camera**

**Tony Kremer—Audio 1**

**Shelley Hoffmann—
Producer**

**Leigh Rivers—Prompter**

**Vinnie Sinopoli—
Floor Manager**

**Cory Rory—Audio 2**

**Wendy Waxman—
Set Director**

**Marni—Wardrobe**

**Meredith Carlin—
Production Manager**

**Rick Hamilton—Lighting**

**Young Sun Huh—
Food Stylist**

# THE GUY FIERI ROAD SHOW

One of the greatest events in the country for food and wine is the South Beach Wine and Food Festival. It's a multiday, sophisticated affair where people spend hundreds on tickets to watch demos and meet chefs, wineglasses in hand. So one day I was doing a demo up on one of the stages and I cut loose and got a little wild—and the crowd went nuts. It was a hot day and everybody in the audience looked uncomfortable, so I squirted a bottle of water into the fan that blew onto the crowd. They went bananas! I thought, *Wow, even this wine crowd wants to get a little crazy.*

So . . . I decided to get it going the next year. I came with a little more action planned, and eventually I had a five-gallon margarita machine onstage. I slipped the sound guy a twenty and my iPod and came onstage to Lynyrd Skynyrd singing, "Hey there fella with your hair color yella!" instead of the elevator music they had picked for my intro. I called it a rock 'n' roll food show. The crowd continued to go nuts.

Next thing I knew I was chatting with Michelle "Michi" Bernstein at William Morris Endeavor, and she asked, "That show you do—is what you're doing intentional?" I was thinking, *I'm about to get the hook.* . . . But she said, "It's amazing—why do you do that?" I said I do it because I want to do a rock

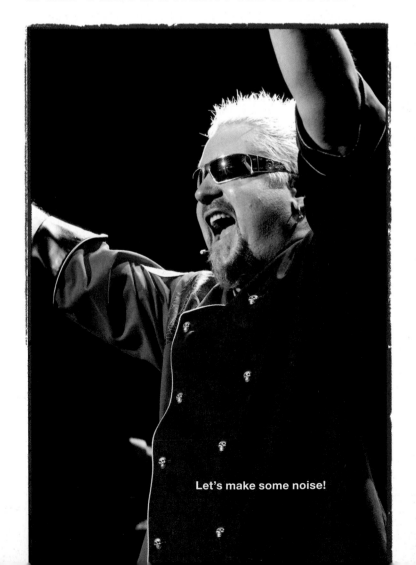

Let's make some noise!

The three amigos: Kleet, Guid, and Dirty.

This is the badge you need to have!

FOOD MEETS ROCK

Guy Fieri ROA'D SHOW

VIP

STG PRESENTS
GUY FIERI
DEC II    8 PM

OFFICE

ONE WAY

ONE WAY

PAY TO PARK

PREVOST

We rock at eight!

'n' roll food show across the country, to entertain people using the premise of food. Well, it just so happens that Michi is the queen of all concerts—from The Eagles to Lady Gaga, she's put them all on. So we took a year to plan and form a tour: twenty-one cities in thirty days, starting outside of Boston with a finale in Vegas. There were two tour buses, a semi, and a full crew with a $150,000 set that included backdrops and cooking stations, and a DJ booth. We did food, rock 'n' roll, and cocktails, just like I do at home when we fire up the jukebox and a bunch of my friends show up. We took it to the road and did it for up to 5,000 people at a time. I brought some of my best buddies, Kleetus and Dirty, Stretch from Grinders, Gorilla from Gorilla BBQ , Panini Pete from Panini Pete's in Alabama, and the crazy DJ Cobra. It was the craziest thing we've ever done.

When we started off the tour, we arrived a day early to rehearse—and it started to sink in that this was a major, full-blown production, not just a 45-minute demo at a food and wine festival. As we sat there and discussed the operation, it was a little overwhelming and I definitely got the butterflies. That first night it was full steam ahead: lights, camera, my cues, music cues, stage managers, and choreography. It probably took us four or five performances to fully get our sea legs, rally together, and fortify the performance.

What really made it so unique was the travel we did. Every town we went to, we brought in ProStart culinary students to do mise en place work with the team. Because we had to shop in every town, there were a lot of moving parts, plus each city had its own nuances. Kleetus and Dirty were responsible for sorting that out. In the meantime I was doing interviews and VIP meet and greets for 150 to 200 people; then rolling into six o'clock a guest chef would show up, get the walk-through, and go on at 6:30. Next up was Woody the flair bartender, then we'd turn up "Kickstart My Heart" from Mötley Crüe (one of my all-time favorite bands) for a full-blown rock 'n' roll entry. Kleetus and Dirty would shoot T-shirts to the audience with a T-shirt gun; then we'd go into an orchestrated cooking program with two different dishes and four elaborate stories, then an encore and bow. I'd have five minutes to hang out in the green room, take off my sweaty chef jacket, and go out to the merchandising booths for autographs—which took between forty-five minutes and two hours. By midnight we were piling back on the bus.

The caterer would provide food, but I always wanted to go local, so I would pre-order food from local restaurants that we'd researched. We'd drive through the night to our next location, check in at the hotel, and shower and sleep till two or so, then get up and do the same routine. In the process we played for more than 35,000 fans, and it was part of what took my second *DD&D* book to #1. It was the toughest, most mentally and physically strenuous thing I've done, but also one of the most rewarding.

People have said that Guy Fieri is a rock star who doesn't play guitar, he plays the griddle. I see it as a chance to lead the fight for the industry. Professional cooks and celebrity chefs can do more than make great food—a lot more. I threw down the gauntlet, bit off too much the way I always do, and guess what? The rock 'n' roll tour will ride again.

P.S. Big thanks to all the fans that made it possible. . . . See ya next year!

Kleet, Guid, and my favorite young chef—my son Hunter.

Recognizing and rewarding kids is one of my favorite things to do!

# Notes from Kleetus:
# Top 10 Rules for Cooking with Guy

1. **"You could lose a finger."** Do not eat off the cutting board!

2. **"Pizza, anyone?"** If you think it's done, it probably is. Don't burn it or it's take-out time.

3. **"I hate dishes."** If you're the chef, you don't have to do dishes.

4. **"Practice is advised."** Be able to laugh, carry on a conversation, take direction, give direction, pick music, and not get cut all at the same time.

5. **"Be fast."** Know all your cut options—julienne, dice, chop, mince, shreds, etc.—and do it quickly.

6. **"Don't let it burn."** Always keep an eye on the burners, ovens, BBQs, and pizza ovens—something may need to be flipped, stirred, or pulled! (Refer to #2.)

7. **"Eat it."** Be prepared on any given day to prepare something you have never done before *and* eat it.

8. **"Just cook."** Don't be intimidated by cooking with a celebrity chef. Do what you do best. Learn, listen, and be proactive.

9. **"Learn it once; know it forever."** If you don't know what you're doing, ask, ask, and ask again.

10. **"Laugh every day."** Last but not least, being best friends with Guy (Guido)—cooking, camping, traveling, eating, and just hanging out every day—is a lesson learned. Guy is all about teaching and not just about cooking. Life is about lessons, and being good at life makes for a happy life.

All eyes on the delivery of the Jambalaya Sandwich.

Cowboy, the resident floor cleaner.

Korina, culinary director of Knuckle Sandwich, teaches Dirty how to cook and tango!

Gorilla has twenty bucks that Dirty will cut himself.

A focused Jedi.

The famous Jambalaya Sandwich (page 148).

The Spaniard knows how to eat—and do makeup.

# IN THE KITCHEN WITH KORINA
## The Girl Behind the Guy

## Guy

To generate as many recipes as I have to over the course of a year—for shows, for demos, for articles—I can't download it all with just anybody; I need a partner to help orchestrate the madness. But in the same way that some people sing a certain way and other people write in a specific style, I've only ever found a couple people who cook the way I cook. Meet Korina McAlister. Like writing a song, I'll throw a few culinary notes out there and Korina will give a few back, and sooner or later we've created a symphony, and we're dancing through food.

Korina understands me—what I like and don't like, how something works and doesn't work. The energy we share is much more than recipe development—it's about having the same respect for things. I love that when Korina gets excited she'll pinch my arm and wiggle and say, "You have *got* to try *thiiiiiis!!!*" She'll show up at my house with to-go food to sample or she'll walk in and start jerking pots and pans out of my drawers to make something she's discovered. She's not overly structured by too much training, and she knows how to translate my psychosis. The greatest compliment I had in the last few years was when Korina's husband (who's a good friend of mine) said, "Thank you for what you do for my family." I did everything I could not to tear up. Thank *you* for coming on the ride.

## Korina

*Picture yourself in a room. It's loud, the lights are bright, and there are twenty hungry eyes fixed on your every action. Someone is writing down everything you cook, dogs are bouncing off your legs, and toddlers and teenagers are begging for a bite. Then imagine you have to bake something (anything) without the benefit of measuring utensils, a food scale, or even an oven you can turn on without lying on the kitchen floor to do so. Not to mention that the stovetop has only half the knobs in place (because it's toddler proof). This is the amazing kitchen I entered to cook in with my old friend Guy.*

*It all started because I bring food wherever I go. It's in my nature; I don't ask, I just do it. One day, as*

1113

My sista from another mista!

my husband and I were hanging out at Guy's house, Guy asked me, "What do you do?" His wife, Lori, said, "What do you mean, what does she do? She's a mom!" Guy proposed that we start working together a bit, bouncing recipe ideas off each other. Well, that part-time job went full-time pretty fast.

Suddenly I found myself in this glorious, tantalizing Guy-created mayhem. I've worked almost every job one can do in a restaurant, at everything from five-star Bay Area spots to Jersey Shore "wing dives," but nothing truly prepared me for Guy's kitchen except my palate and my fearless abandon. I'm not classically trained—not even close—but I've always been first to ask about what somebody has created, and have no reservations about trying new concepts and ideas.

These days I cook and research all day when I'm not on the road helping Guy do an event. When it comes to food, there could be twenty people in the room and Guy and I can still zone into that little twin wonder-power matrix, no problem. Our research and development is an insane mix of finishing each other's sentences and sauces and holding blind tastings with family and friends. I have a twelve- and a nine-year-old, Mason and Dixie, and their palates are great, so they get in there and help sometimes, too. My patient family and friends never eat the same thing twice and rarely before nine P.M.—and I applaud them for having my back in this endeavor!

There's never a dull moment in Guy's life, and thankfully never in mine. Is there a drawback to this dream job? Maybe one—now nobody will cook for me! Well, except Guy . . .

INTRODUCTION ................. 33

# GUY'S KITCHEN

*If you go to a Nascar driver's home garage, you expect to find every possible variety of tools related to cars. Makes sense—the dude races cars. Well, I cook, and **I try to have every single piece of equipment I can imagine, here at my fingertips.** I had it all before I was on TV. It wasn't given to me, and I didn't come by it easily. I just had to have the rockin' kitchen. I didn't build it to be my personal stage, however. Cooking is my favorite way to hang with my friends and family, so I wanted my kitchen to be set up so that six people can be cooking at once, and there's a long counter facing the action for everybody else to hang out at.*

*Here's a rundown of my arsenal.*

## Top 5 Equipment

### Tongs

In my view, tongs are the quintessential kitchen utensil. It's a grabber-poker-flipper-stirrer and even a mini ladle—the most versatile tool that that you can use, hands down. If I could cut and grate with them, I'd be Rambo.

### Knives

Some people have guitar collections; I have thirty-one knives. Like tennis pros have a favorite racket or golf pros a favorite club, chefs have their knives, which are basically an extension of their arms. Each one to his own, but my favorite is an 8- to 10-inch French knife. I had the Guy Fieri Knuckle Sandwich knives built the way I wanted them to be: with properly sized handles, great blades, and a rock-star cool.

The starting lineup.

## Spice Grinder

If you like the way a ground spice tastes right out of a container, just think how good it will taste if you take the whole spice, toast it a little, then grind it up. I think it's way better!

When I came back from barbecue camp one time, I toasted up some Thai chiles, knocked them out in the spice grinder, and made a rub. Everything tasted awesome, and I cleaned out the spice grinder really well—but neglected to mention my technique to Lori. The next morning when she went to make coffee she did her routine, grinding the beans and brewing it . . . and then thought the coffee was poi-sonous! (The residual oils from the peppers really made the coffee taste weird.) Now we have two grinders.

## Squirt Bottles

I'm so tired of taking off lids and then losing them. Being able to transfer something to a squirt bottle makes it quick and easy. Just label it . . .

## Cast-Iron Pan

You can beat it, burn it, blacken it, bake it, and bomb it, and it will be there for you through thick and thin. Just don't wash it with soap and water!

"GORILLA" IN THE MIDST.

← MY BUDDY EMERIL.

MY CULINARY DOJO!

# 𝕿𝖔𝖕 5 𝕻𝖆𝖓𝖙𝖗𝖞 𝕴𝖙𝖊𝖒𝖘

### Olive Oil and Evoo

The right oil for the right job is key, and olive oil is my super-versatile go-to oil. It plays the middle of the road really well. It has a low smoke point, so ya gotta be careful, but you gotta dig the flavor. Canola is the heavy hitter when you're gonna go really hot.

### Apple Cider Vinegar ("ACV")

I use vinegar in a lot of foods, and ACV is my multi-purpose choice for everything from salad dressings to marinades to brining liquids. It's just right, not too harsh or too sweet.

### Soy Sauce ("The Super Salt")

I've been a soy junkie since I was a kid. Soy lends a nice roasted, mellow, balanced saltiness to a dish that's not overdone or too intense. I don't think people loop it into their arsenals enough because their expectation is that it's used only in Asian recipes. Trust me—its uses are multiethnic. Not all soy sauces taste the same. Find the one you like—then you can trust how it will support your dishes.

### Sriracha Sauce

Here's another Asian product that people under-utilize. Sriracha transcends any stereotyped use by being not overly hot, with a little touch of sweetness. It has a nice viscosity and a beautiful color, and works

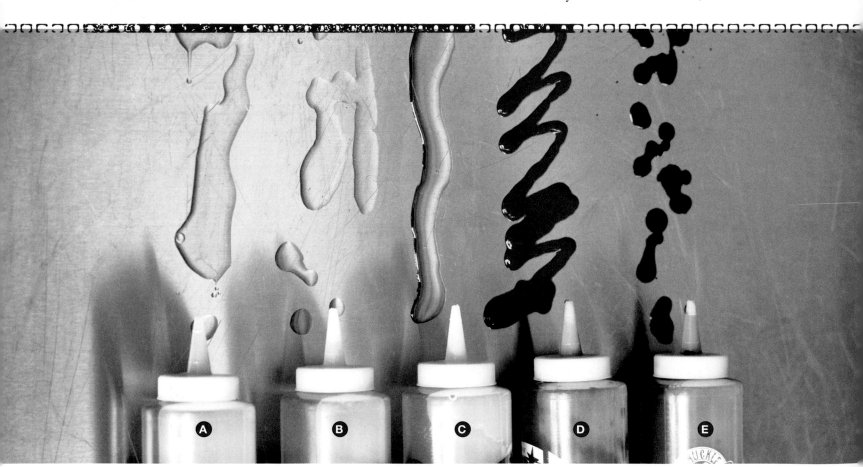

**Time for a quiz—name these!**
A. Evoo, B. ACV, C. Canola oil, D. Sriracha, E. Soy

as a condiment, in marinades, as a basting liquid, in soups—the list goes on.

### Agave Nectar ("The Super Sugar")

Because agave doesn't come from sugarcane, it doesn't have the granules that have to cook down. So you've got nothing but smooth, golden liquid sweetness that's not as cloying or pronounced as honey and mixes well with others.

# Appliances

- Two ovens (gas is my *only* way to go)
- Warming drawer
- Two refrigerators
- Four refrigerated drawers
- Three sinks with foot pedals
- Three trash cans
- Three recycling bins
- One compost pot
- Two dishwashers

# Equipment

### Utensils

- Knives: cleavers, a sushi knife (first knife I ever owned), one with a deer antler handle, one that Bobby Flay gave me during *The Next Food Network Star,* one by famous knife maker Ken Onion, a prime rib and roast cutting knife, boning knife, bendable fish knife, good serrated knives, steak knives . . . the list goes on and on.

- Lots of strong metal tongs, short and long
- Wooden salad tongs
- Flat-headed wooden spatulas (a close second to the tongs)
- A couple of plastic utensils (for delicate nonstick pans)
- Bamboo spoons
- Wooden spoons
- Metal spoons
- Slotted spoons
- Garlic press
- Pizza cutter
- Utility shears
- Potato peelers (that create julienne)
- Baster
- Zester
- Hay hooks (for my 10-gallon jambalaya pot, which has to be kept indoors so it doesn't rust)
- Bench knife
- BBQ mop
- Fry skimmer
- Crab crackers
- Shrimp deveiners
- Parmesan cheese wheel breakers
- Pasta forks
- Ravioli cutting wheel

## Pots, pans, and everything else

- Mix of my old-school Vollrath aluminum-blend pans that we used in restaurants and All-Clad and Viking pans
- Calphalon pans (from college)
- 11 sauté pans, from nonstick to stainless steel (a good nonstick is invaluable)
- Three heavy stockpots in various sizes
- Roasting pans in every size
- Sheet pans
- Pyrex casseroles
- Roasting racks
- Wok (from college)
- Ceramic wok
- 2 paella pans
- Pressure cookers
- Cutting boards (9 synthetic rubber)
- Muffin tins in every size
- Soufflé cups
- China cap strainers
- Hand colanders
- Fine mesh colanders
- Mesh wire steaming inserts
- Bamboo steamers
- Bamboo spiders
- Squirt bottles—all the essentials
- Lots of lighters
- 1 Butane torch
- Couple different thermometers for oil and candy
- Pizza peel
- Pizza stone
- Salad spinner
- Stainless steel bowls in every size possible
- Glass and plastic mixing bowls
- Two sizes of mortar and pestle
- Volcanic mortar and pestle
- Meat grinder
- Falafel maker
- Tostone cup maker
- 1800s nutmeg grinder
- Microplanes (3 different sizes)
- Ginger grater
- Cheese grater
- Mandolin
- Pepper grinders for white, black, and mélange
- Spice grinder
- Fruit presses
- Potato ricer
- Two or three tenderizers
- Cheesecloth
- Butcher twine
- Pastry bag and points
- Sushi mat
- Himalayan salt block (for fish or meat)
- Tortilla pan
- Tortilla press
- Tortilla warmer
- Pasta dryer
- Ravioli molds
- Mofongo pilon
- FoodSaver
- Butcher's metal scabbard
- Serving bowls
- French press coffeemaker
- To-go cups
- Water bottles
- Paper towels in two or three different spots
- 50,000 cloth towels

## Electronics

- Juicer
- Meat slicer
- Immersion blender
- High-speed Vitamix
- KitchenAid mixer
- Cuisinart
- Pasta machine
- Breville espresso machine/coffeemaker
- Rice cooker
- Waffle maker
- Air popper

## Outside equipment

- Gas grill
- Charcoal grill
- Pizza oven
- Propane smoker
- Wood smoker
- Six- by four-foot whole hog smoker
- Big dehydrator

# The Juicer

I don't think most of us are packing our bodies with enough raw fruits and vegetables. So I'd like you to meet my little friend, the juicer. When Lori was pregnant with Hunter and I was busy in the restaurant business, we juiced like crazy. Once Hunter was born, we kept it up, and he has never stayed home sick from school. We've juiced through it all!

My day hasn't started until I've had my juice, so even when I'm on the road shooting *DD&D, Minute to Win It,* or *Guy's Big Bite,* we pack a juicer. The crew and I juice a combo of carrots, celery, pomegranates, beets, and Swiss chard—you name it—every morning. Now they've all gone out and bought their own juicers. Try it, you'll find yourself addicted—in a good way!

One of my production assistants, Fraggle, has been in charge of juicing on the set at *Triple D* these days. We usually start with a base of these fruits and veggies and riffs from there:

| | |
|---|---|
| 3 Granny Smith apples | 2 pears |
| 10 to 12 carrots | 1 bunch large-leaf spinach or chard |

This way you get the full impact of nutritious vegetables married with a sweet base of apples and pears. For variety, change it up each morning by adding more fruit to the mixture, anything from strawberries to raspberries, cantaloupe, mango, and so on. Note that blueberries can be added to just about anything, plus they're high in antioxidants.

All the recipes below should fill a 2-quart pitcher.

## One popular juice is:

| | |
|---|---|
| 3 apples | 1 bunch spinach |
| 2 pears | 3 ripe mangos |
| 10 to 12 carrots | 2 beets (ideally the golden ones) |

Here's a juice combination that everybody except one of our producers, Bryna, liked (she hates celery):

| | |
|---|---|
| 3 pears | ½ celery head |
| 2 apples | 1 cucumber (optional) |
| 10 carrots | 1 honeydew melon |
| 2 beets (or 1 bunch spinach) | |

## And here's another rockin' combo:

| | |
|---|---|
| 3 apples | 1 full bunch celery |
| 10 carrots | 1 pineapple |
| 1 bunch spinach or chard | 2 pints blueberries |

# Pantry

*Here's what I currently have in my arsenal (give or take a few, depending on the time of year). If you find you have a lot of items in your pantry, try this trick: use a marker to write what the item is on the top of the cap so you can find it easily in a drawer.*

### Oils, vinegars, liquids, and sauces

- Extra virgin olive oil
- Olive oil
- Canola oil
- Grapeseed oil
- Truffle oil
- White vinegar
- White wine vinegar
- Rice wine vinegar, seasoned and unseasoned
- Balsamic vinegar
- White balsamic vinegar
- 75-year-old balsamic vinegar
- Sherry wine vinegar
- Red wine vinegar
- Red pepper vinegar
- Italian wine vinegar
- Cabernet sauvignon vinegar
- Organic unpasteurized Bragg's apple cider vinegar
- Double black soy sauce

YEP...NINE PEPPER GRINDERS AND FIFTEEN SQUIRT BOTTLES... I KNOW, A LITTLE OVER THE TOP!

WITH HUNTER (THREE) AT A COOKING DEMO

HUNTER'S REPORT CARD

- Bragg's liquid aminos
- Fish sauce
- Clam juice
- Oyster sauce
- Beef stock, canned
- Demi-glace
- Vegetable broth
- Ten different barbecue sauces
- Coconut milk
- Red curry paste
- Real vanilla extract
- Organic honey
- Maple syrup
- Pomegranate glaze
- Pomegranate liqueur
- Agave nectar
- Banana sauce
- Molasses

- Apple cider syrup
- Coffee syrup

### Herbs and spices

- Kosher salt
- Sea salt
- Smoked sea salt
- Seasoned salt
- Himalayan salt
- Celery salt
- Garam masala
- Black and green cardamom pods
- Fennel seed
- Turmeric
- Horseradish
- Coriander seeds
- Paprika

- Nutmeg
- Black and white sesame seeds
- Saffron
- Dry mustard
- Curry powder
- Sage
- Star anise
- Five spice powder
- Tarragon
- Dill weed
- Thyme
- Allspice
- Whole cumin
- Arrowroot
- Rosemary
- Dark and light chili powder
- Sweet basil
- Whole cloves

- Italian seasoning
- Bay leaves
- Ground ginger
- Adobo seasoning
- Juniper berries
- Vanilla beans
- Savory
- Parsley
- Lemon pepper
- Mustard seed
- Black and white truffle salt
- Oregano
- Granulated garlic
- Garlic pepper
- Pickling spice
- Annatto seed
- Crab boil

### Hot stuff!

- Chipotle peppers
- Ground chipotle
- Achiote paste
- Hot sauce
- Ancho powder
- Chipotle powder
- White pepper
- Crushed chiles
- Cayenne
- Sicilian peppers
- Canned chiles
- Tabasco
- Dried wasabi

### Canned and packaged goods

- Caramelized ginger
- Orange peel
- Canned corn
- Capers
- Canned tomato soup
- Chicken noodle soup
- Cannellini beans
- Kidney beans
- Tuna
- Refried beans
- Pinto beans
- Black beans
- Sweet peas
- Sliced beets
- Espresso beans
- Tomato paste
- Anchovies
- Chow mein noodles
- Tempura batter
- Fire-roasted tomatoes
- Red bell peppers
- Cherries
- Beef jerky
- Saltines
- Marcona almonds
- Toasted soy nuts
- Graham crackers
- Raspberry preserves
- Organic peanut butter
- Applesauce
- Emergen-C

### Grains, starches, sugars, and baking supplies

- Semolina flour
- Rice flour
- Unbleached all-purpose flour
- Tapioca flour
- Masarina
- Masa
- Double O flour
  (high-gluten flour from Italy)
- Scone mix
- Grain blends
- Oatmeal
- Jasmine rice
- Arborio rice
- Basmati rice
- Long grain brown rice
- Rice noodles
- Rice sticks/pasta
- Oriental vermicelli
- Arrow root
- Short brown rice
- Dried black beans
- Quinoa
- Red quinoa
- Tapioca paper
- Instant grits
- Whole grits
- Cornstarch
- Polenta
- Cornmeal
- Italian bread crumbs
- Bread crumbs
- Panko
- Brown sugar
- Organic sugar
- Confectioners' sugar

Hands down, one of the greatest pieces of equipment I've ever owned and cooked with. Nothin' like wood-fired!

- Baker's sugar
- Turbinado sugar
- Yeast
- Baking soda
- Baking powder

# Refrigerator

## Refrigerated sauces and condiments

- Muffaletta olive spread
- Salsa
- Pesto
- Horseradish
- Hot horseradish
- Blue cheese dressing
- Beef au jus
- Hoisin sauce
- Fish sauce
- Soy sauce
- Light soy sauce
- Peanut satay sauce
- Chile garlic sauce
- Sriracha
- Hot chile oil
- Char siu paste
- Tamarind paste
- Kung pao sauce
- Hot black bean paste
- Sweet chile sauce
- Ponzu
- Pickled ginger
- Harissa
- Green curry paste
- Jerk seasoning

- Lemon juice
- Pepperoncinis
- Hot chile peppers
- Dill pickles
- Sweet pickles
- Italian giardiniera
- Italian peppers
- Pickled peppers
- Pickled carrots
- Artichoke hearts
- Pickled jalapeños
- Greek olives
- Anchovy paste
- Pomegranate juice
- Flaxseed oil (best kept in the refrigerator)
- Sesame oil (ditto)
- Chicken base
- Truffle honey
- Whole-grain mustard
- Sweet and hot mustard
- Dijon mustard
- Ginger wasabi mustard
- Chipotle mustard
- Jalapeño mustard
- Stone-ground jalapeño mustard

## Meats, cheese, and dairy

- Milk
- Cream cheese
- Sour cream
- Mascarpone
- Crème fraîche
- Heavy cream
- Feta cheese
- Mozzarella

- Parmigiano-Reggiano
- Pepper Jack
- Horseradish Jack
- Cheddar cheese
- Brie
- Double brie
- Stravecchio
- Salamento
- Guanciale
- Pancetta
- Salami
- Soppressata
- Italian salame
- Lardo
- Pepperoni
- Spanish chorizo
- Applewood-smoked thick-cut bacon

## Miscellaneous

- Tortillas
- Egg roll wrappers
- Virginia peanuts
- Marsala
- Sherry

## Fruits and vegetables

- Bean salad
- Baby carrots (real ones, not "baby cut")
- Green onions
- Organic blueberries
- Fresh thyme
- Fresh oregano
- Heads of garlic
- Lemons

- Limes
- Oranges
- Aji peppers

## Freezers

- Edamame
- Walnuts
- Petite whole onions
- Abalone
- Andouille sausage
- Smoked sausage
- Ham steak
- Pine nuts
- Pineapple
- Raspberries
- Blueberries

- Cornish game hens
- Tortellini
- Sourdough bread
- Wheat bread

## Garden

- Purple-leaf sage
- Bergamot mint
- Spearmint
- Verbena
- Lemongrass
- Thyme
- Marjoram
- Oregano

- Rosemary
- Lavender
- Basil—Thai, purple, sweet
- Swiss chard
- Kale
- Dino kale
- Romaine lettuce
- Red leaf lettuce
- Cabbage—red and green
- Beets—white and red
- Garlic
- Celery
- Parsley
- Italian parsley
- Cilantro
- Green onions

TOP-NOTCH TILE WORK BY JOHNNY "SIZZLE SHANKS" QUINLAN.

KILLER HANDMADE IRON PIZZA PEEL FROM THE BLACKSMITH SHOP IN FERNDALE. THE BOMB.

OVEN WRAPPED IN COPPER BY MY BUDDY GABE DUNN.

# Playin' It Safe

Most of us can probably remember our moms thawing frozen chicken in a baking dish on the countertop as we prepared for school in the morning. That was how things were done. And don't tell me you didn't have a moment in college when pizza left out overnight didn't taste better than it did the night you ordered it. We somehow manage to convince ourselves that the laws of bacteria formation cease to exist in our own kitchens!

When it comes to food safety, cross-contamination is one of the biggest unseen culprits. I've been an instructor for the National Restaurant Association's Serve Safe program for years, and I have certified all my managers in Johnny Garlic's and Tex Wasabi's. Here are a few important tips to keep you and your family out of the Food Contamination Danger Zone!

- I'm a big fan of placing raw meat in a sealable bag, then into a container before placing it in the fridge because of the potential for leaks. The fridge is the correct place to thaw out that meat. You can do it under cold (under 70°F) running water, but that's wasteful, so just think ahead a bit more! (For a large turkey that's three days out.)

- There's a 4-hour window for proteins when they're in the temperature danger zone. The clock starts as soon as it's above 40°F and below 140°F, so pay close attention.

- Use separate cutting boards and knives for raw meat, and wash your hands and any contaminated surfaces with soap and hot water when moving from working with raw meat to any other task.

- Cook food to the correct minimum internal temperature (see the chart below) and make sure stuffed or reheated foods are cooked to 165°F.

- If you want to use a marinade as a basting sauce after it's been used on raw meat, be sure to bring it to a boil for 3 to 4 minutes before it touches cooked meat for serving.

## Purchasing Guidelines

### Fish

- **Should smell like seaweed, not ammonia**

- **Eyes should be clear and not sunken**

- **Flesh should bounce back when pressed with your thumb**

### Clams, mussels, and oysters

- **When raw, if shells are open they should close with a tap; throw out the open ones**

- **After cooking, the shells should be open; throw out the closed ones**

### Other protein

- **Should not be sticky or smell of ammonia**

## Cooking Guidelines

| meat | internal temp. | meat | internal temp. |
|---|---|---|---|
| Beef | 145°F | Pork | 160°F |
| Lamb | 145°F | Fish | 145°F |
| Chicken | 165°F | Ground meat | 160°F |
| Duck | 165°F | Leftovers | 165°F |
| Turkey | 165°F | | |

CAST-IRON SKILLET FROM ONE OF MY FAVORITE CHICKEN JOINTS, PRINCE'S IN NASHVILLE.

"THE" LINE!

## Restaurant CSI

We have to be more cautious about how we're treating our food, and a digital thermometer is one of the most valuable tools in the kitchen. When people say they got sick at a restaurant, I always get the urge to do the CSI on their experience. Here's a case study: You go to lunch with friends from the office and order a hot crab and cheddar melt on a croissant, but you don't eat all of it ('cause it's huge). So you take it back to the office, where it sits on your desk until you remember to put it into the office refrigerator, which is opened and closed about 90,000 times a day. So 5:30 rolls around and you bring your sandwich out to the car. You do a little grocery shopping, then pop the sandwich in your fridge at home. The next day you decide to bring it back to work for lunch, so it goes into your bag, and you stop to get coffee on the way to work, then place the sandwich in the office refrigerator again. Here it comes, ladies and gentleman, the moment of truth. . . . Will that sandwich be safe to eat?

Somehow we seem to believe that keeping food in our possession will magically protect us. *False.* The key is to head on over to the microwave and heat that sandwich up until it reaches the temperature that makes it edible again. In order to kill bacteria, the item must reach 165°F for at least fifteen seconds. Another tip is to let the food sit for a couple minutes after zapping it so that the heat will radiate out and heat the food thoroughly.

Just something for you to think about . . .

As a kid, I never really got the concept of appetizers. Calling them "finger foods" never made any sense to me either, because **they didn't resemble fingers.** So I called them "early food" since they came before dinner. My true awakening to the potential of this course came at my Aunt Patty's wedding, when I was nine or ten years old. My mother, with complete foresight, warned me not to fill up on all the appetizers, but needless to say, I mowed down a buffet of teriyaki chicken wings. Wow, **fun-to-eat food,** and just my size! I couldn't control myself around it and thought, *It's a teaser!* Thus, a lightbulb went off, and I suddenly understood that these were **appe-teasers**. And that became my name for my new obsession.

To be honest, I still think in the appe-teaser realm most of the time. I really enjoy small plates, a little of this and a little of that. **Why not have eleven different things at one sitting,** with no boundaries and no set ethnicity? You can move all over the board to different countries and be as eclectic as you like. We call it "tapas" now. **The freedom is unparalleled.** Of course, you don't want to have hot and spicy Buffalo wings and then move on to yellowtail sashimi, but it's all about free rein. After all, **who wants to go to Disneyland and only ride the Matterhorn?** I want a huge profile of flavors. So I carry this idea into my show *Guy's Big Bite,* and at home I'll always serve a range of appetizers. (By the time we get to the main course, people are shocked to find out we aren't done already.) So these days, I'm down with **appe-tapas.**

# PEPPER GUY'D

Peppers are so alive and powerful that nothing matches their intensity, and eating them is like an adventure. To keep the heat level appropriate, it's useful to know how hot peppers are before throwing them into your next recipe. Heat is measured in something called Scoville units. To give you an idea, the lightweight bell pepper comes in at zero units while the mighty habanero can top out at a hefty 570,000. Pick the right pepper for the right job.

1. **Bell Pepper:** 0 Scoville units
2. **Pepperoncini:** 100 to 500 Scoville units
3. **Pimento:** 100 to 500 Scoville units
4. **Cherry:** 100 to 500 Scoville units
5. **Sweet Banana:** 500 Scoville units
6. **New Mexico/California:** 1,000 to 1,500 Scoville units
7. **Pasilla/Poblano:** 2,000 Scoville units
8. **Ancho:** 2,000 Scoville units
9. **Anaheim:** 2,500 Scoville units
10. **Guajillo:** 2,500 to 5,000 Scoville units
11. **Jalapeño:** 5,000 Scoville units
12. **Chipotle:** 8,000 Scoville units
13. **Serrano:** 25,000 Scoville units
14. **Tabasco:** 30,000 to 50,000 Scoville units
15. **Piquin:** 100,000 to 140,000 Scoville units
16. **Thai Bird:** 150,000 Scoville units
17. **Scotch Bonnet:** 325,000 Scoville units
18. **Habanero:** 325,000 to 570,000 Scoville units

# Confetti Mashed Potato Flautas with Hot Tomatillo Sauce

*Veggie flautas? Are you kidding me? Nope,* **these are money,** *and full of flavor. Go big and* **make a double batch!**

*Triple.*

**1.** In a medium saucepan over medium heat, boil the potatoes in salted water just until tender, about 10 minutes. Drain.

**2.** Roast the pasilla or poblano chiles over a gas stove or under the broiler. Cool, peel, seed, and slice the chiles into 32 long, thin strips. Reserve.

**3.** In a large skillet over medium-high heat, heat the olive oil and cook the onion, ¾ cup of the red bell pepper, and the serrano chile for 3 minutes or until softened. Add the garlic and cook for 1 minute more. Turn off the heat and add the corn.

**4. To make the mashed potato filling,** in a medium bowl, mash the potatoes with a potato masher until smooth. Fold in the sour cream, cream cheese, pepper Jack, salt, and pepper. Gently stir in ½ of the green onions and the pepper-onion mixture. Season to taste with salt and pepper. Keep warm.

**5.** Set a wire rack in a baking sheet and place it in the oven. Preheat the oven to 250°F. In a Dutch oven, heat the canola oil to 350°F. Have the tortillas, beans, potato mixture, roasted chile peppers, avocado, and toothpicks at hand, as well as a plate lined with paper towels for draining.

**6.** Place a tortilla on a dry work surface. Lay about 3 tablespoons black beans along one side, then about ⅓ cup of potato mixture. Top with 2 strips each of roasted chile and avocado.

3 large russet potatoes, peeled and cubed

2 large pasilla or poblano chiles

1 tablespoon olive oil

½ cup small-diced yellow onion

1 cup small-diced red bell pepper

1 serrano chile, cut into small dice

2 tablespoons minced garlic

¾ cup canned low-sodium corn, drained well

½ cup sour cream

¾ cup cream cheese, at room temperature

1½ cups grated pepper Jack cheese (about 6 ounces)

1 teaspoon fine sea salt, plus more for seasoning

1 teaspoon freshly cracked black pepper, plus more for seasoning

1 bunch green onions, sliced

6 cups canola oil

Sixteen 8-inch flour tortillas

*(cont.)*

One 15-ounce can black beans, rinsed and drained well

1 avocado, pitted, peeled, and cut into 32 thin strips

Tomatillo (see page 227)

Grated cotija cheese, for garnish

⅓ cup chopped cilantro, for garnish

*Special Equipment:*
Potato masher, toothpicks

**7.** Roll tightly, tucking the ends in, and secure with a toothpick. Repeat with the rest of the tortillas and filling.

**8.** Check the oil temperature and gently add the flautas to the oil, a maximum 3 at a time so as not to crowd them. Turn frequently and watch carefully, because they will brown quickly, about 1 to 2 minutes per side. Drain each batch briefly on paper towels, remove the toothpick, and lightly sprinkle with salt. Keep warm in the oven.

**9. To serve as appetizers,** place 3 tablespoons of tomatillo on a small plate. Cut a flauta in half on the diagonal, laying one piece on its side on the plate and standing one up. Sprinkle cotija cheese on top and garnish with the cilantro and the remaining green onions and red bell pepper.

**10. For a main course,** serve on a large plate, double the sauce underneath, and stand 4 flauta halves in the sauce. Garnish and serve.

After the filling is laid, roll tightly.

Tuck the edges in and secure with a toothpick. Repeat.

Place in oil and watch carefully, because they will brown quickly.

# Irish Nachos

As you'll see in this book, **I don't believe nachos are only for Mexican food. . . . We all need a nacho in our life.** *I use waffle fries here because the nooks and crannies let the sauce and cheese get into every bite. Cook them according to the package directions—the crispier the better!*

**1.** Preheat the oven to 375°F.

**2.** Shred the corned beef. In a small bowl, combine the sour cream, mustard, and horseradish. Add 1 teaspoon of the black pepper and salt to taste, if desired.

**3.** Cook the waffle fries according to package directions.

**4.** On an oven-safe serving platter or a baking sheet, spread the fries in an even layer. Cover the fries evenly with the corned beef. Top with the cheeses and bake for 15 minutes or until the cheese is bubbly and just starting to brown.

**5.** Evenly sprinkle with the peppers, sauerkraut, green onions, and the remaining black pepper. Drizzle with the sour cream–mustard sauce and serve immediately.

½ pound cooked corned beef

½ cup sour cream

2 tablespoons whole-grain mustard

1 tablespoon prepared horseradish

2 teaspoons freshly ground black pepper

Fine sea salt

One 22-ounce bag frozen waffle-cut fries

1 cup shredded Irish white cheddar cheese

⅓ cup grated fontina cheese

¾ cup Peppadew peppers, seeded and diced (Whole Foods has these in their olive bar)

½ cup sauerkraut (squeezed and drained)

½ cup sliced green onions

Ain't nothin' but a chicken wing—
and a darn good one at that.

# Firecracker Wings

*I gotta tell ya, **I used to think that wings had to be fried.** (Probably because most grilled wings are burned and chewy and lack flavor.) So I set out to make some that will rock 'n' roll without getting fried.*

**1.** Cut the wings apart at the joints and discard the tips. In a large glass bowl, combine the water, kosher salt, ¼ cup of the chili-garlic sauce, and ¼ cup of the honey. Stir until the salt is dissolved. Add the wings and refrigerate for 30 minutes or up to 4 hours.

**2. To make the basting and dipping sauce,** in a small bowl, combine the remaining chili-garlic sauce, the soy sauce, sweet soy sauce, sriracha, the remaining honey, vinegar, and ginger and mix well. Set aside half of the sauce for serving in order to avoid contamination.

**3.** Preheat a grill to medium-high. Drain the wings and season them with sea salt and pepper. Grill the wings until golden, 15 to 20 minutes, turning as needed. When the wings reach the right color, continue cooking over indirect heat until they're at the desired doneness, then baste them with the sauce, turning as needed until the wings are glossy and well coated. Garnish the wings with the sesame seeds and green onion and serve with the reserved dipping sauce.

5 pounds chicken wings

6 cups water

¼ cup kosher salt

⅓ cup chili-garlic sauce

1 cup honey

2 tablespoons soy sauce

½ cup Sweet Soy Sauce (page 85 or find in Asian markets)

3 tablespoons sriracha sauce

¼ cup apple cider vinegar

¼ cup minced ginger

1 teaspoon ground sea salt

1 tablespoon freshly cracked black pepper

1 teaspoon sesame seeds, toasted*

1 tablespoon minced green onions

*\*To toast the sesame seeds, just put them over low heat in a dry skillet and watch them carefully!*

# Petaluma Paté

1 tablespoon olive oil

⅓ cup very finely diced red onion (about ½ small onion)

1 tablespoon minced garlic

¼ cup minced shallot

1 tablespoon tomato paste

⅓ cup Chicken Stock (page 362 or low-sodium store-bought)

1 pound applewood smoked bacon

½ pound best-quality chicken livers

1 pound ground pork loin*

2 tablespoons kosher salt

1 teaspoon freshly cracked pepper, plus more for serving

1 teaspoon Herbes de Sonoma (page 370)

1¼ cups fresh sourdough bread crumbs (no crusts)

3 eggs

⅓ cup Cognac

3 bay leaves

2 thyme sprigs

One 24-inch baguette, for serving

Dijon mustard, for serving

Cornichons, for serving

Olives, for serving

*Ask your butcher for chili grind, ground with a medium die.*

*As an exchange student in France, I got a chance to enjoy some really righteous paté. This is my spin, and **you're gonna wow your krew with this one!***

**1.** Preheat the oven to 350°F.

**2.** In a small skillet over medium heat, heat the olive oil and add the onion, garlic, and shallot. Cook until just soft, about 3 minutes. Add the tomato paste and cook for 3 minutes. Whisk in the chicken stock and simmer, stirring occasionally, for 8 to 10 minutes, until almost all of the liquid is gone. Remove from the heat, spread on a small plate, and set aside to cool.

**3.** In a food processor, pulse half of the bacon 5 or 6 times, until finely ground. Transfer to a large bowl. Put the chicken livers in the food processor and pulse 2 or 3 times, until they are finely ground as well. Add the livers and ground pork to the bacon in the bowl. Season with the salt, pepper, and herbes de Sonoma. Add the bread crumbs and mix together gently. Stir in the eggs, Cognac, and cooled tomato paste mixture.

**4.** In a large loaf pan (11½ by 4 by 3 inches), lay the remaining bacon strips across the bottom and up the sides, gently stretching if necessary. Add the paté mixture, pressing it lightly so that there are no air pockets. Fold the ends of the bacon over the paté and lay an extra piece or two to cover the top completely. Place the bay leaves and thyme sprigs on top. Place the loaf pan in a larger pan and pour an inch or so of water into the larger pan to create a water bath. Bake for 1 hour and 30 minutes or until the internal temperature is 165°F.

**5.** Remove from the water bath and let the paté come to room temperature. Cover with plastic wrap. Place a sheet pan over the paté and top with heavy cans to press down on the paté. Refrigerate for at least 18 hours.

**6.** Remove from the refrigerator and run a thin knife or spatula around the loaf pan.

**7.** Remove the bay leaves and thyme sprigs. Turn the pan upside-down onto a cutting board. Remove the bacon slices and discard. Cut the paté into about 7 or 8 slices. Cut each slice into 4 to 6 strips and serve with a good baguette, mustard, cornichons, fresh cracked pepper, and olives.*

*The tightly wrapped and refrigerated paté will keep for up to ten days.*

# 3P "Pepperoni Pizza Partay"

## PIZZA SAUCE

1 tablespoon olive oil

¼ cup finely chopped onion

1 tablespoon minced garlic

¼ teaspoon red chili flakes

One 28-ounce can crushed tomatoes (I recommend Muir Glen Fire-Roasted)

1 tablespoon finely shredded fresh basil, plus a sprig for garnish

1 teaspoon dried marjoram

1 teaspoon dried oregano

½ teaspoon fine sea salt

½ teaspoon freshly ground black pepper

## PIZZA TOPPINGS

1 tablespoon olive oil

1 cup pepperoni matchsticks

½ cup red bell pepper, seeded and cut into ¼-inch dice

1 tablespoon minced shallot

½ cup sliced cremini mushrooms

1 cup diced fresh mozzarella cheese

¼ cup grated Parmesan cheese

*I dig takin' the food we all enjoy and servin' it in different formats and styles. Call it deconstruction, crazy, whatever—**the 3P rocks!***

**1.** Preheat the oven to 350°F.

**2. For the pizza sauce,** in a 12-inch skillet over medium heat, heat the olive oil. Add the onion and cook until translucent, about 2 minutes. Add the garlic and chili flakes and cook for 1 minute more. Add the tomatoes and reduce the heat to a simmer. Cook for 25 minutes, stirring occasionally, until thickened.

**3.** Add the basil, marjoram, oregano, salt, and pepper. Simmer 15 minutes more. Remove from the heat and adjust the seasoning, if necessary.

**4. For the toppings,** in a large skillet over medium-high heat, heat 1½ teaspoons of the olive oil. Add the pepperoni and cook until just crisp, 4 to 5 minutes. Drain on a paper-towel-lined plate. Heat the remaining 1½ teaspoons olive oil over medium-high heat and add the red bell pepper. Cook until just starting to soften, about 2 minutes. Add the shallot and cook for 1 minute more. Add the mushrooms. Lower the heat to medium and cook for 4 to 6 minutes or until the mushrooms are soft and lightly browned. Remove from the heat.

**5. For the bottom layer,** in a medium bowl, combine the cream cheese, ricotta, Parmesan, egg, garlic, oregano, chili flakes, salt, and pepper. Spread the mixture evenly in a 2-quart casserole dish or a 9-inch pie pan.

**6.** Spread the pizza sauce over the bottom layer. Sprinkle with the pepper-mushroom mixture, then the pepperoni. Top evenly with the mozzarella and bake for 20 minutes or until the mozzarella is melted and the pepperoni is crisped.

**7.** Remove from the oven and sprinkle with the Parmesan. Garnish with julienned basil and serve hot with pizza dough strips or crackers.

With Morgan serving appe-teasers in 1977. No wings here—we probably ate them all!

**BOTTOM LAYER**

8 ounces cream cheese, at room temperature

⅔ cup ricotta cheese

⅓ cup grated Parmesan cheese

1 egg, slightly beaten

½ teaspoon minced garlic

1 teaspoon dried oregano

½ teaspoon red chili flakes

½ teaspoon fine sea salt

½ teaspoon freshly ground black pepper

Julienned basil leaves, for garnish

Baked pizza dough strips or crackers, for serving

# Buffalo Balls

## SERVES 8 TO 10

2 pounds boneless, skinless chicken thighs

3 cups crumbled Ritz crackers (about 3 small sleeves)

1 tablespoon freshly cracked black pepper

1 tablespoon paprika

1 tablespoon dried basil

1 teaspoon celery salt

1 teaspoon ground cumin

½ teaspoon ground white pepper

¾ teaspoon cayenne pepper

2 cups crumbled blue cheese

Canola oil, for frying

1 egg

¼ pound (1 stick) unsalted butter

1 garlic clove, minced

1 tablespoon minced pickled jalapeños

1½ cups hot sauce (I recommend Crystal)

1 celery head, cut into matchsticks

*It's really cool to **find inspiration by seeing something from a new perspective,** and that's how this recipe came about. Through my affiliation with Nabisco, I was asked to make some original recipes using Ritz crackers for the Super Bowl. I didn't want to go with the usual idea of what you can do with cheese and crackers—**I had to go big.** Now, one of my favorite tailgate foods is Buffalo wings . . . question was, how to combine them? Ahaaa . . . this is my solution.*

**1.** In a meat grinder with a medium die, grind the chicken thighs to "chili grind," or have your butcher do it for you. In a large bowl, combine the chicken, 1½ cups of the Ritz crackers, the black pepper, paprika, basil, celery salt, cumin, white pepper, half the cayenne pepper, and 1 cup of the blue cheese. Mix well to incorporate. Cover and refrigerate for at least 4 hours and up to 24 hours.

**2.** Preheat the oven to 275°F. Pour 2 inches of canola oil into a large, deep skillet and heat the oil to 350°F over medium-high heat. Set a cooling rack over a baking sheet.

**3.** Form the chicken mixture into walnut-size balls and set them aside on a plate. Beat the egg in a shallow bowl and place the remaining 1½ cups crackers in another bowl. Dip each ball in the egg and then roll it in the crackers, covering it thoroughly. Add the balls to the hot oil (in batches so as not to crowd them) and fry until golden brown, about 2 minutes. They cook very quickly, so working with a few at a time will help. As they finish cooking, place the balls on the rack over the baking sheet. When all the balls are fried, place the baking sheet in the oven and bake for 10 minutes.

**4.** Meanwhile, in a small saucepan over low heat, melt the butter. Add the garlic and jalapeños and cook 2 minutes. Stir in the hot sauce and keep warm over low heat.

**5.** To serve, drizzle the hot sauce over the Buffalo balls or serve it as a dip on the side. Celery sticks and the remaining blue cheese make a cooling addition.

# Louisiana BBQ Shrimp

### ⮔ SERVES 4 TO 6 ⮔

½ pound (2 sticks) unsalted butter, cold

¼ cup minced onion

1 tablespoon chopped garlic

½ teaspoon ground cumin

1 teaspoon dried thyme

1 teaspoon dried basil

½ teaspoon cayenne pepper

1 teaspoon paprika

1 pound shrimp (21/25 count), peeled (leave tail on) and deveined

One 12-ounce bottle Abita beer or other light-style Pilsner

1 cup seafood stock* (I recommend Kitchen Basics)

Kosher salt

Freshly ground black pepper

Fresh lemon juice

Hot sauce

¼ cup thinly sliced green onions

*Or simmer the shrimp shells with ¾ cup water and ¾ cup clam juice until reduced to 1 cup–about 5 to 10 minutes. Strain.*

*My good friend Dr. Jerry Chesser and I got to know each other while sitting on the board of directors for the California Restaurant Association's Educational Foundation. Jerry's a good ol' Southern chef who's incredibly knowledgeable about food in every facet, and we became the best of buddies. So I had him over to dinner, or should I say to cook, and it turned into a kitchen melee. We were in there cooking it up, going after it, and (this is not a joke)* **by the time we were done there was not a single clean pot or pan left** *(and I have a lot of pots and pans). It got to the point that Lori had to get out the beach towels and lay things out to dry on the counters. It probably took her two hours. So Lori said to Jerry, "I loved it—the food was fantastic—but* **you're not allowed to come back and cook with Guy.**" *Ha ha . . . (Jerry, she was just kidding. Come back soon.)*

**The meal really was incredible,** *and one of the dishes was this Louisiana BBQ shrimp. Everybody wants it to be on the grill, but it's not!*

**1.** Preheat the oven to 350°F.

**2.** In a medium saucepan, melt half the butter over medium heat. Add the onion and cook for 3 minutes or until just translucent. Stir in the garlic, cumin, thyme, basil, cayenne, and paprika and cook for 2 minutes, taking care not to burn the garlic.

**3.** Arrange the shrimp in one layer in a 9 by 13-inch baking pan. Pour the butter over the shrimp. Bake for 4 to 5 minutes or until the shrimp are almost (three-quarters of the way) cooked through. (Do not overcook or you'll have rubbery shrimp.)

**4.** Use a slotted spoon to transfer the shrimp to a warm plate, cover, and keep warm. Transfer the liquid to a saucepan and add the beer and seafood stock. Cook over high heat until the liquid is reduced to one-third the original amount.

**5.** Reduce the heat to medium. Cut the remaining cold butter into pats and whisk it in, 2 or 3 pats at a time, until the mixture is slightly thick and glossy. Remove the sauce from the heat and adjust the seasoning with salt, pepper, lemon juice, and hot sauce to taste. Arrange the shrimp, 4 to 6 per plate, be generous with the sauce, and garnish with green onions.

# Fire-Roasted Shrimp Cocktail

## ⮞ SERVES 12 ⮜

### SHRIMP

1 tablespoon dried oregano

1 tablespoon cumin seeds

1 garlic clove, crushed

½ teaspoon coarse sea salt

½ teaspoon freshly cracked black pepper

1 tablespoon olive oil

1 teaspoon hot sauce

1 pound shrimp (21/25 count), peeled, deveined, and butterflied

### COCKTAIL MIXTURE

1½ cups Grilled Ketchup (page 364) or regular ketchup

12 ounces orange soda

⅓ cup fresh lime juice

3 tablespoons hot sauce

1 English cucumber, peeled and cut into ½-inch dice (about 2 cups)

2 avocados, pitted, peeled, and cut into ½-inch dice

1 cup ½-inch-diced red onion

3 tablespoons chopped cilantro

Lime and saltine crackers for garnish

*Sometimes a regional food has been done one way for so long that no one thinks about its potential.* In Northern California, your typical "Mexican" shrimp cocktail is pulled together with bottled ketchup, cucumber, and avocado. But my style is **never to settle for processed** when it's worth doing something from scratch, as it can have a profound impact on the flavor and quality of the overall dish. **Here the idea was to take something I love and make it better**, so I tossed out the processed ketchup. And I love shrimp, but I'm not a boiled shrimp kinda guy—I like the texture that grilling or sautéing gives them. This is my spin, and it's proved to be pretty successful, even among the loyalists.

**1. For the shrimp,** mix all the ingredients except the shrimp in a resealable 1-gallon plastic bag. Add the shrimp and marinate in the refrigerator for at least 1 hour or up to 6 hours.

**2.** Preheat the grill to medium-high. Remove the shrimp from the marinade and drain well. Discard the marinade. Grill the shrimp until opaque, about 3 to 5 minutes. Remove from the heat and refrigerate immediately.

**3. For the cocktail mixture,** combine the ketchup, soda, lime juice, and hot sauce in a large bowl and mix until blended. Gently mix in the cucumber, avocado, onion, and cilantro.

**4.** Cut each shrimp into 4 pieces (in half, then each half in half). Stir the shrimp into the cocktail mixture.

**5.** Serve in martini glasses with slices of lime and saltine crackers.

A view from the high dive at the Flavortown pool!

# Bacon-Jalapeño Duck

### ⟿ MAKES 16 PIECES, TO SERVE 4 TO 6 ⟿

**BRINE**

2 cups water

2 tablespoons kosher salt

2 tablespoons chopped chipotle pepper in adobo

5 black peppercorns

2 garlic cloves, smashed

One 2-inch piece ginger, peeled and smashed

2 boneless, skin-on duck breast halves (8 to 12 ounces total)

**DUCK**

8 to 10 thick-cut applewood-smoked bacon slices

16 pickled jalapeño rings

Dipping Sauce (recipe follows)

*Special Equipment:* **Four 8-inch long bamboo skewers**

*I think I wasn't a big fan of duck as a kid because I ate too many wild ducks that still had shotgun pellets in them. But farm-raised is right on. And hey,* **when you wrap bacon around it, you can't go wrong.** *Give it a shot (without the pellets, of course).*

**1.** In a resealable 1-gallon plastic bag, combine all the brine ingredients except the duck and mix until the salt is dissolved. Add the duck and refrigerate for 1 to 2 hours or up to 8 hours.

**2.** Remove the duck and pat it dry. Remove the skin (fatty layer) and silverskin from the duck breast. Discard the silverskin. Slice the duck into 1½ by 1½-inch pieces (you need 16) and cut the skin into 2-inch pieces, and set aside.

**3.** In a skillet over medium-high heat, cook the bacon until cooked halfway, about 3 minutes. Reserve the bacon fat. Cut the strips in half crosswise.

**4. To assemble the duck skewers,** place a jalapeño ring on top of a piece of duck, wrap with a piece of the bacon, and spear on a skewer at the seam of the bacon. Repeat using 4 duck pieces per skewer ½-inch apart.

**5.** In a heavy-bottomed 12-inch skillet over medium-high heat, cook the duck skin, stirring, until the fat has rendered completely, 10 to 15 minutes. Remove and discard the duck skin pieces. (Add reserved bacon fat if more fat is needed.)

**6.** Put the skewers in the pan and cook on both sides, 3 to 4 minutes per side or until the bacon is crisp. Transfer to a platter and baste with some of the dipping sauce to coat. Serve with additional dipping sauce drizzled over the top and on the side.

# Dipping Sauce

**MAKES 1 CUP**

**1.** In a small saucepan over medium heat, heat the canola oil. Add the ginger and chili flakes and stir for 1 minute. Add the remaining ingredients, heat through, and set aside until needed.

1 teaspoon canola oil

1 tablespoon minced ginger

½ teaspoon red chili flakes

1 teaspoon minced chipotle pepper in adobo

¾ cup plum sauce

1 tablespoon Sweet Soy Sauce (page 85)

1 tablespoon rice vinegar

# Rojo Onion Rings

## ⤙ SERVES 4 ⤚

1 quart canola oil

¾ cup hot sauce
(I recommend sriracha)

1 tablespoon granulated garlic

1⅓ cups ketchup

1 cup buttermilk

½ cup all-purpose flour

4 cups panko bread crumbs

2 large sweet onions,
preferably Vidalia, Walla Walla,
or Maui, cut ⅜-inch thick and
separated into rings, very
center cores discarded

1 teaspoon fine sea salt

*These bad boys have been **rockin' the menu at Johnny Garlic's and Tex Wasabi's.** Hope they do the same for you at your casa!*

**1.** In a heavy-bottomed skillet or deep fryer, heat the oil to 360°F. Line a plate with paper towels and have a baking sheet handy.

**2.** In a shallow bowl, combine the hot sauce, garlic, ketchup, and 2 teaspoons of water until blended. Place the buttermilk, flour, and panko into three separate bowls and place them in this work order: buttermilk, flour, sriracha mixture, panko.

**3.** Soak the onion rings in the buttermilk for at least 30 minutes. Dip the onion rings into the flour, then the sriracha mixture, and finish them with the panko and set them aside on the baking sheet as you finish. Let them set up for 10 to 20 minutes in the refrigerator before frying. (The batter sticks better that way!)

**4.** Working in batches, deep-fry the onion rings for about 3 minutes or until starting to brown. Turn as needed. As you finish, transfer them to the paper-towel-lined plate and sprinkle with sea salt. Serve immediately.

**Gotta go for da Rojo!**

# Jimmy's Favorite Garlic Bread

*I named this one after one of my first* Guy's Big Bite *producers, Jimmy Zankel.* **I made it, he loved it, and it was named!** *You're gonna dig this.*

**1.** Preheat the oven to 350°F.

**2. For the garlic butter,** slice the tops off the garlic heads and place them cut side up on a piece of foil. Drizzle with olive oil and season with salt and pepper. Enclose the garlic completely and roast for 1 hour or until soft. Set aside to cool.

**3.** Squeeze the roasted garlic cloves into medium mixing bowl. Add the remaining ingredients through the ¼ cup grated Parmesan cheese and combine thoroughly. Refrigerate until ready to use.

**4.** When you're ready to prepare the garlic bread, preheat the oven to 400°F.

**5.** Spread the garlic butter generously over each half of the bread and set the bread on a baking sheet. Bake until light golden brown, 8 to 12 minutes.

**6.** Top with basil, tomatoes, and the remaining 1½ tablespoons Parmesan. Cut into 2-inch slices and serve.

## GARLIC BUTTER

2 garlic heads

Olive oil

Salt and freshly ground black pepper

½ pound (2 sticks) unsalted butter, at room temperature

½ cup mayonnaise

Pinch paprika

1 tablespoon Italian seasoning

1 tablespoon chopped flat-leaf parsley

1 teaspoon ground sea salt

1 teaspoon red chili flakes

¼ cup grated Parmesan cheese, plus 1½ tablespoons for sprinkling

One 24-inch sourdough bread loaf, split in half

Basil leaves

½ chopped sun-dried tomatoes

1½ tablespoons grated Parmesan cheese

# Shrimp-n-Potato Spinach Tostados

## TOSTADAS

Two 10-ounce packages frozen spinach, thawed

1 tablespoon finely diced red bell pepper

1 teaspoon finely diced seeded serrano pepper

4 garlic cloves, minced

2 large eggs

⅓ cup panko bread crumbs

⅓ cup grated Parmesan cheese

1 teaspoon freshly cracked black pepper

½ teaspoon ground sea salt, plus more for sprinkling

¼ teaspoon cayenne pepper

3 tablespoons olive oil

## TOPPING

2 tablespoons sour cream

½ teaspoon grated lime zest

2 medium russet potatoes (about 1 pound)

*(cont.)*

*In memory of the time my parents freaked out all my friends with spinach pasta back in '78, I am makin' some tostadas outta spinach. (Pssst . . . don't tell anyone I'm making healthy alternatives. . . . )*

**1.** Preheat the oven to 250°F.

**2. To make the tostadas,** place the spinach in a colander and press down to remove as much water as possible. Transfer the spinach to a double layer of paper towels and press and squeeze to remove any remaining water. Chop the spinach and combine it in a medium bowl with the remaining tostada ingredients except the olive oil. The mixture should be very well combined and moist but not wet.

**3.** Line a baking sheet with parchment paper. Divide the mixture into 12 equal portions and form into flat patties about 3 inches in diameter and ¼-inch thick, or as thin as you can without the patties breaking apart. Arrange the patties on the baking sheet and press down until very firm. This can be done ahead, but be sure to refrigerate the patties.

**4.** In a large nonstick skillet over medium-high heat, heat the oil. Working in batches, cook the patties about 2 minutes on one side, and then gently flip them and cook the other side for 1 to 2 minutes. They will be slightly browned. Place them on a paper-towel-lined baking sheet, sprinkle with a pinch of salt, and hold in the warm oven. Set the skillet aside, but do not wash it yet!

**5.** In a small bowl, combine the sour cream and lime zest.

**6.** Peel the potatoes and put them in a saucepan of salted water. Bring to a boil and cook until just fork tender. Drain and cut into ½-inch dice.

**7.** In the same pan the patties were cooked in, reheat the oil over medium-high heat. Add the shallot and cook until translucent, about 2 minutes. Add in the tomatoes, potatoes, and capers and stir to combine. Add the shrimp and stock and cook until shrimp turn pink, 3 to 4 minutes. Stir in the pepper and the parsley and remove from the heat.

**8.** Remove the patties from the oven and transfer them to a serving platter. Portion the shrimp mixture on each patty, sprinkle with ½ teaspoon feta, top with a drizzle of the sour cream mixture, and serve immediately.

**1 tablespoon finely diced shallot**

**1½ cups seeded and diced Roma tomatoes**

**2 tablespoons drained capers**

**½ pound (21/25 count) shrimp, peeled, deveined, and cut into ½-inch pieces**

**¼ cup Chicken Stock (page 362) or low-sodium store-bought**

**1 teaspoon freshly cracked black pepper**

**1 tablespoon chopped flat-leaf parsley**

**2 tablespoons finely crumbled feta cheese**

# Garlic-Onion Tortilla Stack

### ⊱ SERVES 6 TO 8 ⊰

⅔ cup canola oil

4 cups small-diced red onion
(about 2 pounds)

3 tablespoons unsalted butter

2 tablespoons sugar

¾ cup roasted garlic
(see page 71)

5 tablespoons grated
Parmesan cheese

¼ cup mayonnaise

3 tablespoons minced cilantro

Kosher salt and freshly ground
black pepper

Twelve 8-inch flour tortillas

2 tablespoons balsamic vinegar

*When we learned Lori was pregnant with Hunter, we went over to my parents' house to tell them the news. As we arrived, my mom said, "You have to try this—it's called an onion cake." **I responded, "I don't like cake, I don't think I'll like it."** I'd had onion tarts in France and don't care so much for flaky pastry tart shells. I prefer more texture and chew. But my mom insisted, so we ate it. **Without question, it was great.** I thought, If I add garlic, this is really something that I'd like to have on the menu when I open my restaurant. **It sounded odd, but looked and tasted great.** The Onion Stack turned out to be one of the number-one-selling appetizer at Johnny Garlic's.*

*This recipe isn't difficult, but be sure to allow yourself enough time.*

**1.** In a large skillet over medium heat, heat the oil. Add the onion and cook for 5 minutes, stirring regularly, until lightly browned but not overly dark. Add the butter and sugar and cook until the onion has thoroughly browned, about 20 to 25 minutes. Remove from the heat, transfer to a medium bowl, and set aside to cool.

**2.** Add the garlic, Parmesan, mayonnaise, cilantro, and salt and pepper to taste and stir to combine. Cover and refrigerate for at least 4 hours.

**3.** Reserve one-third of the mixture in the refrigerator to use to make the dipping sauce. Evenly spread the remaining mixture on the top of 11 of the tortillas. Stack the tortillas on top of one another and top with the remaining tortilla. Wrap the tortilla stack in plastic wrap and refrigerate for 12 to 24 hours to set up.

**4.** Preheat a grill to medium. Cut the stack into 16 wedges. Using tongs, grill each wedge on all sides until it is warmed and grill marks appear.

**5.** Mix the reserved onion mixture with the balsamic vinegar to make a dipping sauce; season to taste.

**6.** Serve the wedges with the dipping sauce.

# Bacon-Wrapped Shrimp with Chipotle BBQ Sauce

SERVES 4 TO 6

10 bacon slices, cut in half crosswise

20 shrimp (21/25 count), peeled (leave tail on) and deveined

**SAUCE**

½ cup my Kansas City BBQ sauce

¼ cup canola oil

3 tablespoons fresh lemon juice

1 tablespoon Dijon mustard

1 chipotle pepper, diced, plus 2 tablespoons adobo sauce

½ teaspoon red chili flakes

¼ teaspoon cayenne pepper

¼ teaspoon freshly ground black pepper

*Special Equipment:* Five (10- to 12-inch) bamboo skewers

*This recipe's a grilling dream machine.* Par-cooked bacon bastes the shrimp as it cooks; then the pair get their sweet-salty characteristics full throttled with some spicy chipotle BBQ sauce. **Someone should write a song about this.**

**1.** Soak the skewers in water for 30 minutes, to keep them from burning during grilling. Preheat the grill to medium.

**2.** In a large skillet, cook the bacon halfway to crispy but still pliable. Set aside on paper towels to cool.

**3.** Wrap a piece of bacon around each shrimp and skewer the shrimp through the point where the bacon ends meet, to keep it intact. Spear 4 shrimp per skewer.

**4.** Combine all the sauce ingredients in a blender and puree. Divide the sauce in half, one batch for basting and one batch for dipping.

**5.** Grill the shrimp skewers until the shrimp begin to turn pink, about 5 minutes. Then baste with the sauce until the shrimp are cooked through, about 6 to 8 minutes in all. Serve the shrimp with the reserved sauce on the side.

Grillin' and thrillin'.

# Sangria-Glazed Shrimp

## SERVES 4 TO 6

*The movie trailer voiceover to this recipe might be: "The dude that brought you Bloody Mary Flank Steak and the ever-popular mojito chicken now blows it up with Sangria-Glazed Shrimp—opening tonight in a kitchen near you!"*

**1. For the glaze,** in a small saucepan, combine all the ingredients except the cornstarch. Simmer over medium-high heat and reduce to about 1 cup of rich red, syrupy liquid, about 20 minutes.

**2.** In a small bowl, whisk the cornstarch and 1½ tablespoons water. Whisk the cornstarch mixture into the hot wine mixture. Turn the heat to low and simmer until thickened, about 5 minutes or until it coats the back of a spoon. Keep warm.

**3. For the shrimp,** in a medium skillet over medium heat, melt the butter. Add the onion, pepper, and apple and cook until tender but not browned, about 3 minutes. Remove from the pan and keep warm.

**4.** Heat the canola oil in the same pan. Season the shrimp with the paprika. Add the garlic and shrimp to the pan and cook until the shrimp turn pink, about 2 minutes per side. Cook in batches as needed so that the pan isn't crowded and the shrimp get good color.

**5.** To serve, pour the sauce onto a rimmed platter and arrange the shrimp over the sauce. Scatter the apple mixture on top. Garnish with mint. Serve with rice, if desired.

### GLAZE

⅔ bottle full-bodied red wine (Burgundy or Zinfandel; about 2¼ cups)

¼ cup apple juice

¼ cup orange juice

¼ cup dry sherry

2 tablespoons dark brown sugar

2 tablespoons honey

1½ teaspoons cornstarch

### SHRIMP

1 tablespoon unsalted butter

½ cup diced red onion

1 red bell pepper, diced

1 Granny Smith apple, cored and diced (do not peel)

1 tablespoon canola oil

1 pound shrimp (21/25 count), peeled (leave tail on) and deveined

1 teaspoon paprika

1 tablespoon minced garlic

Mint sprigs, for garnish

Cooked rice, for serving (optional)

# Chicken Lettuce Cups

2¼ cups canola oil

5 wonton wrappers

1 iceberg lettuce head

1 teaspoon minced ginger

⅓ cup ¼-inch-diced red onion (about ½ small onion)

⅓ cup ¼-inch-diced red bell pepper (about ¼ pepper)

⅓ cup ¼-inch-diced carrot (about ½ medium carrot)

⅓ cup ¼-inch-diced celery (about ½ celery stalk)

⅓ cup ¼-inch-diced sugar snap peas (about 10 peas)

1 teaspoon minced garlic

½ cup sliced stemmed shiitake mushrooms

⅓ cup mung bean sprouts, cut into 1-inch pieces

1 pound boneless, skinless chicken thighs, ½-inch diced

Plum Sesame Sambal Sauce (recipe follows)

2 tablespoons sliced green onion

1 tablespoon minced unsalted peanuts

½ teaspoon black sesame seeds

*I was making lettuce cups way before we realized they could be **an alternative to a bun for low-carb fans.** I had my fair share of them, and even the bad ones were not so bad, but I wanted my own great version, and this was it. I do a lot of recipe testing over a propane stove up at our cabin in Northern California. Just imagine the scene—there's no electricity or running water, and everyone is just sitting around eating lettuce cups. . . . Crazy. By the way, **these are a big hit at Tex Wasabi's!***

**1.** In a heavy saucepan, heat 2 cups canola oil to 350°F over medium heat, or until a bit of wonton wrapper sizzles when added. Add the wonton wrappers and fry for about 35 seconds, until lightly browned. Drain on a paper-towel-lined plate. Crush the wrappers and set aside.

**2.** Cut the lettuce in half from top to bottom, remove the core, and carefully remove the 10 nicest leaves. Wash the lettuce in cold water and pat dry with paper towels. Stack the lettuce cups on a plate and refrigerate.

**3.** In a medium wok or large skillet over high heat, add 2 tablespoons canola oil. When the oil is hot, add the ginger, onion, and bell pepper. Cook 3 minutes, then add the carrot and celery and cook 2 minutes. Add the snap peas, garlic, shiitake mushrooms, and mung bean sprouts and cook 2 minutes more. Remove the vegetables from the wok and set aside. Add the remaining 2 tablespoons of oil to the wok. When the oil is hot, add the chicken and cook, constantly stirring, until cooked through, about 6 to 8 minutes. Return the vegetables to the wok with the chicken, then immediately add ¼ cup of the Plum Sesame Sambal Sauce and stir, scraping up any browned bits. Cook for 30 seconds, or until the sauce thickens.

**4.** Transfer the chicken and vegetable mixture to a serving bowl and top with the green onion, crushed wontons, peanuts, and sesame seeds.

**5.** Serve by spooning chicken mixture into lettuce cups. Serve the remaining Plum Sesame Sambal Sauce alongside. Unused portion will last refrigerated for 14 days.

## Plum Sesame Sambal Sauce

**MAKES ¾ CUP**

**1.** Combine all the ingredients in a jar with a lid. Shake well before serving.

**PLUM SESAME SAMBAL SAUCE**

1 teaspoon toasted sesame seeds*

½ cup soy sauce

1 tablespoon minced garlic

1 tablespoon minced ginger

1 tablespoon chili-garlic sauce

1 tablespoon plum sauce

2 tablespoons rice vinegar

1 tablespoon hoisin sauce

1 teaspoon minced cilantro

¼ teaspoon sesame oil

1 tablespoon mirin (sweetened rice wine)

*To toast sesame seeds, shake them in a skillet over medium-high heat until golden brown.*

# Rhode Island Calamari

## ⤙ SERVES 4 ⤚

¾ pound cleaned calamari

1 quart canola oil

½ cup olive oil

¼ pound (1 stick) unsalted butter

½ cup chopped red onion

1 cup sliced drained pepperoncini

1 teaspoon red chili flakes

¼ cup minced garlic

½ cup white wine

¼ cup clam juice

One 12- to 14-inch sourdough bread loaf

½ teaspoon seasoned cornstarch

2 cups all-purpose flour

1 tablespoon seasoned salt

½ teaspoon cayenne pepper

⅓ cup seeded, diced Roma tomatoes

⅓ cup chopped green onion

*Lori and I had been married about five years when we went to this packed old-school restaurant in her home state of Rhode Island. As we were seated in a patent leather booth, a guy walked up and said, **"Calamarialamama?" I responded, "What?" He stated, "Two calamarialamamas,"** and just walked away. I looked at Lori like he must be from another planet. So the guy came back with two big bowls of fried calamari in a pepperoncini sauce. **I looked at him and said, "I didn't order this." Then I ate both bowls** . . . I showed him. . . .*

**1.** Cut the calamari tubes into ¼-inch-thick slices; leave the tentacles intact. Refrigerate until you're ready to cook. In a deep pot, heat the canola oil over medium heat to 350°F. Preheat the oven to 350°F.

**2.** Meanwhile, in a large skillet over high heat, combine the olive oil and butter. And the red onion and cook about 5 minutes, then add the pepperoncini and chili flakes and cook about 2 minutes. Add the garlic and cook until tender, about 1 minute. Add the wine, stir, and cook until slightly reduced, 4 to 6 minutes. Stir in the clam juice and lower the heat to a simmer for 5 minutes. Keep warm.

**3.** Slice off the top of the bread, core out the middle, and toast the bread bowl lightly in the oven. Keep warm.

**4.** In a medium bowl, mix the cornstarch, flour, seasoned salt, and cayenne.

**5.** Toss the calamari in the flour mixture and shake off the excess. Fry the calamari in the canola oil until golden brown and crispy, about 3 minutes, working in batches to give the calamari room to cook. Drain briefly on paper towels. Toss the fried calamari with the sauce and pour it into the toasted bread bowl. Garnish with the tomatoes and green onion and serve. . . . And yes, eat that bowl!!!

# Ahi Won Tacos

## ⤙ SERVES 4 ⤚

### TACOS

1 cup canola oil

16 round potsticker skins or wonton wrappers

½ pound sashimi-grade ahi tuna, ¼-inch diced

1 cup Mango-Jicama Salsa (recipe follows)

½ cup Sweet Soy Sauce (recipe follows)

1 cup Wasabi Cream (recipe follows)

¾ pound pea shoots, heavy stems removed

¼ cup eel sauce

### MANGO-JICAMA SALSA

1 cup ¼-inch-cubed mango

¼ cup ¼-inch-diced jicama

¼ cup ¼-inch-diced red onion

1 tablespoon minced cilantro

1 tablespoon sweet chili sauce

1 teaspoon seeded, finely diced jalapeño

¼ teaspoon fine sea salt

*I first created Ahi Won Tostadas during my cooking adventure with Sammy Hagar* (see page 129). *We were cooking Red Rocker Chicken that day at the restaurant, and I was thinking about having eaten sashimi and tacos down in Cabo, so I started pulling these things together into one dish.*

Just like Sammy, these rock!

1. In a deep-fryer or heavy-bottomed pot, heat the canola oil to 350°F. Fold the potsticker skins to create a taco shape. Using tongs, holding one side, fry one at a time until crispy, 7 to 10 seconds per side, turning once. Set aside on paper towels to cool.

2. In a small bowl, gently toss the tuna, Mango-Jicama Salsa, and Sweet Soy Sauce. Fill the taco shells with the tuna mixture and top with a drizzle of the Wasabi Cream.

3. To serve, arrange 4 tacos per serving over a bed of the pea shoots and drizzle the whole plate with the eel sauce.

## Mango-Jicama Salsa

**MAKES 1½ CUPS**

1. In a small bowl, gently combine all the ingredients. Allow the flavors to marry for 20 minutes before serving.

## Sweet Soy Sauce

**MAKES 1 CUP**

1. Whisk all ingredients in a small bowl until well combined. Refrigerate for 15 minutes, or until you are ready to serve.

## Wasabi Cream

**MAKES 1¼ CUPS**

1. Combine all the ingredients in a mixer fitted with a paddle. Beat on high until the mixture forms stiff peaks, about 5 minutes. This is best if served immediately after making, but refrigerate until needed if necessary.

**SWEET SOY SAUCE**

1 cup soy sauce

2 tablespoons sesame oil

1 teaspoon minced garlic

1 teaspoon minced ginger

½ teaspoon red chili flakes

¼ teaspoon wasabi powder

**WASABI CREAM**

1 cup heavy cream

2 tablespoons sour cream

2 tablespoons wasabi powder

2 tablespoons rice vinegar

2 tablespoons sugar

1 teaspoon fresh lemon juice

¼ teaspoon fine sea salt

# Chicken-Avocado Egg Rolls

**SERVES 12**

2 tablespoons canola oil

½ cup finely minced red onion

¼ cup finely minced red bell pepper

2 tablespoons minced ginger

1 tablespoon minced garlic

¼ cup sliced bamboo shoots

¼ cup finely chopped celery

2 cups ½-inch-diced boneless, skinless chicken breast (about 1¼ pounds)

¼ cup soy sauce

Kosher salt and freshly ground black pepper

1 cup thinly shredded green cabbage

½ cup shredded carrots

1 quart canola or rice bran oil, plus more as needed

15 egg roll wrappers (3 extra for mistakes)

2 Hass avocados, pitted, peeled, and sliced into 12 pieces each

1 egg

1 tablespoon milk

Sweet chili sauce, for dipping

*I've always been an egg roll junkie, and I don't believe there are very many good frozen egg rolls; they have to be made fresh. So when I began creating egg roll recipes, I thought, **Why do they have to be stuffed only with traditional items?** I started popping different things into egg rolls and seeing how they came out—everything from cheese steak to sauerkraut.*

*Avocado becomes incredibly soft when cooked, almost like vegetable butter, so when I threw it in with cabbage and carrot, it produced a great creamy texture that you don't necessarily expect (but are happy to find) in an egg roll. I'm kinda like the Christopher Columbus of egg rolls! Ha ha.*

**1.** In a skillet over high heat, heat the 2 tablespoons canola oil. Cook the onion and bell pepper for 2 minutes or until the onion is translucent. Add the ginger, garlic, bamboo shoots, celery, and chicken, reduce the heat to medium-high, and cook for 5 minutes, stirring occasionally. Add the soy sauce, stir well, and set aside to cool. Season to taste with salt and pepper.

**2.** In a large bowl, combine the cabbage, carrots, and the warm chicken mixture.

**3.** In a medium saucepan, heat the 1 quart canola or rice bran oil to 350°F. The oil needs to be deep enough to keep the egg rolls from touching the bottom of the pan; add more oil if needed. Prepare a baking sheet with a cooling rack on top.

**4. To create the egg rolls,** lay an egg roll wrapper on your work surface with one corner facing you. Place about ⅓ cup of the mixture on the wrapper and place 2 pieces of avocado on top. Whisk together the egg and milk for the egg wash. Fold the top corner down over the filling, then fold in the two

In a large bowl, combine the cabbage, carrots, and chicken mixture.

Lay an egg roll wrapper with one corner facing you. Place about 1/3 cup of the mixture on the wrapper and place 2 pieces of avocado on top.

Fold the top corner over the mixture, then fold one of the side corners over the mixture.

Brush some of the egg wash on the top corner.

Roll the egg roll upward firmly, taking care not to tear the wrapper.

Each egg roll should be 4 to 5 inches long.

Dredge each egg roll in the egg wash, then fry three at a time . . .

. . . until golden brown.

All right, who took a bite?

side corners over the filling. Brush some of the egg wash on the top corner. Roll the egg roll upward firmly, taking care not to tear the wrapper. Each egg roll should be 4 to 5 inches long. Repeat with the remaining ingredients.

**5.** Dredge each egg roll in the egg wash, allowing the excess to drip off. Fry the egg rolls, 3 at a time, until golden brown, about 3 to 4 minutes. Drain on the cooling rack. Slice the egg rolls on the diagonal. Serve with sweet chili sauce.

# Ginger Pork Potstickers

6 ounces medium grind ground pork

¼ cup finely diced white onion

2 tablespoons minced ginger

1 tablespoon minced garlic, plus more for garnish

¼ cup thinly sliced green onion, plus more for garnish

1 teaspoon soy sauce

¼ teaspoon sesame oil

Pinch salt and freshly ground black pepper

12 to 18 round wonton wrappers or potsticker skins

1 egg, beaten

1 teaspoon canola oil

Ponzu or soy sauce, for dipping

*Long before I was on Food Network, I helped a Japanese restaurant owner with her business, and she wanted to pay me. I told her I didn't want any money, but that I'd like **to learn firsthand how to make some traditional Japanese dishes**. She said she didn't know because she was raised in the States, but she introduced me to a friend who did. Her friend, who spoke very limited English, came over and we proceeded to make potstickers together.*

*I had a million things going on—Hunter was asking me questions, and the phone was ringing off the hook—and she was waiting there patiently. Finally she looked at me and explained that **when I'm cooking Japanese food, I need to dedicate myself to making the food at a focused pace**. She very gently and diligently showed me her method. It was killing me. I thought, Let's get the food processor and chop that ginger! But that wasn't how it was done. Working with her gave me a lot of perspective about how food is respected in Japan. **It was a very calming experience**, and that's part of what makes Japanese food work and come together so beautifully.*

**1.** In a medium sauté pan over medium heat, heat the canola oil. Add the pork, white onion, ginger, and garlic and sauté until the pork is cooked, about 3 minutes. Add the ¼ cup of green onion, soy sauce, sesame oil, salt, and pepper, mix, and set aside to cool.

**2.** In a medium stockpot, bring 2 quarts water to a boil over medium-high heat. Place a cooling rack over a baking sheet.

**3.** Place 1 tablespoon of the filling in the middle of a wonton wrapper. Brush the edges of the wrapper with the egg and fold it in half to create a half-moon shape, pinching the edges closed as you go. Repeat with the remaining wrappers.

**Place 1 tablespoon of the filling in the middle of a wonton wrapper. Brush the edges of the wrapper with egg.**

**Fold it in half to create a half-moon shape, pinching the edges closed as you go.**

**Place the potstickers in the boiling water for 1 minute.**

**Fry without moving them until the bottoms are browned, then flip to brown all over.**

**Plated.**

**4.** Using a slotted spoon, place the potstickers in the boiling water for 1 minute or until they float to the top. Remove and place the potstickers on the cooling rack.

**5.** When the potstickers have cooled completely, heat the canola oil in a large skillet over medium-high heat. Add the potstickers and cook without moving them until the bottoms are browned, 4 to 5 minutes. Carefully remove the potstickers with a spatula. Serve with ponzu or soy sauce and garnish with sliced green onion.

**Potsticker paradise!**

# Cilantro-Wrapped Shrimp with Spicy Pickled Pineapple

## MAKES 24 PIECES, TO SERVE 8

*I so dig these that I usually scarf down seven or eight before I tell everyone they're ready. It's the crunch of the sweet cilantro shrimp, countered by the pickled pineapple. (My mouth is watering just reading this!)*

**1.** In a medium skillet, heat the oil over medium-high heat. Add the jalapeño and onion and cook for 1 to 2 minutes, just until softened. Add the vinegar, pineapple, honey, lemon juice, and salt and pepper to taste and cook for 3 minutes. Chill for 1 hour in the refrigerator.

**2.** Pour 2 inches of canola oil into a large, heavy pot and heat it to 350°F over medium-high heat.

**3.** Season the shrimp with salt and pepper. In a small bowl, whisk the milk and eggs.

**4.** Dip a wonton wrapper in the milk mixture, then place 1 piece of shrimp in a corner of the wrapper. Add 2 whole leaves of cilantro and 2 pieces of red pepper and roll up the wrapper like a cigar. Fry until light brown, 1 to 2 minutes, working in batches as needed. Drain on paper towels and serve with the spicy pickled pineapple.

Pickled pineapple . . . get it?

### SPICY PICKLED PINEAPPLE

1 teaspoon olive oil

2 tablespoons minced seeded jalapeño

2 tablespoons finely diced white onion

6 tablespoons rice vinegar

1 cup drained crushed pineapple

2 tablespoons honey

2 tablespoons fresh lemon juice

Kosher salt and freshly ground black pepper

### CILANTRO SHRIMP

Canola oil, for frying

12 shrimp (21/25 count), cut lengthwise in half, shelled and tail removed

1 cup milk

2 eggs

24 square wonton wrappers

⅓ cup loosely packed cilantro leaves

1 red bell pepper, seeded and cut into 48 strips (12 strips per quarter pepper—micro-julienne)

# No Can Beato This Taquito

¼ cup olive oil

1 large red onion, diced

1 red bell pepper, seeded and cut in thin strips

2 jalapeños, seeded and diced

2 medium red potatoes, cut in ½-inch cubes

2 tablespoons minced garlic

2 pounds boneless, skinless chicken breasts, cut in 1-inch strips

1 tablespoon dried oregano

1 teaspoon ground cumin

Kosher salt and freshly ground black pepper

3 ounces tequila (your favorite)

Juice of 1 lime (3 tablespoons)

2 tablespoons minced cilantro

24 corn tortillas

Canola oil, for frying

Guacamole Sauce (recipe follows)

Tomatillo Salsa (recipe follows)

*Special Equipment:* Toothpicks

*On* Triple D, *I've seen taquitos made all across the country, and it's given me a good foundation as a fan and taquito creator myself. If you're going to take that jump and make them, I think that* **simply sticking ground beef in them is a waste of effort.** *If you're going to go to the trouble,* **make high-quality taquitos, with texture, character, and dignity!** *The name came out of joking around, but to me it's true—no one can beato these quality taquitos. Some may come close, but* **these, my friends, are damn good.**

**1.** In medium skillet over medium-high heat, put the olive oil, onion, red pepper, jalapeños, potatoes, garlic, and chicken. Cook, stirring occasionally, until chicken is cooked through and vegetables are soft, about 15 minutes. Add the oregano and cumin and season with salt and pepper to taste.

**2.** Add the tequila and lime juice, stir, and let simmer until liquid is almost evaporated, 3 to 4 minutes. Set aside to cool.

**3.** Shred the chicken with two forks and let cool again. Stir in the cilantro.

**4.** Wrap the tortillas in damp paper towels and microwave for 2 minutes to make them pliable. Place about 3 tablespoons of filling down the center of 1 tortilla and roll it tightly. Seal the taquito by gently weaving a toothpick like a needle through the seam side. Repeat with the remaining tortillas and filling.

**5.** In a large cast-iron skillet, heat ½ inch of canola oil to 350°F. Add the taquitos to the hot oil, seam side down, working in batches to make sure there's enough room for the taquitos to cook. Fry 2 minutes or until golden brown, then gently turn over and fry on the other side.

**6.** Remove the taquitos with tongs and drain on paper towels. Remove the toothpicks and serve the taquitos with guacamole sauce and salsa.

# Guacamole Sauce

**MAKES 2 CUPS**

**1.** Place all the ingredients in a blender and puree.

**2.** Refrigerate, covered. (Use within 2 hours.)

# Tomatillo Salsa

**MAKES ABOUT 3 CUPS**

**1.** Heat a grill to high.

**2.** Rub the tomatillos with olive oil and grill until browned all over.

**3.** Alternatively, broil on a sheet pan until blackened.

**4.** Place the tomatillos in a blender with the onion, diced tomato, garlic, cilantro, vinegar, hot sauce, and water and puree. Season with salt and pepper to taste and pour into a serving bowl. Top the salsa with the sour cream and chopped tomatoes.

## GUACAMOLE SAUCE

3 ripe Hass avocados, pitted and flesh scooped out

1 jalapeño, seeded and minced

¼ cup finely diced red onion

¼ cup seeded ¼-inch diced fresh tomato

½ cup of your favorite beer

¼ cup sour cream

Juice of 1 lime

¼ cup cilantro leaves

Kosher salt and freshly ground black pepper

## TOMATILLO SALSA

8 tomatillos (about 1½ pounds), husks removed

2 tablespoons olive oil

½ cup diced red onion

⅔ cup diced fresh tomato

1 peeled garlic clove, chopped

1 teaspoon chopped cilantro

1 tablespoon distilled white vinegar

2 tablespoons hot sauce (I recommend Tapatio)

¼ cup water

Kosher salt and freshly ground black pepper

2 tablespoons sour cream

½ tomato, chopped, for garnish

Soup to me is a bit like pizza. **When it's good it's really great, and when it's bad it's still kind of good.** For example, most kids ate Campbell's chicken soup. It is what it is, and it often holds a fond place in our memories.

But homemade chicken noodle soup with meat pulled off a freshly roasted chicken and chicken stock made from the bones, with some really nice pasta added at the correct time, is incomparable. **There's a lot that can make a soup great, and it starts with good ingredients.** But there's also the cooking method, the timing, the garnish, and the passion of the cook. Soup may not always get the respect it deserves, but I'm always looking for new recipes to try. It was my go-to comfort food growing up, from chili to chowder, broth to noodle soup, and **I still like it so much that I'll never turn it down.** I'll happily eat a piping hot bowl on a hot day.

# Good Pho You

## SOUP

2 pounds beef knuckle bones

2 pounds beef neck bones

2 pounds beef marrow bones

2½ pounds beef chuck, fat trimmed, cut into 2-inch pieces

2 yellow onions

One 4-inch piece ginger

⅓ cup fish sauce

2 tablespoons dark brown sugar

2 tablespoons coriander seeds

5 whole star anise

5 cloves

3 dried Thai chiles

1 cinnamon stick

8 black peppercorns

One 8-ounce package fresh rice sticks (noodles), 1/16-inch thick

## GARNISH

1 cup fresh bean sprouts

¼ cup thinly sliced green onion

1 serrano chile, seeded and minced

*(cont.)*

*I coulda given this recipe a million names. **"Go Pho It," "U Can't Pho Get-taboutit"** . . . but this name's the best. (Okay, so pho is actually pronounced closer to "fa"—but it's still fun.) **We're talking flavor, seasoning on point, and righteous veggies**. Enjoy, and it really is "good pho you"!*

**1.** Place the bones and chuck in a large stockpot and add water to cover. Bring to a boil over high heat and boil rapidly for 6 minutes.

**2.** Meanwhile, fill another large stockpot with 7 quarts cool water and bring to a boil over high heat.

**3.** When meat and bones have finished boiling, remove them with tongs and place them in the second stockpot. Bring the water back to a boil, then lower the heat to medium-low. Simmer, skimming off any foam that collects at the surface. Discard the first pot of boiling water.

**4.** While stock is simmering (about 15 minutes), place onions and ginger on a hot grill, skin intact. Over an open gas flame, or under a broiler, turn to char on all sides. When they are evenly charred, let them cool. Remove the skins. Rinse the onions and ginger well under running water, then roughly chop them. Add the onion, ginger, fish sauce, and brown sugar to the simmering beef stock. Let simmer 1 hour.

**5.** One spice at a time, toast the coriander, star anise, cloves, and Thai chiles in a small dry skillet over low heat until fragrant. Set each aside to cool.

**6.** Wrap the cinnamon, peppercorns, and toasted spices in a piece of cheesecloth and tie closed with kitchen twine. Add to the stock and simmer 1 hour longer.

¼ cup daikon radish matchsticks

¼ cup thinly sliced red onion

½ cup chopped loosely packed cilantro

¼ cup chopped loosely packed mint

¼ cup loosely packed Thai basil or regular basil

2 limes, cut into 8 wedges

Nuoc cham sauce (found in Asian markets), for serving

Sriracha sauce, for serving

Hoisin sauce, for serving

¼ pound beef sirloin (prime), shaved very thin across the grain (have your butcher do this)

**Special Equipment:**
Cheesecloth, kitchen twine

**7.** Transfer the chuck pieces to a medium bowl and let cool. Shred the meat with a fork. Remove and discard any sinew or fat. Set aside, covered with foil, to keep warm.

**8.** Strain the stock into a clean pot and discard the bones and solids (including the cheesecloth). Bring the strained stock back to a boil over medium-low heat.

**9.** Heat the soup bowls you will be using in a 200°F oven. Prepare the rice sticks (noodles) according to the package directions.

**10.** To serve the pho, assemble the sprouts, green onion, serrano, daikon, red onion, herbs, and limes and the three sauces in small dishes for guests to use as garnishes. Place ¾ cup rice sticks (cooked noodles) in a soup bowl and top with a thin slice of the raw sirloin and 1 cup of shredded beef. Carefully ladle 2 cups boiling hot broth over the rice sticks. (The boiling stock will cook the raw sirloin immediately.) Allow guests to garnish their pho as desired.

# Cheddar Trans-Porter Soup

➤ SERVES 6 ➤

*This isn't the chunky, clumpy, gloopy "did I just eat nacho cheese" soup. This is* ***big, warm flavor for any time of year***.

**1.** In a large Dutch oven over medium-high heat, melt the butter in the oil and cook the onion and celery until soft and transparent, about 5 minutes. Season with half the salt and black pepper. Add the carrots, red pepper, and jalapeño and cook until tender but still a little crisp, 5 to 7 minutes. Add the garlic and cook for 1 minute more. Stir in the chicken stock. Bring to a boil, reduce the heat to medium-low, and simmer for 15 minutes.

**2.** In a large bowl, toss the grated cheddar with the flour, dry mustard, and white pepper.

**3.** Blend the stock mixture well with a stick blender or transfer in batches to a blender and puree until smooth. Add the cheese mixture and blend again. Add the Worcestershire and beer. Return the soup to the pan over low heat and cook it at a low simmer for 20 minutes, stirring frequently.

**4.** Season to taste with the remaining salt and pepper. Serve with pretzels and beer!

1 tablespoon unsalted butter

1 tablespoon grapeseed or olive oil

1 cup diced sweet onion (about ½ large onion)

1 cup diced celery (about 4 stalks)

1½ tablespoons kosher salt

1½ tablespoons freshly cracked black pepper

1 cup diced carrot (about 2 medium)

1 cup diced red bell pepper (1 large)

2 tablespoons chopped, seeded jalapeño (1 large)

¼ cup chopped garlic (4 to 5 cloves)

8 cups Chicken Stock (preferably homemade, page 362, using Italian seasoning option, or low-sodium store-bought)

¾ pound cheddar cheese, grated (about 3¼ cups)

½ cup unbleached all-purpose flour

1 tablespoon dry mustard

½ teaspoon ground white pepper

1 tablespoon Worcestershire sauce

1½ to 2 cups porter-style beer

Pretzels and beer, for serving

# Grilled Chicken Tortellini Soup

### ～ SERVES 8 TO 10 ～

*Grill it, chop it, pull it, sauté it, and cook it in some stock.* **This bad boy is "stocked" full of flavor!**

**1.** Preheat a grill to medium-high.

**2.** Season the chicken pieces with salt, pepper, granulated garlic, and paprika. Grill the chicken until golden, about 15 minutes (do not worry about cooking it completely through; the chicken will simmer in the stock later). Grill the Roma tomatoes until they just start to blacken, 8 to 10 minutes.

**3.** Meanwhile, heat the stock in a large stockpot over medium-high heat. Add the chicken and tomatoes, bring to a boil, lower the heat to medium-low, and cook at a strong simmer for 20 minutes.

**4.** Remove chicken and tomatoes and set aside to cool. Skin and dice the tomatoes. Remove the skin, bones, and fat from the chicken and shred or chop the meat into bite-size pieces.

**5.** Heat a small skillet over medium-high heat and add the olive oil. When hot, add the leeks and cook until just tender, about 3 minutes. Add the shallots and cook for 2 minutes more. Add the leeks and shallots to the stock.

**6.** Return the chicken and tomatoes to the stock and add the beans, chard, and tortellini. Bring the soup to a low simmer over medium-low heat and simmer for 3 to 5 minutes, until the tortellini are cooked through and chard stems are tender. Season to taste with salt and pepper.

**7.** Serve garnished with parsley and Parmesan.

## CHICKEN AND TOMATOES

One 5-pound chicken, cut into 8 pieces (see page 186)

1 tablespoon kosher salt

1 tablespoon freshly ground black pepper

1 tablespoon paprika

1 tablespoon granulated garlic

4 Roma tomatoes (about ⅔ pound)

## SOUP

12 cups Chicken Stock (page 362, or low-sodium store-bought)

2 tablespoons olive oil

2 cups ¼-inch diced leeks (white and light green parts)

½ cup diced shallots

Two 14.5-ounce cans cannellini beans, drained and rinsed

4 loosely packed cups 1-inch-thick shredded Swiss chard

One 8-ounce package sausage-filled tortellini (frozen or fresh)

Kosher salt

Freshly cracked black pepper

¼ cup chopped flat-leaf parsley

¼ cup grated Parmesan cheese

# Chicken Pozole

### ～ SERVES 6 TO 8 ～

.04 ounce dried guajillo peppers (about 4), stemmed and seeded

½ cup boiling water

1 tablespoon canola oil

One 4- to 5-pound chicken, cut into parts (see page 186), insides reserved

1 tablespoon freshly cracked black pepper

1 tablespoon kosher salt

4 garlic cloves, smashed

1 large onion, cut in half

1 teaspoon red chili flakes

4 cups Chicken Stock (page 362; use Mexican option, if desired, or low-sodium store-bought)

6 cups water

2 large carrots, cut in half

2 celery stalks, trimmed and cut in half

One 28-ounce can hominy, drained and rinsed

1 tablespoon epazote or dried oregano, Mexican if possible

(cont.)

*As a kid, I spent a lot of time with a vegetarian family my family was close to, and **swore I'd never eat hominy again**. That is, until I had my buddy Gus's pozole at Old Mexico Restaurant in Santa Rosa. After that **I knew I had to make my own**. Dive in!*

**1.** In a small bowl, add the guajillo peppers and boiling water (love the guajillo pepper), weigh down, and soak for 1 hour.

**2.** In a large stockpot, heat the oil over medium-high heat. Season the chicken with salt and pepper. Add the chicken parts, including the neck, heart, and liver, browning them in batches about 5 minutes. Add the garlic, onion, and chili flakes and cook for 1 to 2 minutes longer. Add the chicken stock and scrape up the brown bits. Then add the water and chicken parts, carrots and celery. Lower the heat to medium and simmer, uncovered, for 30 minutes.

**3.** Transfer the chicken pieces with tongs to a plate to cool. (Leave the neck, heart, and liver in the stock.)

**4.** When the chicken is cool, use a fork to pull chicken meat away from the bones. Reserve the meat, discard the skin and fat, and return the bones to the stockpot. Simmer the bones in the stock for another 30 minutes.

**5.** Skim the foam and excess fat from the surface of the stock. Strain the stock and return it to the stockpot. Discard the solids.

**6.** Remove the guajillo peppers, reserving soaking liquid, and chop into ½-inch pieces. Add liquid and peppers to a blender and blend until smooth. Set the puree aside.

**7.** Puree half the hominy in the blender with 1 cup of the strained stock. Pour the pureed hominy back into the stock and add the whole hominy and epazote. Add the guajillo puree 2 tablespoons at a time, until desired heat is reached. Return to a simmer and simmer for 25 minutes.

**8.** Meanwhile, place the garnishes in decorative bowls or arrange them attractively on a large serving platter.

**9.** When ready to serve, shred or chop the chicken into bite-size pieces, discarding any sinew, and add it back to the stockpot. Adjust the seasonings to taste.

**10.** Serve the pozole in individual shallow bowls and allow guests to garnish as they please. Serve with tortilla chips.

**GARNISHES**

1½ cups thinly sliced green cabbage

1 cup ¼-inch-diced, seeded fresh tomato

¼ cup ¼-inch-diced red onion

½ cup loosely packed cilantro leaves

2 Hass avocados, pitted, peeled, and diced

¾ cup grated queso fresco

½ cup thinly sliced red radishes

2 limes, cut into wedges

⅓ cup chopped jalapeños (fresh or pickled)

Freshly fried tortilla chips, for serving

# Shrimp and Chicken Tom Kai Gai (Tom Korina Guy)

1 lemongrass stalk

8 cups Chicken Stock (homemade preferred, page 362, or low-sodium store-bought)

2 pounds boneless, skinless chicken breasts, cut into 1- by 2-inch pieces

2 cups sliced stemmed shiitake mushrooms

1 to 3 fresh red Thai chiles, seeded and minced

¼ cup grated ginger

One 13.5-ounce can coconut milk

2 tablespoons agave nectar

2 tablespoons fish sauce

¼ red bell pepper, seeded and sliced in ¼-inch strips

1 pound shrimp (21/25 count), peeled, deveined, and butterflied

⅓ cup fresh lime juice

¼ cup chopped cilantro

¼ cup sliced green onion

*(cont.)*

*Tom Kai Gai may be the official name of this soup, but I think **it stands for Tom (my manager), Korina (my culinary director), and Guy (me!)**. So it's gotta be good.*

**1.** Trim the bottom end of the lemongrass stalk and cut the stalk 2 to 3 inches above the bottom. Reserve the top intact. Smash the lower portion of the stalk with the back of your knife, discard the tough outer layer, and then mince it.

**2.** In a large soup pot over medium-high heat, combine the chicken stock and the reserved lemongrass top. Bring to a boil, then add the chicken and mushrooms. Bring back to a simmer and add the minced lemongrass and fresh chile. Boil 5 to 8 minutes, until the chicken is cooked through.

**3.** Remove and discard the lemongrass stalk and skim any fat that has risen.

**4.** Lower the heat to medium. Add the ginger, coconut milk, agave, half of the fish sauce, and the red bell pepper and stir to combine. Bring back to a gentle simmer.

**5.** Add the shrimp and cook for 2 minutes or until just cooked through. Stir in the lime juice and taste for balance. Adjust the seasoning with the remaining fish sauce for saltiness, more agave for sweetness, and additional lime juice for tartness.

**6.** For guests to garnish, serve with the cilantro, green onion, Thai basil, mint, bean sprouts, and chili-garlic paste for additional heat.

¼ cup shredded Thai basil

¼ cup shredded mint

¼ cup fresh bean sprouts, cut into 1-inch pieces

Chili-garlic paste, for serving

# Grilled Chicken Tortilla Soup with Tequila Crema

### SERVES 4 TO 6

**MARINADE**

2 tablespoons vegetable oil

2 ounces silver tequila

Juice of 2 limes

1 chipotle pepper in adobo

1 tablespoon ground cumin

1 tablespoon chili powder

4 garlic cloves

1 teaspoon dried Mexican oregano

1 teaspoon kosher salt

1 teaspoon freshly cracked black pepper

4 bone-in, skinless chicken thighs (approximately ¾ pound)

**SOUP BASE**

1 jalapeño

2 tablespoons vegetable oil

1 yellow onion, diced

4 garlic cloves, minced

*(cont.)*

*Marinate, grill, and shred!* That's gonna kick off the super flavor of this go-to soup.

**1.** For the marinade, put everything except the chicken in a small food processor or blender and blend until smooth. Pour the marinade into a resealable 1-gallon plastic bag and add the chicken. Seal the bag and refrigerate for 6 to 8 hours.

**2.** Preheat a grill or grill pan to medium-high. Grill the jalapeño until the skin is well charred. Transfer the jalapeño to a small bowl and cover with plastic wrap to loosen the skin. When cool enough to handle, remove the stem, skin, and seeds, then finely mince.

**3.** Heat a large, heavy-bottomed pot over medium-high heat and pour in the vegetable oil. Once hot, add the onion and cook until it just starts to brown, 5 to 7 minutes. Add the garlic, jalapeño, chili powder, cumin, and salt and pepper to taste. Cook, stirring, 3 to 4 minutes, taking care not to burn the mixture.

**4.** Add some of the chicken stock and scrape up any brown bits from the bottom of the pan. Add the remaining chicken stock, tomatoes, lime juice, and strips fom the 1 tortilla. Bring the mixture to a boil, then lower the heat and simmer, uncovered, for 30 minutes. Taste and adjust the seasoning.

**5.** Meanwhile, heat a grill or grill pan to medium-high. Remove the chicken from the marinade and grill it on both sides until cooked through, about 14 to 18 minutes. Transfer the chicken to a large plate. When cool enough to handle, remove the bones and shred the meat. Keep warm.

1 teaspoon chili powder

1 teaspoon ground cumin

Kosher salt and freshly ground black pepper

2 quarts chicken stock (I recommend Kitchen Basics)

One 14.5-ounce can crushed fire-roasted tomatoes (I recommend Muir Glen)

Juice of 1 lime

1 corn tortilla, cut into ¼-inch strips

**FOR SERVING**

2 cups vegetable oil, for frying

8 corn tortillas, cut into ¼-inch-wide strips

1 teaspoon kosher salt, plus more for seasoning

Pinch chili powder

¾ cup sour cream

1 ounce tequila

Grated zest of 1 lime

1 teaspoon freshly cracked black pepper

1 Hass avocado, pitted, peeled, and diced

½ bunch cilantro, roughly chopped

Lime wedges, for garnish

**6.** When you're ready to serve, heat the vegetable oil in a deep skillet to 350°F. Add the tortilla strips in batches and fry until golden brown. Transfer to a paper-towel-lined plate and season with the teaspoon of salt and a pinch of chili powder.

**7.** Combine the sour cream, tequila, and lime zest in a small bowl and season with salt and pepper.

**8.** To serve, put some of the shredded chicken in the bottom of each bowl and pour in the hot soup base. Top with diced avocado, fried tortilla strips, the tequila crema, and cilantro. Garnish with lime wedges and serve.

# Heirloom Nitro Tomato Soup

#### ⇌ SERVES 8 ⇋

8 cups diced seeded heirloom or organic tomatoes (about 3½ pounds)

½ cup diced onion

¼ cup diced carrot

¼ cup diced celery

5 jalapeños, seeded and chopped

2 tablespoons chopped garlic

Olive oil, as needed

2 teaspoons kosher salt

1 tablespoon freshly cracked black pepper

12 tablespoons (1½ sticks) unsalted butter

¾ cup all-purpose flour

2 tablespoons ground cumin

½ cup finely chopped cilantro

2 cups heavy cream

*The better the base ingredients, the better the outcome of your dish. It's kind of like a foundation on a house. Find those heirloom tomatoes if you can. If not, find the best tomatoes available—or wait for summer when heirlooms are cheaper and easier to find. The key with cooking the roux of butter and flour is to remove the raw flour taste by cooking and stirring—but be sure not to burn it. And as always, it pays to toast and grind your own cumin seeds if you can!*

**1.** Preheat the oven to 425°F.

**2.** Place the tomatoes, onion, carrot, celery, jalapeños, and garlic on a rimmed baking sheet and drizzle them with olive oil. Season with 1 teaspoon of the salt and 1 teaspoon of the pepper. Roast the vegetables for 15 to 20 minutes, or until they've started to brown. Set the vegetables aside.

**3.** In a Dutch oven, melt the butter over medium-high heat. Add the flour and stir constantly for 5 minutes, until the mixture is light golden brown. (This is the roux.) Immediately add the vegetables and any pan juices and stir until incorporated. Season with the cumin and the remaining 1 teaspoon salt and 2 teaspoons pepper. Lower the heat to medium-low and simmer for 30 minutes. Carefully transfer to a blender in batches and puree until smooth, adding a touch of water, if necessary, to thin to the desired consistency. Return the soup to the Dutch oven.

**4.** Reduce the heat to low and add the cilantro and cream. Stir to combine. (Do not return to a boil once the cream has been incorporated.) Adjust the seasoning if necessary.

# Ginger Carrot Soup

**What a dynamic duo.** *Spicy ginger and sweet carrot rock 'n' roll so well together. You should double the recipe now!*

**1.** In a heavy Dutch oven (preferably enameled cast iron) over medium-high heat, add the olive oil. When hot, add onion. Sprinkle with the salt and cook for 10 minutes, until the onions just start to brown. Add the garlic and ginger and cook for 2 minutes, taking care not to burn the mixture. Stir in the carrots, potato, and stock. Bring to a simmer, reduce the heat to medium-low, cover, and cook until the carrots and potato are very tender, 15 to 18 minutes. Keep warm.

**2.** In a small skillet over high heat, lightly toast the pine nuts. Set aside to cool.

**3.** In a small bowl, combine the yogurt, honey, thyme, and black pepper.

**4.** With a stick blender or in a standard blender in batches, puree the carrot mixture. Adjust the seasonings with salt and pepper to taste. Place in individual serving bowls, swirl in 2 tablespoons of the yogurt mixture and 2 teaspoons of pine nuts per bowl, and serve immediately.

*Note: You can prepare the soup 3 or 4 days ahead, keep refrigerated, and add the pine nuts and the yogurt mixture when ready to serve.*

2 tablespoons olive oil

1 cup chopped sweet onion

½ teaspoon kosher salt, plus more for seasoning

1 tablespoon minced garlic

1 tablespoon minced ginger

2 pounds carrots, chopped into even 1-inch pieces

1 medium russet potato, peeled and chopped into 1-inch pieces

1 quart Chicken Stock (homemade preferred, page 362, or low-sodium store-bought) or vegetable stock

¼ cup pine nuts

1⅓ cups plain yogurt

1 teaspoon honey

1 teaspoon minced thyme leaves

½ teaspoon freshly cracked black pepper, plus more for seasoning

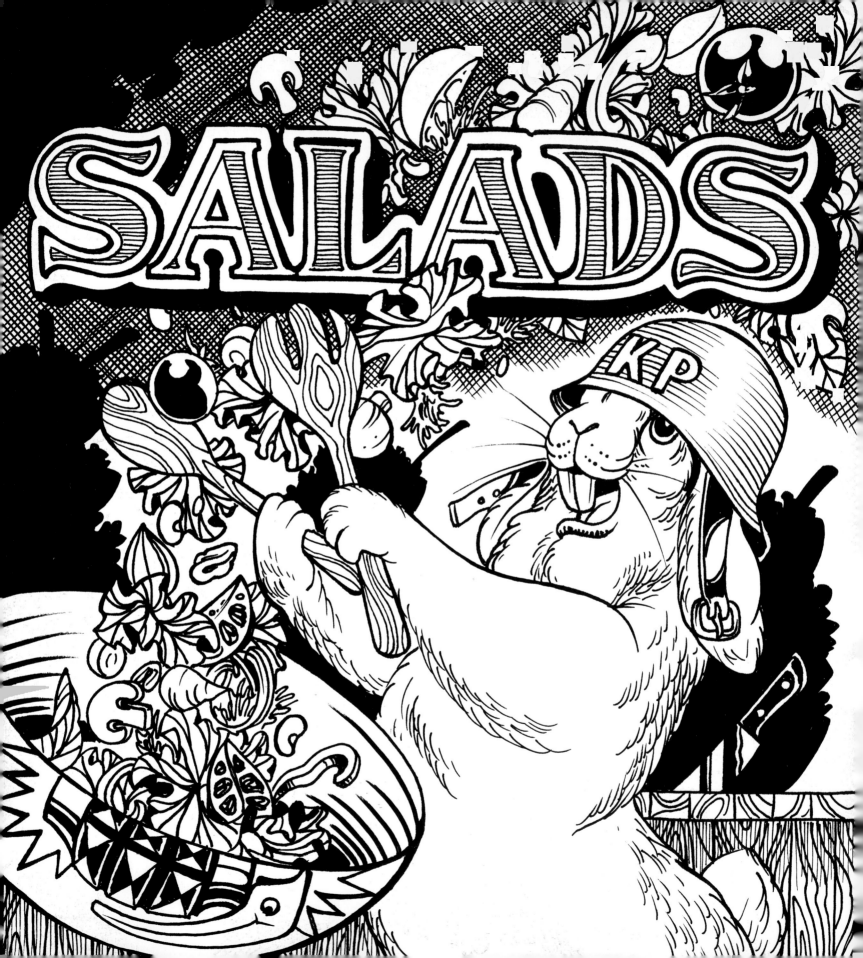

My mom and dad are great cooks and **the queen and king of super salads. They knock them out of the park**, and while growing up it was often the salads that got me past the bulgur and steamed vegetables they might be experimenting with. But my take on salads is a bit different. I've never been a huge fan of the ever-popular soft lettuces like baby greens, red leaf, or butter. Give me hearts of romaine, radicchio, endive, iceberg, and *cabbage,* as **I am the king of crunch.** I've always enjoyed **texture and snap.** For example, taco salad was my absolute favorite as a kid, and I couldn't get enough of Caesar, chopped, and BLT salads. These days I like some textural variation, such as adding beans or fruit, but I have **a few strict salad rules**:

1. No junky croutons—nothing outta the box.

2. Do not predress or overdress your salad.

3. Inspect your lettuce thoroughly.

4. Wash *and* dry your lettuce
   (there's nothing worse than wet lettuce).

# Grilled Romaine with Blue Cheese-Bacon Vinaigrette

SERVES 6

4 tablespoons extra virgin olive oil

¾ cup finely diced red onion

½ pound bacon, ¼-inch diced

½ cup balsamic vinegar

3 romaine lettuce heads, cores removed and leafy ends trimmed, cut in half lengthwise

½ cup crumbled blue cheese

Freshly cracked black pepper

*You gotta dig opening up the **big flavors** of this salad. The romaine is **nice and sweet** when warmed up.*

**1.** Preheat a grill or indoor grill pan for to high.

**2.** Heat 1 tablespoon of the olive oil in a large skillet over high heat. Add the onion and bacon and cook until the bacon is crispy. Remove onion and bacon from pan. Add the balsamic vinegar and 1 tablespoon of the olive oil to the skillet and reduce for 2 to 3 minutes. Remove from heat and set aside.

**3.** Brush the romaine with the remaining 2 tablespoons olive oil. Place on the grill cut side down and quickly sear until grill marks are visible. Set aside.

**4.** For each serving, place a half head of romaine cut side up on a plate and drizzle the balsamic dressing on top. Sprinkle with blue cheese and the bacon and onion, and garnish with cracked black pepper.

# Waka Waka Salad

*My parents are one of the biggest influences on my cooking, so I always treat what they make with a lot of respect. But one day my mom showed up with this salad that had uncooked ramen noodles in it, and I thought,* You've got to be kidding me. Those noodles are going to be too dry. *Then **Mom knocked out a dressing using the ramen seasoning packet**. So I took a bite of it, crunching down on the Spanish peanuts, and **I just about died**. I ate the whole bowl and couldn't stop talking about it. So I did my thing to it and made it a bit more refined. I made it for my sister, served it as an appetizer, and **people loved it, but this crazy salad still didn't have a name.***

*Back in the day, the best way to promote Johnny Garlic's was to do demonstrations at events. One time I was cooking in front of about 100 people (that was a big crowd then) and showing how to slice cabbage really thin, which is key—I think it tastes less bitter. A woman raised her hand and asked what the salad was called. I responded, "I don't know . . . **wha, wha, what is the name** . . . waka . . . waka . . . waka salad! **It's waka waka salad, that's the name of it, lady!**" And it stuck.*

**1.** In a large bowl, combine the oil, vinegar, garlic, ginger, ramen seasoning, salt, and pepper.

**2.** In a separate large bowl, mix the cabbages, onions, carrots, and cilantro. Whisk the dressing and pour it over the cabbage mixture. Toss thoroughly. (Dress the salad no more than 10 minutes before serving.)

**3.** Divide the fried wonton wrappers among serving plates and top with the salad. Sprinkle with ramen pieces and chopped peanuts. Serve immediately.

---

1 cup canola oil

1 cup red wine vinegar

1 teaspoon minced garlic

1 teaspoon minced ginger

½ packet oriental seasoning from a ramen noodle packet

Pinch salt and freshly ground black pepper

½ Napa cabbage head (¾ pound), sliced ⅛-inch thick

¼ red cabbage head (½ pound), sliced ⅛-inch thick

½ green cabbage head (¾ pound), sliced ⅛-inch thick

2 medium red onions, thinly sliced

2 large carrots, shredded

¼ cup chopped cilantro

24 wonton wrappers, fried (see page 351)

3 packets ramen noodles, broken into small pieces

¾ cup finely chopped Spanish peanuts

# My Super Thai Beef Salad

### ⤙ SERVES 6 ⤚

**MARINADE**

1 tablespoon minced garlic

¼ cup oyster sauce

2 tablespoons soy sauce

1 teaspoon fish sauce

1 teaspoon rice vinegar

1 tablespoon fresh lime juice

1 tablespoon agave nectar

1 tablespoon freshly cracked
black pepper

1 pound flank steak (or
chateaubriand, sliced to
½-inch thick against the grain)

**DRESSING**

2½ tablespoons mild fish
sauce

⅓ cup fresh lime juice

2 tablespoon soy sauce

1 teaspoon chili-garlic paste

2 tablespoons agave nectar

¼ cup finely chopped cilantro

*(cont.)*

You don't see enough beef and salad combos out there! **The thinner you cut the meat, the better**, so that it doesn't weigh the whole show down.

**1.** Combine all the marinade ingredients except the steak in a small bowl. Adjust the seasoning to taste. Place the steak in a resealable 1-gallon plastic bag and add the marinade. Set in a shallow bowl (to catch any leaks) in the refrigerator to marinate for at least 2 hours and up to 4.

**2.** Whisk the dressing ingredients together in a small nonreactive bowl. Refrigerate for 1 hour to allow the flavors to marry, stirring occasionally.

**3.** Remove the steak from the refrigerator to allow it to come to room temperature. Preheat a grill to high.

**4.** Remove the steak from the marinade and discard the marinade. Grill the steak about 4 minutes on each side, until medium to medium-rare or until it reaches 140°F internally. Let the steak rest, lightly covered, for 6 to 8 minutes.

**5.** Adjust the flavors in the dressing as desired: more lime juice to balance saltiness, more fish sauce to add saltiness, more agave for sweetness.

**6.** For the salad, toss the greens with the basil and mint leaves. Arrange the greens on a platter and top with the bean sprouts. Slice the beef across the grain as thin as you can (the thinner the better), then cut into bite-size pieces with the grain. Lay the steak on the greens and top with the papaya and watermelon and garnish with the cashews.

**SALAD**

**6 cups baby mixed salad greens**

**¼ cup (lightly packed) torn Thai basil**

**¼ cup (lightly packed) torn mint**

**1 cup fresh bean sprouts**

**1½ cups cubed peeled papaya**

**1½ cups cubed seedless watermelon**

**3 tablespoons chopped cashews, for garnish**

# Green Papaya Salad with Lemongrass Chicken

## ⇴ SERVES 6 ⇴

### LEMONGRASS CHICKEN

1 cup minced lemongrass
(about 5 stalks)

3 tablespoons minced ginger

1 tablespoon minced garlic

½ cup dry white wine
(sauvignon blanc or
chardonnay)

3 tablespoons fish sauce

2 tablespoons soy sauce

2 tablespoons fresh lemon
juice

6 boneless, skinless chicken
thighs, cut into ¾-inch strips
(1 to 1¼ pounds)

½ lemon, to finish

Chopped peanuts, for garnish

Chopped green onions, for
garnish

### PAPAYA SALAD

3 cups thin matchsticks green
(unripe) papaya

1 cup thin matchsticks carrot

*I can hear it now—"What, green papaya? Guido, you're nuts!"* **Just try it, Mikey, you'll like it.** *And it ain't Life cereal—it's better (and Mikey does like it). The sweet crunch of the papaya is amazing.*

*P.S. **It's so worth all the work**—just get yourself a great mandoline and start the chicken marinating the day before, if you have time!*

**1. To make the chicken,** place the lemongrass, ginger, garlic, wine, fish sauce, soy sauce, and lemon juice in a resealable 1-gallon plastic bag. Add the chicken, seal, and marinate for 4 to 24 hours in the refrigerator.

**2. To make the papaya salad,** combine all the ingredients in a large bowl, toss with the vinaigrette, and refrigerate for 30 minutes.

**3. To make the vinaigrette,** whisk all the ingredients except the olive oil in a medium bowl. Slowly whisk in the olive oil. Refrigerate until chilled.

**4.** Preheat a grill to medium-high.

**5.** Remove the chicken from the marinade (discard the marinade). Skewer the chicken lengthwise onto bamboo skewers and grill on both sides until marked and cooked through, about 12 minutes. Place the skewers onto a serving platter and squeeze the lemon over the chicken. Garnish with the peanuts and green onions, and serve the salad alongside the chicken.

1 English cucumber, seeded and cut in thin matchsticks

1 cup fresh bean sprouts

1 cup thin matchsticks daikon radish

3 green onions, cut in 2-inch-long matchsticks (white and green parts)

¼ cup finely shredded mint leaves

### ASIAN VINAIGRETTE

¼ cup rice vinegar

3 tablespoons mirin

½ teaspoon sesame oil

1 tablespoon soy sauce

2 tablespoons fish sauce

1 teaspoon Chili Sauce (page 368)

¼ cup olive oil

*Special Equipment:* Ten 12-inch bamboo skewers, soaked in water for 20 minutes

# Queen Korina's Salad

### ⟿ SERVES 4 TO 6 ⟾

## MEAT

One 1½- to 2-pound flank steak

3 tablespoons dried Mexican oregano

2 teaspoons ground cumin

Coarse sea salt and freshly ground black pepper

3 cups beef stock (I recommend Kitchen Basics)

2 cups water

4 garlic cloves, smashed

1 sweet onion, quartered

3 bay leaves

12 black peppercorns

## VINAIGRETTE

5 tablespoons distilled white vinegar

5 tablespoons fresh lime juice

1 tablespoon juice from pickled jalapeños

3 tablespoons dried Mexican oregano

1½ teaspoons fine sea salt

1 teaspoon freshly ground black pepper

½ teaspoon ground cumin

1 cup extra virgin olive oil

**(cont.)**

*I love cooking challenges, like the day Korina, my culinary director, told me she could make **a killer beef salad**. . . . Yeah, right! Of course, we challenged her to prove it. She made it, we tried it, it's written down here, and **you're gonna dig it**. It's a GBB fave.*

**1. To make the meat,** rub the flank steak with the oregano, cumin, and salt and pepper.

**2.** Cover and allow to rest at room temperature for 20 minutes. Place the steak, beef stock, water, garlic, onion, bay leaves, and peppercorns in a large pot and bring to a boil over medium-high heat. Reduce the heat to medium-low and simmer for 1½ hours or until the meat comes apart easily with a fork. (Add more beef stock or water if needed while cooking.) Set the pot aside for the liquid to cool to room temperature, about 20 minutes.

**3.** Cover the pot and refrigerate for 1 to 3 hours. Trim the meat of any remaining fat, cut the meat into 4 pieces across the grain, and use 2 forks to shred it. Place the meat back into the cooking liquid until you're ready to serve.

**4. To make the vinaigrette,** whisk all the ingredients except the olive oil in a medium bowl. Whisk in the olive oil in a steady stream until incorporated.

**5. For the salad,** toss the lettuce, tomatoes, cilantro, and red onion with the vinaigrette. Drain the meat (discard the cooking liquid) and arrange it on the salad. Serve garnished with radishes, avocados slices, and tortilla chips around the bowl.

## SALAD

**4 romaine hearts, cored and cut crosswise into ¼-inch strips**

**4 large tomatoes, cut in 1- to 1½-inch wedges**

**1 bunch cilantro, leaves only, coarsely chopped**

**1 medium red onion, thinly sliced**

**2 bunches radishes, trimmed**

**4 avocados, pitted, peeled, and sliced**

**Favorite corn tortilla chips**

# Guy's Caesar Salad

1 large egg, coddled*

1 teaspoon Worcestershire sauce

2 garlic cloves, minced

2 tablespoons fresh lemon juice

1 teaspoon anchovy paste

1 cup extra virgin olive oil

Salt and freshly ground black pepper

2 romaine lettuce heads

⅓ cup grated Parmesan cheese, for garnish

*To coddle the egg, immerse the (uncracked) egg in boiling water for 10 minutes.

As flambé captains (see page 244), one of the main things we'd make was Caesar salad. People came to see the anchovies muddled together with garlic and Dijon, the coddling of the egg, the ritual of it all. I'd been making Caesar salad since I was seventeen, and as time went on, everywhere I'd go **people would ask me to make my Caesar salad—the way a lounge singer is famous for a particular song**. To this day you can find me making it at home, just like the old days.

I like that my recipe is not as emulsified, not as creamy, as a blender method. **What can I say? It just makes it good.**

**1.** Beat the egg in a large mixing bowl. Add the Worcestershire, garlic, lemon juice, anchovy paste, and olive oil and whisk to combine. Season with salt and pepper to taste.

**2.** Core the stems off the romaine and trim the top ½ inch off the leaves. Fan the leaves out on a serving platter. Sprinkle the Parmesan over the lettuce and drizzle the dressing on top. Serve immediately.

# Long Beach Coleslaw

*When I lived in Long Beach, California,* **there was a restaurant in Belmont Shores that we would go to specifically for a salad** *they made with cabbage, iceberg lettuce, and blue cheese. Even after I moved I'd make sure to go back for it, so when I discovered they'd closed and torn the place down, it was heartbreaking. Naturally, I was put to the task of trying to figure out how they'd made it all those years. I like to think that* **this version may even improve upon the original.** *These days, we make Long Beach slaw in my family at least three or four times a month. The tangy vinegar, sweet blue cheese, crunch of green iceberg, and softer crunch of the wilted purple cabbage is* **a beautiful combination for the eyes as well as the taste buds.**

2 tablespoons extra virgin olive oil

½ red onion, thinly sliced

2 tablespoons minced garlic

½ small red cabbage head, trimmed and cut into ⅛-inch shreds

1 tablespoon freshly ground black pepper, plus more as needed

1 teaspoon fine sea salt

1 cup red wine vinegar

2 iceberg lettuce heads, trimmed and cut into 1-inch squares

1 cup thick and chunky blue cheese salad dressing (I recommend Marie's)

**1.** In a medium skillet over medium-high heat, combine the olive oil, onion, and garlic and cook for 2 minutes (do not brown). Add the cabbage, pepper, salt, and vinegar. Mix thoroughly and cook for 3 to 5 minutes, until the cabbage is tender. Transfer to a bowl and refrigerate until cool.

**2.** In a large salad bowl, toss the lettuce with the blue cheese dressing. Drain the cabbage and lightly mix with the iceberg and dressing. Add pepper to taste. Serve immediately.

SALADS ......................... **125**

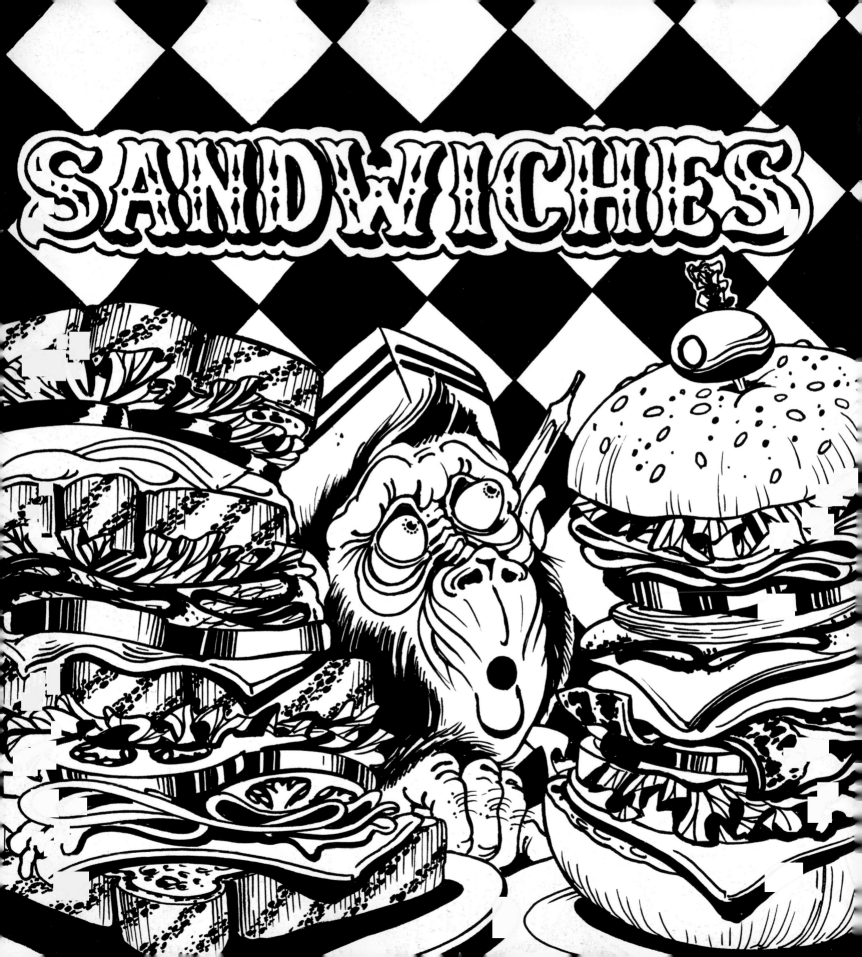

Sandwiches have always been a big mainstay in my life, but not your run-of-the-mill varieties. I can't remember ever having a bologna sandwich in my lunch bag, but good salami or pastrami were common. There wasn't a store-bought loaf of presliced white bread to be found at our house, but **my mother would bake sourdough rolls and an eclectic variety of nut- and grain-based breads that seemed like the essence of the earth, they were so hearty**. In retrospect, my parents were preparing foods that were more adult than kid-friendly, and I was just fine with that. But when my dad made things, even sandwiches, he'd go wild. One morning when I was in third grade, my dad prepared a sandwich on a piece of grain-and-nut-loaded bread that was cut about two inches thick on one side and ¼-inch thick on the other. It was as if he'd cut it with a camping axe, it was so uneven. Next, he pulled some turkey left over from dinner and slathered on Dijon mustard with hunks of lettuce and a big wedge of tomato. I tried to eat this creation at school, and it fell apart. I complained to my dad that night, and he responded, **"Fine, you don't like the sandwich, I'm sorry about that. Next time I'll let you take care of it."** At school the next day, I reached inside my lunch bag to find a couple of slices of bread, a pile of turkey, a wedge of lettuce, a tomato, and way down at the very bottom, a full jar of Dijon and a butter knife. This was my first experience with a dish being deconstructed. **It was just like him—if you didn't like something, it was up to you to fix it.**

So from that day on, every morning I'd go to the kitchen and prepare my sandwich for school. I've carried on this tradition with my sons. Hunter's been making his own sandwiches for school since the fourth grade, and I believe it's helped him learn to appreciate food.

Sandwiches are too often underappreciated. Made with stale bread and bad ingredients, they cry out for help, so here are a few tips. I'm a big fan of canoeing bread (scooping out the middle) and toasting it for a good crust, then preparing the sandwich with minimal or no fat such as mayonnaise, which I think of as food lube. If the ingredients are top-grade, like juicy tomatoes, fresh lettuce, and tender avocado, then you just don't need it. Same theory goes for a burger—it's not always necessary to use mayonnaise or ketchup if you build it the right way. The sweetness of ketchup can be replaced by slices of ripe tomato, and the acid factor by dill pickle. I'll concede that the sharpness of mustard is a nice counterbalance and might be more critical, but add super crunchy lettuce and a juicy burger with enough fat and you're on the road. It's all about the correct proportions, such as never overloading it with cheese. Another rule of thumb is to store all the ingredients separately until you're ready to make your sandwich. If you keep all the deli meats in one container, for example, then each meat loses its individual flavor identity, resulting in a more boring bite. Remember, a sandwich is a portable meal, not to be served too hot or too cold, and all the flavors will open up at the proper temperature. Follow these simple rules, then go for it.

# Red Rocker Margarita Chicken

## ⟷ SERVES 4 ⟷

*I'm a rocker, so of course I'm a Sammy Hagar fan. The "Red Rocker"
is the Man, and **boy, does he enjoy good food**. As a restaurateur in Northern California, I found the chance to meet him a couple of times over the years,
and **he was always so cool, totally the real deal**. After the Food Network events went down, Sammy found out that I was cooking with his Cabo
Wabo tequila, doing flambés and things like that. So we decided that he'd
come up to Johnny Garlic's from where he lives in Marin County one Saturday
morning to talk about tequila. I pulled up in my new Corvette just as Sammy
pulled up in his GT500. So we immediately went over to each other's cars and
started covering the specs. It was so cool, like I'd known him all my life.*

**With the Red Rocker.**

*After rappin' a bit we got down to what he likes to eat (which is like him ask-
ing me what music I like), and we started jamming out a couple dishes together.
One was the Ahi Won Tacos (page 84) and the other turned out to be this Red
Rocker Margarita Chicken. We had a great time, and by the end everyone was
late for appointments, but we swapped cars in the parking lot and rolled over to
Tex Wasabi's. Once there, we stood on the
balcony overlooking the restaurant and bar
and the conversation turned to age. I com-
mented, "I'm going to be forty, and I can't
believe it; it doesn't make mathematical
sense to me." He responded, "Listen to me,
Guy." (Everything he says sounds like a
rocker.) "There's no way you thought you'd be
rolling into forty like you're rolling now." Which
is, of course, so true.*

*Currently Sammy and I are looking
into some restaurant projects together. It's not a dream come true,*

2 jalapeños, cut into thin rounds

3 tablespoons cilantro leaves

¼ cup tequila (I recommend Cabo Wabo Reposado)

1 tablespoon minced garlic

1 teaspoon red chili flakes

1 teaspoon ground cumin

1 tablespoon dried oregano

Juice of 2 limes (about ¼ cup)

2 teaspoons kosher salt

4 boneless, skinless chicken breast halves

2 roasted red bell peppers, cut into thin strips*

1 cup all-purpose flour

1 teaspoon granulated garlic

2 cups canola oil

4 kaiser rolls

¼ cup mayonnaise

¼ green cabbage head, very thinly sliced

¼ red onion, very thinly sliced

4 ounces thinly sliced provolone cheese

*Roast bell peppers over an open flame or under the broiler, turning to char on all sides. Skin and seed them.

because I never would have fathomed it could be possible. He's a great friend for advice about anything in the industry, from agents and attorneys to being in the spotlight and keeping it real.

**The Red Rocker Margarita Chicken came out so well that we ran it on the restaurant menu.** So just like a tune that ends up on an album, here it is in the book as a tribute to Sammy.

**1.** In a medium bowl, combine the jalapeños, cilantro, tequila, minced garlic, chili flakes, cumin, oregano, lime juice, and 1 teaspoon of the salt. Place the chicken and red bell peppers in a resealable 1-gallon plastic bag and pour in the marinade. Marinate the chicken in the refrigerator for 4 to 8 hours.

**2.** In a small mixing bowl, combine the flour, the remaining 1 teaspoon salt, and the granulated garlic.

**3.** Preheat a grill to high. In a medium heavy-bottomed pot, heat the canola oil to 350°F.

**4.** Remove the chicken from the marinade. (Leave the roasted peppers in the marinade.) Grill the chicken until cooked through, turning several times to prevent burning, about 12 minutes in all. Cover the cooked chicken and let sit for 5 minutes. Thinly slice the chicken across the grain.

**5.** Remove the roasted peppers from the marinade, dredge them in the flour mixture, and fry in the oil until crispy, 2 to 3 minutes, working in batches as needed. Drain on paper towels.

**6.** Split and lightly toast the rolls. Spread mayonnaise (food lube) on the bottom halves. Stack each roll evenly with the cabbage, onion, chicken breast, fried peppers, and cheese.

# DLT 44

*What do you do with duck confit aside from the expected classics? You got it, you make a* **duck confit, lettuce, and tomato sandwich**—*and cook it in the West Wing Mess of the White House, of course! (True story.)*

½ cup mayonnaise

2 tablespoons minced capers, drained

2 tablespoons fresh lemon juice

¼ teaspoon cayenne pepper

1 teaspoon freshly cracked black pepper

¼ cup bacon fat, rendered and strained*

2 cups Duck Confit (page 203), shredded

12 slices whole-grain bread

2 heirloom tomatoes (¾ pound total)

4 Bibb lettuce leaves

2 Hass avocados, pitted and peeled

*Special Equipment:*
**Long sandwich picks**

*\*When you cook bacon, strain and reserve the fat and keep in an airtight jar in your refrigerator for future use.*

**1.** In a small bowl, combine the mayonnaise, capers, lemon juice, cayenne, and black pepper. Add salt to taste (capers can vary in their saltiness, so taste the mixture before adding the salt).

**2.** In a medium nonstick skillet over medium-high heat, melt the bacon fat and heat until shimmering. Pat the duck into four equal patties and place in the bacon fat. Cook for 3 minutes on each side or until just crisp. Remove and drain on a paper-towel-lined plate.

**3.** Lightly toast the bread, cut the tomatoes in ½-inch-thick slices, tear the lettuce into bread-size portions, and slice the avocados.

**4.** Assemble the sandwich: Spread the caper mayonnaise on one side of each bread slice. Top three slices of bread as follows: duck patty, avocado, another slice of bread, tomato, lettuce, and the final slice of bread.

**5.** Skewer each sandwich in the four corners with picks and slice into four triangles. Serve immediately.

# Sloppy Joes with Maui Onion Straws

## ⤜ SERVES 8 ⤛

¼ cup canola oil

½ red bell pepper, ¼-inch diced

½ green bell pepper, ¼-inch diced

½ red onion, ¼-inch diced

1 pound ground beef (80/20 lean)

1 pound medium grind ground pork

2 tablespoons minced garlic

¼ cup red wine

¼ cup red wine vinegar

1 tablespoon seeded, deveined, diced jalapeño

1 teaspoon cayenne pepper

1 tablespoon paprika

1 teaspoon ground cumin

1 teaspoon dry mustard

¾ cup tomato paste

1½ cups tomato sauce

3 tablespoons packed light brown sugar

¼ cup Worcestershire sauce

2 tablespoons freshly ground black pepper

1 tablespoon kosher salt

*(cont.)*

*As a kid, sloppy Joes were one of my super favorites. This is my adult spin on it.* **I hope it takes you back to grade school lunch**—*in a good way!*

**1.** In a large straight-sided skillet over medium-high heat, heat the oil. Add the peppers and onion and cook for 5 minutes or until softened. Add the beef and pork and cook thoroughly, breaking up the meat while cooking, about 6 minutes. Add the garlic and continue cooking for 2 minutes. If there is a lot of grease in the pan, drain it off. Stir in the wine and add the remaining ingredients except the rolls and onion straws. Reduce the heat to medium-low, cover, and simmer for 20 to 30 minutes, until mixture thickens.

**2.** Serve on toasted rolls, topping the meat mixture with Maui Onion Straws.

# Maui Onion Straws

**MAKES 4 CUPS**

**1.** In medium heavy-bottomed pot, heat the oil to 350°F.

**2.** Whisk together the eggs and milk in a medium bowl. Mix the flour, cayenne, paprika, garlic powder, pepper, and salt in another bowl.

**3.** Soak the onion slices in the egg-milk mixture for 10 minutes. Shake the excess liquid from 4 or 5 onion slices at a time and dredge them in the flour mixture. Add them to the oil and cook until golden brown, about 3 minutes. Remove with a slotted spoon and drain on paper towels. Repeat with the remaining onion slices.

8 kaiser rolls or quality hamburger buns, split and toasted

Maui Onion Straws (recipe follows)

**MAUI ONION STRAWS**

1 quart canola oil

2 eggs

1 cup milk

2 cups all-purpose flour

2 teaspoons cayenne pepper

2 teaspoons paprika

2 teaspoons garlic powder

2 teaspoons freshly ground black pepper

2 tablespoons fine sea salt

3 cups ⅛-inch slices (cut into half-moons, not into rings) Vidalia onions or similar sweet onion

# Texas Hold'em

2 cups warm water (110°F)

1 tablespoon active dry yeast (about 2 packets)

1 tablespoon agave nectar

2 tablespoons finely ground cornmeal

4 to 5 cups all-purpose flour, plus extra for dusting

1 tablespoon fine sea salt

¼ cup grapeseed or canola oil

½ pound bacon, chopped

1 cup ¼-inch-sliced sweet onion (about ½ onion)

¼ cup mayonnaise

2 tablespoons Chili Sauce (page 368)

1 tablespoon minced chipotle pepper in adobo

½ cup finely chopped cilantro

4 cups shredded or chopped leftover "Bring It On" Beef Brisket (page 240)

½ cup thin strips roasted red bell pepper (see page 130)

¼ cup shredded Havarti cheese

*(cont.)*

*In the spirit of the Earl of Sandwich, **this bad boy's a real-deal sandwich** that won't take you away from the card game.*

**1.** In a large glass bowl, combine the water, yeast, agave nectar, and cornmeal. Let sit in a warm place for 10 to 15 minutes, until foamy. Stir in 4 cups of the flour, the sea salt, and the oil. Turn the dough out onto a lightly floured board and knead just until all ingredients are well incorporated and dough is smooth. (Add more flour as needed if sticky). Lightly oil a large glass bowl and place the dough ball into it. Cover the bowl and set aside in a warm place to rise for 1 hour.

**2.** In a medium skillet over medium-high heat, cook the bacon until just crisp. With a slotted spoon, transfer the bacon to a paper-towel-lined plate. Add the onion to the rendered fat and cook for 15 to 20 minutes, until soft and deep brown.

**3.** In a small bowl, combine the mayonnaise, chili sauce, chipotle, and ¼ cup cilantro and blend well. Refrigerate until needed.

**4.** Preheat the oven to 375°F. Lightly grease and flour a 9 by 5-inch loaf pan.

**5.** Turn the dough onto a floured surface, sprinkle it with flour, and knead gently until smooth, folding over several times. Flour a rolling pin and roll the dough into a rectangle about 12 by 9 inches.

**6.** Spread the dough generously with the chipotle mayonnaise. Cover with the brisket, then the onion, roasted pepper, and bacon. Sprinkle evenly with the Havarti, the remaining cilantro, and cracked pepper.

**7.** From the short side, gently roll up the dough "jelly roll" style, tucking in the ends as you go. Place the dough roll in the prepared loaf pan, brush with the melted butter, and sprinkle the top with the dry Jack. Bake for 1 hour 25 minutes, until dark golden brown. You should hear a slightly hollow sound when you tap the bread.

**8.** Cool for a full 30 minutes in the pan on a wire rack. Then remove from the loaf pan and slice into 1-inch thick slices. Enjoy immediately.

1 teaspoon freshly cracked black pepper

2 tablespoons unsalted butter, melted

2 tablespoons grated dry Jack cheese

# Pepperoni Burger

### ~ SERVES 4 ~

*I first made this burger for Boo (Hunter's nickname) when we were having lunch at Johnny Garlic's in Santa Rosa. You see,* **he didn't know if he wanted a burger or pizza.** *He loved what he got. . . . Hope you do, too!*

⅔ pound ground beef (80% lean)

⅓ pound medium grind ground pork

1 teaspoon kosher salt

1 tablespoon freshly cracked black pepper

2 tablespoons olive oil

1 cup pepperoni matchsticks

½ cup diced onion

1 tablespoon minced garlic

¼ cup diced seeded tomatoes

Four 1-inch slices fresh mozzarella

¼ cup ice cubes

4 ciabatta rolls

**1.** In a medium bowl, gently combine the beef and the pork. Form the mixture into four 1-inch-thick patties, season them with salt and pepper, and refrigerate.

**2.** In a cast-iron skillet over medium-high heat, heat the olive oil. When it's shimmering, add the pepperoni. Cook, stirring frequently, for 5 minutes or until just crisp. Transfer to a paper-towel-lined plate.

**3.** Cook the onion in the same skillet for 5 to 6 minutes, until they just start to color. Add the garlic and cook for 1 to 2 minutes more. Add the tomatoes and pepperoni and cook for 2 minutes. With a slotted spoon, transfer everything to a bowl, leaving the oil in the skillet.

**4.** With the heat still at medium-high, cook the burger patties for 5 minutes on one side and 3 on the other for medium-rare. Top each patty with one-quarter of the pepperoni mixture and cover with a slice of mozzarella. Add the ice cubes to the pan and cover tightly for 3 minutes to allow the cheese to melt and cover the patties.

**5.** Meanwhile, split and toast the rolls.

**6.** Place a burger on each roll and serve immediately.

# Chicago Italian Beef Sandwich

### ⇒ SERVES 6 LARGE PORTIONS ⇐

**SPICE MIX**

3 tablespoons Italian seasoning

2 tablespoons fine sea salt

2 tablespoons freshly cracked black pepper

1 teaspoon cayenne pepper

1 tablespoon paprika

1 teaspoon red chili flakes

4 pounds beef top round, with fat cap

3 tablespoons bacon fat or canola oil

3 yellow onions, chopped

1 cup garlic cloves, peeled and smashed

½ cup red wine

3 tablespoons Worcestershire sauce

2 cups beef stock (I recommend Kitchen Basics)

2 bay leaves

6 sourdough hero or hoagie rolls, split and toasted

1 cup chopped drained Guido's Hot Italian Giardiniera (page 165)

1 cup jarred red bell peppers, sliced ¼-inch thick

*Through* Diners, Drive-Ins and Dives, *I'm known as somebody who searches for the inside track to really good grub. And the fact is, I've always been that way.* **I'll spend more time looking for what to eat than actually eating.** *One time during a layover in Chicago before my Food Network career I was walking around the airport looking for something to eat for probably about an hour when I came upon this little cluttered stand with so many things on the menu board that I questioned whether they could actually serve good food. Then someone in line spoke up and said,* "**This is the bomb**. *The best Chicago beef is found in the airport." I was like, "Really??" When I got to the window I asked, "What's the best thing you've got?" This older guy looks back at me and says in a thick Chicago accent, "What do you think we got here? Where you from?"* Ooohhhh, *this guy was busting my balls right there. "Italian beef. We've got Chicago Italian beef." I said, "I'll have one of those." And he said, "You want it dipped?" Yeah, I guess. "Can you handle hot peppers?" Yeah, you bet! It went on and on. Finally he made my sandwich, grabbed my credit card, and noticed my name. "Fieri?? You're a paesano and you didn't know what Chicago beef is?" I responded, "I've never been to Chicago," then I took my sandwich, full of humility, and sat down.*

*My mouth is watering just remembering what happened next. With that first bite of salty wet beef, soggy bun, hot pepper, and the crunch of the vinegary, sweet, and salty giardiniera,* **I thought I was going to die. I engulfed the whole thing,** *then went back for another dose of smack from this guy. As I unwrapped my second sandwich on the plane, the aromas wafted out, and let's just say my fellow passengers experienced some major sandwich envy.*

*This sandwich is reason enough to close this book and fly directly to Chicago, or hijack a bus and take all your friends. If I lived there I would weigh 9,000 pounds. Now, whenever I'm in Chicago, I try the hot Italian beef at different places, and over time I've come up with my own interpretation. P.S. One of my favorite Chicago Italian beef sandwiches is at Paradise Pup in Chicago.* **They rock it Big-Time.**

**1.** Combine all the ingredients for the spice mix. Rub the meat with the spice mix, cover tightly with plastic wrap, and refrigerate for 2 to 3 hours. (Store any remaining spice mix in a tightly capped jar.)

**2.** Preheat the oven to 275°F.

**3.** On the stovetop, in a roasting pan over high heat, add the bacon fat. When smoking, add the beef and cook for 15 minutes, turning the meat often, until it is nicely browned on all sides. Add the onions and cook for 5 minutes, then add the garlic and cook for 1 minute. Add the wine, Worcestershire, stock, and bay leaves and scrape up all the browned bits.

**4.** Transfer the pan to the oven and roast the meat about 1 hour 30 minutes, uncovered, until an instant-read thermometer in the center registers 135°F. Remove the meat and let it cool.

**5.** Cool the broth in the roasting pan and remove the fat that rises to the top. Strain.

**6.** When the meat is cool, slice it very thin. Reheat the broth and add the meat.

**7.** Place some meat on each roll, ladle some broth over the meat, and top with giardiniera vegetables and red peppers. (You can use any leftover meat to make the Chicago Beef Pizza on page 164.)

**This should be the state sandwich of Illinois!**

# Baltimore Beef Bad Boy

*~ SERVES 8 ~*

## SPICE MIX

1 tablespoon fine sea salt

Freshly ground black pepper

1 tablespoon onion powder

1 tablespoon garlic powder

2 teaspoons dried oregano

1 tablespoon paprika

1 teaspoon chili powder

2 pounds top round,
cut in 2 equal pieces

## SOUR CREAM–
HORSERADISH SAUCE

½ cup sour cream

½ cup mayonnaise

1 teaspoon fresh lemon juice

½ cup prepared hot
horseradish

1 teaspoon minced garlic

½ teaspoon fine sea salt

16 rye bread slices, lightly
toasted

2 white onions,
sliced paper thin

*The first production producer on my show* Guy's Big Bite *was Jimmy Zankel. Jimmy loved to talk food and was the first person I'd ever met who was in the Bacon of the Month Club. He called me one day, asked if I'd heard of pit beef, and described it. I said no, but I'd had something similar—cooked over open coals, thinly sliced, and served on rye bread. Inspired by his enthusiasm, I started messing with cooking beef over very high heat using a dry rub and then grilling it in softball-size pieces of 6- by 6-inches. My family became my guinea pigs along with my friends Dirty P (Paul Thomson) and Rob "Nob" Myers. **I hand-sliced the beef super thin (so thin it only had one side!)** and served it with sliced white onions on toasted rye bread with horseradish-garlic sauce. **It was so great that we immediately made anther round.** The next day Nob brought over a slicer from his Meyers Restaurant Supply, and we made a third round of pit beef. When I finally made it over to Chap's Pit Beef in Baltimore to try it, I was happy to find that my version still held its ground. My advice: Mortgage your house to get yourself a slicer; it's worth it.*

**1.** Combine the spice mix ingredients in a resealable 1-gallon plastic bag and shake to mix thoroughly. Add 1 piece of meat, shake it around in the bag, remove it, and repeat with the second piece of meat. Add the first piece back to the bag, seal, and marinate for as long as you can in the refrigerator—24 to 48 hours is recommended. But if you can't wait, just go for it. It won't be as over-the-top, but it will still be really good.

**2.** In a medium bowl, combine the sour cream, mayonnaise, lemon juice, horseradish, garlic, sea salt, and pepper. Mix thoroughly and refrigerate for at least 4 hours.

**3.** Twenty minutes before you plan on grilling, remove the meat from the refrigerator and let it sit at room temperature. Preheat a grill or large grilling pan to high.

**4.** Grill the meat for 10 to 15 minutes (7½ minutes per side) or until desired doneness (it's best at medium-rare, about 140° or 145°F). Set the meat aside, cover, and let rest for 5 to 10 minutes.

**5.** Slice the meat paper-thin with a knife or a countertop deli slicer. Divide the meat among 8 bread slices, spread some sour cream–horseradish sauce on each one, then place a few rings of onion slices, and top with the rest of the bread.

**You gotta get one . . .**

**It's okay if your mouth is full-on watering right now. (Mine is . . .)**

# Snake Bite

SERVES 8

¼ pound bacon, cut into ½-inch pieces

4 tablespoons (½ stick) unsalted butter

1 large yellow onion, diced (about 1½ cups)

3 tablespoons minced garlic

½ cup white wine

One 28-ounce can diced tomatoes

2 tablespoons Worcestershire sauce

¼ cup Chicken Stock (page 362 or low-sodium store-bought)

1 tablespoon cayenne pepper

1 tablespoon ground cumin

1 tablespoon granulated garlic

1 tablespoon dried basil

1 tablespoon dried oregano

1 tablespoon freshly cracked black pepper

1 tablespoon paprika

2 tablespoons dried thyme

1 teaspoon ground cinnamon

1 teaspoon fine sea salt

2 pounds shrimp (U15), peeled, deveined, and butterflied

*(cont.)*

*I'm a huge hot rod fan, and* **this dish was invented for and served to the hot rod king Carroll Shelby!**

The best word to describe this is *unctuous.* . . .

**1.** In a large skillet over medium-high heat, cook the bacon until just crisp. Remove from the pan and set aside. In the same pan, over medium-high heat, melt 1 tablespoon butter, add the onion, and cook for 5 to 7 minutes, until the onion is just starting to brown. Add the minced garlic and cook for 2 minutes more. Add ¼ cup of the wine and stir to remove any bits from the bottom of the pan. Add the tomatoes, Worcestershire, and the chicken stock. Simmer the sauce for 20 minutes, stirring occasionally, until thickened.

**2.** In a large bowl, combine the cayenne, cumin, granulated garlic, dried basil, oregano, pepper, paprika, thyme, cinnamon, and salt. Add the shrimp and toss to coat in the spice mix.

**3.** In a separate skillet over medium heat, heat the oil and 2 tablespoons of the butter. (Be careful not to burn the butter!) Add the shrimp (reserving any extra spice mix) and cook for about 90 seconds on each side, or until a bit pink (they won't be fully cooked). Transfer the shrimp to a plate.

**4.** Raise the heat to medium-high, add the remaining ¼ cup wine, and scrape up any browned bits. Add the green onion, reserving 2 to 3 tablespoons for garnish. Add any remaining spice mix and cook until the liquid is reduced by one-third. Add the cream, lower the heat to medium-low, and simmer until reduced by another one-third.

**5.** Meanwhile, spread the rolls with garlic butter and grill or toast them.

**6.** Add the shrimp to the tomato sauce and stir in the reduced cream, cilantro, and basil. Simmer for 3 to 4 minutes, to finish cooking the shrimp. Stir in the remaining 1 tablespoon butter. Garnish with the reserved green onions, piling a generous portion of shrimp and sauce on each of the split rolls and with the top bun offset. Serve immediately.

**1 tablespoon olive oil or grapeseed oil**

**1 cup thinly sliced green onions**

**1 cup heavy cream**

**8 ciabatta rolls, split**

**Garlic butter, as needed (see page 71)**

**¼ cup chopped cilantro**

**3 tablespoons finely shredded basil**

# Morgan's Veggie Patties

## ❧ SERVES 4 ❧

4 tablespoons olive oil

3 tablespoons diced red onion

2 tablespoons diced pitted black olives

2 tablespoons diced red bell pepper

1 teaspoon diced jalapeño

1½ tablespoons diced garlic

1 tablespoon diced jarred artichoke hearts (in water, not marinated)

½ cup drained cooked black beans

½ cup drained cooked chickpeas

½ cup drained cooked white beans

¾ cup rolled oats

½ teaspoon sweet Hungarian paprika

½ teaspoon chili powder

1 teaspoon dried oregano

1 tablespoon minced flat-leaf parsley

½ teaspoon red chili flakes

½ teaspoon ground cumin

½ teaspoon celery salt

*(cont.)*

*A standard veggie patty looks to me like something you'd come across in a field of buffalos.* But if you're a vegetarian like my sister, Morgan, then you're often restricted to such things on a menu. So in tribute to her, I set about compiling ingredients **to take these patties to another level. I wanted great flavor, texture, and chew,** and found it using a combination of oats, beans, seeds, and spices. Morgan has become a fanatic for these, and they've also gone on the menu at Johnny Garlic's. Love ya, Bips! (nickname)

**1.** In a medium skillet over medium heat, heat 2 tablespoons of the olive oil. Add the onion, olives, red pepper, jalapeño, garlic, and artichoke, and cook until the onion is translucent, about 8 minutes. Transfer the mixture to a large bowl and let cool.

**2.** Add the beans and chickpeas to the cooked veggies and mix thoroughly. Add the oats, paprika, chili powder, oregano, parsley, chili flakes, cumin, celery salt, sage, bread crumbs, and egg and again mix thoroughly. Form into four patties, cover, and refrigerate for 30 minutes.

**3.** In a small bowl, mix together the mayonnaise, cilantro, salt, and pepper.

**4.** Heat the remaining 2 tablespoons olive oil in a large skillet over medium-high heat and cook the patties 2 to 3 minutes per side, until nicely browned.

**5.** Serve on the buns with the cilantro mayonnaise.

Wow—she's younger, more beautiful, and smarter than me. . . .

¼ teaspoon ground sage

2 tablespoons seasoned bread crumbs

1 egg

¼ cup mayonnaise

2 tablespoons minced cilantro

¼ teaspoon fine sea salt

¼ teaspoon freshly ground black pepper

4 whole-grain burger buns

# Jambalaya Sandwich

¼ pound thick-cut bacon, diced

1 pound pork butt or pork loin, cut into ½-inch cubes

1 pound smoked sausage, cut into ½-inch slices

½ pound andouille sausage, cut into ½-inch slices

1 cup chopped red onion

1 cup thinly sliced celery stalks

1 cup red bell pepper matchsticks

1 pound boneless, skinless chicken thighs, cut into ½-inch cubes

¼ cup chopped garlic cloves

¼ cup chopped flat-leaf parsley

1 cup chopped green onions

2 teaspoons cayenne pepper, or to taste

Salt and freshly ground black pepper

½ cup water

Two 12-inch sourdough bread loaves

1 pound thinly sliced Havarti cheese

*I learned to make jambalaya from a Cajun buddy of mine named Ron Walker. (We call him "Unyawn.") The first time I saw him make it was at a BBQ class in Houston, Texas. Ron brought in this huge cast-iron pot and set about making his killer jambalaya. I'll never forget it.*

*One day I decided I'd try doing jambalaya for a football game. I realized the plates and utensils were going to be tough to handle while watching the game, so I thought about keeping all that great flavor but substituting bread for the rice. So I started making this sandwich like I make all my food: big and flavorful. It took off and ended up being one of my first really well-known dishes.*

**1.** In a large cast-iron pot or Dutch oven over medium-high heat, cook the bacon until it is crisp and the fat is rendered. Set the bacon aside.

**2.** Add the pork to the fat and cook on medium-high heat until it is browned on all sides, 10 minutes. Add the sausages, red onion, celery, and red pepper and cook until onion is translucent, about 10 minutes. Add the chicken, garlic, parsley, and ¾ cup of the green onions. Cook until chicken is cooked through, 10 minutes more. Add the cayenne and season with salt and pepper to taste. Stir in the water, cover, and let simmer on low for 45 minutes to 1 hour.

**3.** Preheat the oven to 200°F. Split the bread loaves and place the cheese slices on the bread bottoms. Toast lightly in the oven.

**4.** Spoon some of the pork mixture onto the bread bottoms and top with the bacon and the remaining ¼ cup green onion. Finish with the bread tops. Cut each sandwich into 4 pieces and serve immediately.

Oh, you gotta try-a . . . dis jambalaya!

# Saigon Sub

### ∼ SERVES 4 ∼

2 pounds pork butt, cut into 4 pieces

Salt and freshly ground black pepper

¼ cup plus 2 tablespoons soy sauce

⅓ cup water

2 tablespoons chili-garlic sauce (I recommend Tuong Ot Toi Viet Nam)

¼ cup ketchup

½ cup distilled white vinegar

2 tablespoons dark brown sugar

¼ cup dry white wine

½ cup peeled and thinly sliced cucumber

2 tablespoons olive oil

24-inch Italian bread or 4 hero or hoagie rolls, split

1 cup mayonnaise

3 tablespoons sriracha sauce

8 romaine lettuce leaves

1 tablespoon minced mint

1 bunch cilantro

*This is my spin on taking one of my "faves"—pulled pork sandwiches with slaw—and hittin' it with an Asian twist. It'll give your taste buds a round-house kick!*

**1.** Season the pork pieces with salt and pepper. Place in a Dutch oven and add ¼ cup of the soy sauce, the water, chili-garlic sauce, ketchup, and ¼ cup of the vinegar. Simmer over medium heat for about 2½ hours, covered, until fork-tender.

**2.** Use a slotted spoon to transfer the meat to a large bowl. Use two forks to pull it apart into shreds. Add some of the cooking liquid to moisten lightly. Cool.

**3.** While the meat is cooking, in a medium bowl, combine the remaining ¼ cup vinegar, the brown sugar, wine, and the remaining 2 tablespoons soy sauce and stir until the sugar dissolves. Add the cucumber and marinate at room temperature for 10 to 15 minutes.

**4.** Drizzle the olive oil on the bread. Toast the bread lightly, if desired.

**5.** Spread the mayonnaise on the bread and drizzle with sriracha. Arrange the meat on the bread and top with the lettuce, marinated cucumber, mint, and cilantro. Add the top half of the bread, slice the sandwiches in 3-inch sections, and serve.

**Reminds me of the dancing hot dog at the drive-in!**

# THE MOTLEY QUE

I've been barbecuing and smoking everything from mozzarella to beef jerky since my teenage years. It's always been heaven to me. Several years ago I decided I really wanted to take it to another level and learn the core fundamentals of barbecue, so I enrolled in a course taught by Lola and Jim Rice at Klose Pits in Houston.

I'd always been a Houston Oilers fan, so upon arriving I drove over to the Astrodome and asked, "Is this where the Oilers played? Is there a museum?" And they said, "Of what?" The Oilers had been moved to Tennessee, and there was nothing left except the stadium. It wasn't the first time that trip that I'd get a puzzled reaction . . . Next I drove up to Klose Pits (where David Klose makes some of the most outrageous barbecue pits in the world) and got out of the car in my red Dickie shorts, spiked belt, flip-flops, and T-shirt. Some guys in overalls and jeans were standing outside, probably expecting me to ask for directions or something. When I asked them if that was where the barbecue class was, they said, "Yeah." Then looked me up and down and sideways. One dude walked up and asked, "Boy, what are you doing here?" I explained that I was a chef, there for the class. Our teachers, Lola and Jim, had just won the American Royal barbecue competition, which is like winning the Super Bowl of BBQ. This was no casual gathering of students, and it seemed to me as if everyone knew each other at the kick-off reception. That night I first met my friend Ron "Unyawn" Walker over a big pot of Cajun jambalaya.

The next morning I headed to barbecue class. They asked us to break up into groups, and I ended up meeting a big guy named Matt Sprouls. As you may know, I'm known for giving nicknames, and I called this guy Mustard most of the day. I could tell he couldn't figure out why this crazy guy from California was calling him a condiment, but it became clear to him that night when he looked in the mirror. He'd been sporting a big line of mustard on his pants after he'd bumped up against a table early in the day.

So out of that one class I made some great friends: Mustard, who works for AT&T; Robert

A gift from Stretch at Grinders in Kansas City.

("Riley"), who drives a truck out of Missouri; Unyawn, an engineer out of New Orleans; and Mikey Z, a pharmacist out of Detroit. I (the chef from California) was the odd man out, but we had so much fun that we decided we'd all go to the American Royal together. None of us had ever competed, so we cooked with a team called The Habitual Smokers who were competing in the open division that year. Lo and behold, the team won the Reserve Grand Champions title. That was it—we'd already been hooked on the food; now we were all hooked on winning. So we formed our team. Each one of these guys has his own style of cooking, so I named our group the Motley Que, after one of my favorite bands. We're not grand champions yet, but it's been unbelievable, and they're some of my best friends. They'll give you the shirts off their backs in the middle of winter. Our motto is: *Go big or go home.*

**Mustard**  **Unyawn**  **Mikey Z**  **Riley**

**Guido and Mustard**

At Festivus Maximus.

Motley Que wins! Go big!

Getting ready for the presentation at the American Royal.

These are probably two of the most important, ace-in-the-hole comfort foods in my life, so of course I have my point of view on the best ways to go about making them.

## The Lowdown on Pizza

Unfortunately, I think people believe frozen pizza from the store is the answer to a problem. What probably ends up happening is they want to make it cheaper and fresher at home, and they feel like they're making it themselves by pulling it out of the oven. I'm down with the idea of cheaper and fresher, but here's the good news: **real homemade pizza is easy to make and will taste 100 times better,** and you don't have to make scratch dough.

1. Drop twenty-five bucks for a pizza stone; you'll see that the dividends are monster.

2. Go buy some good raw dough from a grocery store or local pizzeria, or see page 157 to make your own. (Don't feel like you're cheating if you buy it—you're not doing anything wrong! Just make sure it's fresh and good.)

3. Place your pizza stone in the oven and crank it to 500°F or as high as you can get it. Let preheat for 1 hour.

4. Work the dough out lightly into a round. It's worth working on your stretching technique; just takes a little practice.

5. Lightly apply the sauce and top-quality cheese and toppings of your choice.

6. I prefer to dust my pizza peel with flour but not too much, as it gets cakey and burns on the crust. To me the absolute key to getting a dynamite crust is to cook it hot and fast on the stone. Let the stone recover its hot temperature for 5 to 10 minutes before you put another pizza on it.

That's it—a few simple techniques, and your pizza is gonna rock. Don't settle for the mediocre pre-cooked frozen boxed stuff! (Until I come out with one! Ha ha!)

1. You know the old theory that pasta waits for no one? That's the truth. Your sauce should be made, the salad done, and everything should be in place before you cook and pull the pasta.

2. Buy good-quality pasta. You get what you pay for. If you buy bargain-basement pasta, you're getting bargain-basement quality. In today's world of low-carb diets, if you're going to eat it, then why not eat something really good? I like the good pasta I buy to look a little dusty, which is just a result of the way it's made and dried.

3. Use an ample amount of water, such as 4 or 5 quarts to a pound of pasta. Cooking 3 pounds of pasta? Then go get that turkey frying pot that you use once a year and cook your pasta in 3 gallons of water!

4. Salt the water. (Use 1 to 1½ tablespoons per gallon.) 1 tablespoon to 1½ of salt per gallon. Salt is essential, to give the pasta life and flavor.

5. Do not overcook pasta. Place it in rapidly boiling water and cook the pasta to al dente. Just when you think it's almost done, drain it quickly. And I don't want to see you rinsing pasta under running water, either—none of that malarkey.

6. Do not let pasta sit, and do not put olive oil in the water or toss oil with cooked pasta to prevent sticking. The sheen left on it by the oil will keep the sauce from sticking to and flavoring the pasta. The only exception I'd make is if the pasta is for a salad and you have to let it cool down.

7. Toss your sauce with the pasta and let it amalgamate, but don't oversauce your pasta. It's not a castle; DON'T SET IT IN A MOAT.

# Pizza Dough

*These two types of dough are the foundation of good pizza.* **You don't build a $10 million mansion on a weak foundation,** *and the same goes for your pizza.*

**1.** In the bowl of a stand mixer, dissolve the sugar in the warm water. Sprinkle the yeast on top and let stand for 10 minutes or until foamy. Add the olive oil and salt to the yeast mixture, then use the dough hook to mix in the all-purpose flour (for the Prime Time recipe) or the whole-wheat flour and 1 cup of the all-purpose flour (for the Whole-Wheat recipe) until the dough starts to come together. Add more flour as needed and allow the machine to knead the dough until smooth.

**2.** If you don't have a stand mixer, you can use a food processor by pulsing the dough until it is smooth and elastic. Or combine by hand in a large bowl.

**3.** Turn the dough onto a floured board and knead until it is smooth, 2 to 3 minutes. Place the dough in an oiled bowl and turn to coat the surface. Cover the bowl with plastic wrap and let stand in a warm place until the dough is doubled in size, about 1 hour.

**4.** Turn the dough out onto a lightly floured surface and divide it in half for 2 large pizzas or into 4 equal pieces for calzones or small individual pizzas. Form into smooth, tight balls, cover loosely with plastic wrap or a well-floured kitchen towel, and set in a warm place to rise again for 30 to 45 minutes.

**5.** Center a quality pizza stone (if using) in the oven and sprinkle a pizza peel lightly with flour. Preheat the oven to 500°F.

### PRIME TIME PIZZA DOUGH

1 teaspoon sugar

1 cup warm water (110° to 115°F)

1 tablespoon active dry yeast (or 2 packets)

2 tablespoons olive oil, plus more for bowl

1 teaspoon fine sea salt

2½ cups all-purpose flour, plus more for dusting

*Special equipment:* Pizza peel and pizza stone (or pizza pan)

### WHOLE-WHEAT PIZZA DOUGH

1 teaspoon brown sugar

1½ cups warm water (115°F)

1 tablespoon active dry yeast (or 2 packets)

1 tablespoon olive oil, plus more for the bowl

1 teaspoon fine sea salt

2 cups whole-wheat flour

1½ cups all-purpose flour, plus extra for dusting

*Special Equipment:* Pizza peel and pizza stone (or pizza pan)

Knead the dough until it's smooth, then let rest for 1 hour in an oiled bowl.

After it has poofed the first time, cut the dough in two or four pieces.

Form the dough into smooth, tight balls.

Let rest, covered under a well-floured kitchen towel for another 35 to 45 minutes.

Tossing it old-school . . . this took practice. (Or you can use a rolling pin . . . the key is evenly thin stretched dough.)

Put a little flour on your peel before putting down the stretched dough so it slides off easily into the oven.

Sauce and top.

Slide it into the oven. Rotate if browning unevenly.

Voilà.

**6.** Press dough with fingers until it's as flat as possible. Then drape it over both of your fists and gently pull the edges outward, while rotating the crust. When the circle has reached the desired size and thickness, place it on the pizza peel (or on a pizza pan that has been sprinkled with flour). Top the pizza as desired and slide the pizza from the peel to the hot pizza stone.

**7.** Bake for 8 to 12 minutes, depending on thickness, until the crust is firm, crisp, and golden at the edges and the cheese (if using) is melted.

---

### Some of my favorite pizza-topping combos

**Au Naturel:** Parmigiano-Reggiano, fresh rosemary, olive oil, cracked black pepper, and sea salt

**Sauceless Mediterranean:** Parmigiano-Reggiano, Kalamata olives, red onions, sun-dried tomatoes, and pine nuts. (Don't add the tomatoes and pine nuts until the last 30 seconds of cooking or they'll burn!)

**The Motley Que Pizza:** Pulled BBQ chicken, my Chipotle BBQ Sauce (page 76), red onions, cilantro, and fontina cheese

**Spicy Hawaiian:** Canadian bacon, pineapple, red jalapeño, marinara sauce, and mozzarella

---

**An air guitar has nothing on my my "Air Pizza Peel."**

# Cajun Crab and Asparagus Pie

~ SERVES 2 ~

Salt

¾ cup sliced large asparagus spears (cut on the bias, ¼-inch thick)

One 10-ounce ball Whole-Wheat Pizza Dough or Prime Time Pizza Dough (½ recipe, page 157)

¾ cup Cajun Alfredo Sauce (recipe follows)

¾ cup fresh crabmeat, drained and well picked for shells

¼ cup grated mozzarella cheese

2 tablespoons diced roasted red bell pepper

Freshly cracked black pepper

¼ cup shaved Parmesan cheese, for garnish

Lemon wedges, for garnish (optional)

1 green onion, sliced, for garnish (optional)

Grated zest of 1 lemon

*Special Equipment:* Pizza peel and pizza stone (or pizza pan)

*This recipe is dedicated to anyone who thinks of pizza only in terms of pepperoni, sausage, and mushrooms.* **Open the door to the wild, wild world of pizza.**

**1.** Place a pizza stone (if using) in a cold oven and preheat the oven to 500°F.

**2.** Bring 1 quart of salted water to a boil in a medium saucepan and fill a large bowl with water and ice. Add the asparagus to the boiling water and cook for 1 to 2 minutes, then immediately drain the asparagus and drop them into the ice water to stop the cooking. Drain again when cool.

**3.** When all the ingredients are ready, roll the dough into a 10½-inch round. Build the pizza in this order: sauce, crab, mozzarella, asparagus, roasted pepper. Add some freshly cracked pepper.

**4.** Bake the pizza according to the directions on page 157 for 12 to 15 minutes, until golden brown.

**5.** Shave the Parmesan onto the pizza, slice it, and serve with a squeeze of fresh lemon and green onion, and half of the lemon zest.

# Cajun Alfredo Sauce

**MAKES 1¾ CUP**

**1.** In a medium skillet over medium-high heat, heat the olive oil. Add the flour and stir constantly for 2 minutes to create a roux. Lower the heat to medium, add the garlic, cayenne, ancho chile, nutmeg, cracked pepper, and paprika and stir for 1 minute. Gradually stir in the cream, whisking constantly until the mixture is thickened, about 10 minutes. Stir in the Parmesan and remove from the heat. Season with salt and pepper to taste.

1 tablespoon olive oil

1 tablespoon all-purpose flour

1 tablespoon minced garlic

⅛ teaspoon cayenne pepper

⅛ teaspoon ancho chile powder

Pinch freshly grated nutmeg

⅛ teaspoon freshly cracked black pepper

¼ teaspoon smoked sweet paprika

¾ cup heavy cream

¼ cup grated Parmesan cheese

Salt and freshly ground black pepper

# The French Pig Pizza

1 tablespoon olive oil

¼ pound pancetta, diced

2 cups leek matchsticks
(2 by ¼ inch, white and light
green parts only)

½ teaspoon freshly cracked
black pepper

Salt

1 Granny Smith or similar tart,
firm apple, peeled and cut into
2 by ¼-inch matchsticks

One 10-ounce ball Whole-
Wheat Pizza Dough or Prime
Time Pizza Dough (½ recipe,
page 157)

4 to 5 ounces Brie cheese with
rind, cut into ¼-inch slices

Balsamic vinegar for drizzling

Extra virgin olive oil, for
drizzling

*Special Equipment:* Pizza peel
and pizza stone* (or pizza pan)

*\*Don't mess with a pizza stone until it
cools! They break easily when hot.*

*Come on now, I could put pancetta, Brie, leeks, and apples **on a flip-flop** and
you would love it . . .*

**1.** Place a pizza stone in a cold oven and preheat the oven to 500°F.

**2.** In a large skillet over medium-high heat, heat the olive oil. Add the pancetta and cook until just crisp. Remove to a paper-towel-lined plate. Remove all but 1 tablespoon of the fat from the skillet and add the leeks. Sprinkle with the pepper and a pinch of salt and cook over medium-high heat, stirring occasionally, until the leeks start to brown, 6 to 8 minutes. Add the apples and cook for 5 minutes more, until the apples are golden but not falling apart. Turn off the heat.

**3.** Stretch the dough into a round as directed in the dough recipe. Top with the apple and leek mixture, then the Brie.

**4.** Bake the pizza for 10 to 12 minutes, until the crust is golden. Sprinkle with the pancetta, drizzle with the vinegar and extra virgin olive oil, slice, and serve.

If you have an extra ball of dough,
jump over to the Dessert chapter
(page 388) and check out my
dessert pizza recipes.

*Oui oui!* My Brie pizza piggy!

# Chicago Beef Pizza with Hot Italian Giardiniera

3 tablespoons sour cream

1 tablespoon prepared horse-radish

1½ teaspoons freshly cracked pepper

One 10-ounce ball (½ recipe) Whole-Wheat Pizza Dough (page 157)

1 cup finely chopped cooked roast beef (page 140, or use your own)

2 teaspoons minced garlic

1½ cups grated pepper Jack cheese

1 cup Hot Italian Giardiniera, drained, cut into ¼-inch dice (recipe follows)

1 tablespoon extra virgin olive oil

*Special Equipment:* Pizza peel and pizza stone (or pizza pan)

*Chinese food, spaghetti with marinara, and Chicago beef pizza are three things I'll eat morning, noon, or night. If you can't get around to making this and you're in Chicago, **you gotta check out Vito & Nick's.** And the giardiniera is also great on sandwiches and in salads.*

*Note that **the giardiniera needs to be made 3 days in advance** (or you can buy it if you gotta have this tonight!).*

**1.** Place a pizza stone (if using) in a cold oven and preheat the oven to 500°F.

**2.** In a small glass or plastic bowl, combine the sour cream, horseradish, and ½ teaspoon of the pepper.

**3.** Stretch out the dough into a round as directed in the dough recipe. Build the pizza layers as follows: horseradish cream, beef, garlic, cheese.

**4.** Bake the pizza according to the directions on page 157 for 12 to 14 minutes, until the cheese is bubbly and melted and the crust is golden.

**5.** Top with the giardiniera, drizzle with the olive oil, and sprinkle the pizza with the rest of the pepper. Slice and serve immediately.

# Guido's Hot Italian Giardiniera

**MAKES 6 PINTS**

*To sterilize the jars, boil the jars and lids fully covered in water for 5 minutes. Remove with tongs to cool on a paper-towel-covered surface.*

**1.** Partly fill a large bowl with the ice, 1 cup of the white vinegar, 1 cup of the apple cider vinegar, and approximately 2 cups of water.

**2.** Fill a large stockpot half full of water and add the kosher salt. Bring to a boil over high heat. Add the peppers, celery, carrots, onions, and cauliflower. Boil for 2 to 3 minutes, then drain the vegetables and plunge them into the vinegar-ice bath. Toss the vegetables until all are cool, then drain.

**3.** In a large bowl, combine the remaining 3 cups white vinegar, 3 cups apple cider vinegar, the sugar, pepper, chili flakes, garlic, and sea salt and stir until the sugar and salt are dissolved.

**4.** Divide the ingredients among 6 pint-size canning jars: vegetables, olives, pimento, and half a serrano pepper for each jar. Fill each jar to the top with the vinegar mixture, cap tightly, and refrigerate for 3 days before enjoying. The giardiniera lasts about 1 month, refrigerated.

1 quart ice cubes

1 quart distilled white vinegar

1 quart apple cider vinegar

¼ cup kosher salt

2 red bell peppers, cut into ½-inch pieces

1 yellow bell pepper, cut into ½-inch pieces

2 celery stalks, cut into ½-inch pieces

2 medium carrots, cut into ½-inch pieces

6 pearl onions, peeled and diced

2 cups cauliflower florets, cut into ½-inch pieces

1 tablespoon sugar

½ teaspoon freshly ground black pepper

1 teaspoon red chili flakes

6 garlic cloves

1 teaspoon fine sea salt

1 cup green or black olives, pitted and quartered

¼ cup minced drained pimento

3 fresh serrano peppers, halved, seeds removed

*Special Equipment:* 6 pint-size canning jars with rings and lids

# Fieri Spaghetti and Meatballs

2 tablespoons extra virgin olive oil

1 cup finely diced red onion

½ cup finely diced red bell pepper

1½ teaspoons red chili flakes

2 tablespoons minced garlic

1 teaspoon kosher salt

1 cup milk

1 cup ½-inch-diced sourdough bread cubes (from about 2 slices, crusts removed)

1 pound ground beef (80% lean)

1 pound ground bulk pork sausage, unseasoned

2 tablespoons minced fresh basil (about 6 leaves)

2 tablespoons minced fresh oregano

1 tablespoon freshly cracked black pepper

2 tablespoons minced fresh flat-leaf parsley

½ cup finely grated Parmesan cheese

2 eggs, beaten

*(cont.)*

*As a chef I'm asked all the time **what I'd eat for my last meal**. Well, there are quite a few choices, but I gotta tell ya, this is the one from my childhood.*

**1.** In a large skillet over medium heat, heat the extra virgin oil. Cook the onion, bell pepper, and chili flakes for 2 minutes. Add the garlic and salt and cook until tender, about 4 minutes. Transfer the vegetables to a large bowl and let cool. (Keep the pan handy.)

**2.** Meanwhile, pour the milk over the bread and let soak for 5 minutes. Drain off the milk and lightly squeeze the bread, so that it is moist but not wet.

**3.** To the bowl with the cooled vegetables, add the beef and sausage, soaked bread, basil, oregano, pepper, parsley, grated Parmesan, and eggs. Mix thoroughly but gently and shape into 2-inch balls. The more gentle you are, the more tender the meatballs will be.

**4.** In the same pan used for the vegetables, heat the oil over medium heat. Cook the meatballs in batches, browning each completely. Continue to cook until the internal temperature reaches 165°F on an instant-read thermometer.

**5.** Bring a large pot of salted water to a boil. Bring the marinara sauce to a simmer over low heat.

**6.** Cook the spaghetti al dente, according to the package directions. Drain and toss with about 2 cups of the marinara sauce. You can either portion to individual plates or pasta bowls, add more sauce and 3 meatballs per person, and garnish with shredded Parmesan, or place the pasta in a large serving dish and top with sauce, meatballs, and Parmesan.

**1 tablespoon olive oil**

**5 to 6 cups Marinara Sauce (page 363)**

**2 pounds spaghetti**

**½ cup shredded Parmesan cheese, for garnish**

**This is as big as it can get—but it's souped up!**

# Dirty Bird Sketti

### ⌘ SERVES 8 ⌘

¼ pound thick-sliced bacon, sliced into ¼-inch pieces

2 teaspoons to 1 tablespoon cayenne pepper (I prefer it spicy)

1 tablespoon ground ancho chile powder

1 tablespoon ground cumin

1 tablespoon granulated garlic

2 tablespoons dried thyme

1 tablespoon dried oregano

1 teaspoon ground cinnamon

1 tablespoon paprika

2 pounds boneless, skinless chicken breasts, cut into ½-inch dice

3 tablespoons unsalted butter

1½ cups ¼-inch-diced white onion (2 medium onions)

3 tablespoons minced garlic

¼ cup dry white wine

4 cups Marinara Sauce (page 363)

2 tablespoons Worcestershire sauce

*(cont.)*

*Cookin', **jammin' the tunes,** and hangin' with friends and family, that's what I'm talkin' about. I created this rockin' dish while my bro Eric Lindell was bustin' out his tune "Dirty Bird."* **Check him out at ericlindell.com—play it and eat it!**

**1.** In a large skillet over medium-high heat, cook the bacon until crispy. Transfer the bacon to a paper-towel-lined plate and reserve the pan with the fat.

**2.** In a small bowl, make a spice blend by mixing the cayenne, ancho chile, cumin, granulated garlic, thyme, oregano, cinnamon, and paprika. Dust the mixture over the chicken pieces and toss to coat evenly. (Store the remaining spice blend in a tightly capped jar.)

**3.** Heat the bacon fat over medium-high heat and add the chicken. Cook until browned on all sides, 10 to 12 minutes. Remove the chicken from the pan and keep warm.

**4.** Melt the butter in the same skillet over medium-high heat. Add the onion and cook 3 minutes. Add the garlic and cook until the onion is translucent, about 1 minute. Stir in the wine, scraping up any browned bits. Add the marinara sauce, Worcestershire, and pepper. Simmer for 20 minutes.

**5.** Add half the green onion, ¼ cup cilantro, the basil, chicken, and bacon. Cook for 5 minutes to warm everything through.

**6.** Meanwhile, bring a large pot of salted water to a boil. Cook the spaghetti al dente, according to the package directions. Serve the sauce over the spaghetti in a serving bowl and top with remaining green onions and cilantro.

**1 tablespoon freshly cracked black pepper**

**1 cup sliced green onion**

**½ cup chopped cilantro**

**2 tablespoons finely shredded basil**

**1 pound spaghetti**

# Linguine and Clams

## SERVES 4

2 tablespoons olive oil

5 pounds littleneck clams, in shell, scrubbed (see below)*

½ cup garlic cloves (about 14), crushed

½ teaspoon red chili flakes

½ cup white wine

½ cup chicken stock (I recommend Kitchen Basics)

Grated zest of 1½ lemons

6 thyme sprigs

1 pound linguine

2 tablespoons unsalted butter

Fine sea salt

1 teaspoon freshly cracked black pepper

1 tablespoon flat-leaf parsley, chopped

1 lemon, cut into wedges, for garnish

*Anudda idea—take the clams outta the shell and make a killer pizza with roasted garlic and extra virgin oil.*

*I love the simple, pure, unquestionably fantastic flavor and texture of linguine and clams.* **This is how you do it!**

**1.** Bring a large pot of salted water to a boil.

**2.** In a deep 14-inch skillet or heavy stockpot over high heat, heat the olive oil. When the oil is hot, add the clams and let cook for 2 to 3 minutes. Add the garlic and chili flakes and cook for 1 to 2 minutes, taking care not to burn them, then add the white wine, chicken stock, and the zest of 1 lemon. Add the thyme sprigs, cover tightly, and reduce heat to medium-high. Cook until the clams have steamed open, 5 to 10 minutes.

**3.** Meanwhile, after the clams have been steaming for 3 minutes, start cooking the pasta to al dente, according to the package directions. The goal is to have the clams and the pasta done at the same time.

**4.** Discard any unopened clams. Add the butter, sea salt to taste, and the pepper and stir to combine. Add the cooked pasta and toss. Garnish with the parsley and remaining lemon zest and wedges.

## Clam Prep

Scrub and inspect clams—they should all be closed. Mix 1 cup of cornmeal and 2 tablespoons of salt with 1 gallon of water. Let clams sit in the water for 30 minutes to 1 hour to flush out any residual sand.

Lori's hands-down favorite!

# Tequila Turkey Fettuccine

### ⟿ SERVES 2 ⟾

*This is the dish that helped bring home the* Next Food Network Star *title.* **Think about a fettuccine alfredo in Mexico during Thanksgiving. . . . "Tequila!"**

**1.** Bring a large pot of salted water to a boil.

**2.** In a large skillet over high heat, heat the olive oil. Add the onion and jalapeño and cook until the onion is translucent, about 3 minutes. Add the turkey and roasted red pepper and mix lightly, taking care not to break up the turkey too much. Add the garlic and cook for 2 minutes.

**3.** Cook the fettuccine al dente, according to the package directions. Drain.

**4.** Pour the tequila around the edge of the pan to deglaze it. Add the cream and let reduce for 2 to 4 minutes. Add the lemon juice, cilantro, and salt and stir to combine. Add the fettuccine and toss, then add the Parmesan and toss again.

**5.** Nest the pasta on a serving plate. Garnish the pasta with sprigs of cilantro and a sprinkle of tomato and freshly cracked black pepper. Serve with lime wedges.

**2 tablespoons olive oil**

**¼ cup ⅛-inch strips of red onion**

**3 teaspoons minced jalapeño**

**5 ounces cooked turkey breast, sliced into ½-inch pieces**

**¼ cup roasted red bell pepper strips**

**1 tablespoon minced garlic**

**9 ounces fettuccine**

**1 ounce white or silver tequila**

**½ cup heavy cream**

**1 tablespoon fresh lemon juice**

**1 tablespoon chopped cilantro, plus 2 sprigs for garnish**

**¼ teaspoon fine sea salt**

**2 tablespoons grated Parmesan cheese**

**2 tablespoons seeded and diced Roma tomato (about ½ tomato)**

**Freshly cracked black pepper**

**2 lime wedges**

# Weird Spaghetti

2 pounds ground beef
(80% lean)

1 onion, finely diced

2½ teaspoons ground
cinnamon

2½ teaspoons ground cloves

2½ teaspoons ground cumin

2½ teaspoons ground ginger

2½ teaspoons dry mustard

1 teaspoon freshly grated
nutmeg or ground nutmeg

½ teaspoon kosher salt

¾ teaspoon cocoa powder
(Dutch process preferred)

1½ cups Marinara Sauce
(see page 363)

1 quart low-sodium beef stock
(I recommend Kitchen Basics)

2 tablespoons apple cider
vinegar

2 tablespoons Worcestershire
sauce

1 pound bucatini pasta or thick
spaghetti

¼ cup freshly grated
Parmigiano-Reggiano

*Looks like an old-school Bolognese pasta, but **you can't judge a book by its cover**. This one is closer to Cincinnati spaghetti. And for a lot of folks outside of Cinci, that's "weird spaghetti."*

**1.** In a large skillet over medium heat, brown the beef, breaking the mass into smaller pieces. While the meat is cooking and still a little pink, add the onion and cook until the beef is browned and the onion is translucent. Remove all the fat from the pan.

**2.** Stir in the cinnamon, cloves, cumin, ginger, mustard, nutmeg, salt, and cocoa and cook for 2 to 3 minutes, then stir in the marinara sauce. Add the beef stock, vinegar, and Worcestershire. Bring to a gentle simmer and cook over low heat for 1 hour to marry the flavors thoroughly.

**3.** Meanwhile, bring a large pot of salted water to a boil. Cook the bucatini al dente, according to the package directions. Drain.

**4.** To serve, put the cooked bucatini in a serving bowl and add the meat sauce. Garnish with Parmigiano-Reggiano and serve.

# St. Pat's Pasta

### ~ SERVES 4 TO 6 ~

**When your family tree is Italian and Irish**, then of course you make a St. Pat's pasta—the best of both worlds.

**1.** In a large skillet over medium-high heat, melt the butter in the oil. Add the carrots and cabbage and cook, stirring occasionally, until just tender and the cabbage starts to brown, about 20 minutes.

**2.** Stir in the shallots and garlic and cook for 3 to 4 minutes. Add the corned beef and pepper and cook until the beef starts to crisp, about 10 minutes. Stir occasionally.

**3.** Meanwhile, bring a large pot of salted water to a boil. Cook the linguine al dente, according to the package directions. Drain.

**4.** Stir in the white wine and scrape up any browned bits. Add the cream, half-and-half, mustards, and horseradish. Simmer until the sauce has thickened a bit, about 5 minutes.

**5.** Stir in the cheddar and adjust the seasonings as needed. Stir in the peas and linguine, then transfer to a serving dish.

**6.** Garnish with the Parmesan and serve immediately.

2 tablespoons unsalted butter

1 tablespoon canola oil

¼ cup ¼-inch-diced carrots

1 cup 1-inch-diced green cabbage

1 tablespoon minced shallots

1 teaspoon minced garlic

2 cups shredded cooked corned beef (about ¾ pound)

1 teaspoon freshly cracked black pepper

1 pound linguine

¼ cup dry white wine

1½ cups heavy cream

1½ cups half-and-half

1 tablespoon Dijon mustard

1 tablespoon whole-grain mustard

1 tablespoon prepared horseradish

2 cups grated Irish white cheddar or extra sharp white cheddar

¾ cup fresh or frozen peas (not canned)

¼ cup grated Parmesan cheese

# VEGAS: GO BIG OR GO HOME

**I drove into Vegas in 1987 in my 1976 280Z with everything I owned** loaded up in the trunk. I had all my clothes, a cutting board snagged from my parents' kitchen (this thing was big and had been built to slide in and out of the countertop!), the family wok, and my first knife. Cruising into town in the August heat, I thought, This is ridiculous, where in the world am I? There were strip malls and Chinese restaurants everywhere, and it looked like I'd landed in sports bar heaven. I was just eighteen, but I was armed with my GED, a year at College of the Redwoods in Eureka, and a year at American River College in Sacramento. I already knew at that point that I wanted to own my own restaurant and was totally confident in my cooking, but my father had very wisely advised me to learn the business side. So I was ready for the big time: the University of Nevada–Las Vegas's Harrah Hotel College. I unloaded at Tonapau Hall, where my buddy Double D (Dan Dawson) had a dorm room where I could crash on his floor until I could find a place to live.

At the time, UNLV was up and coming and Vegas was growing rapidly. You could take a class on just about anything that got you going. I took courses like the history of rock 'n' roll for my music elective, and they had one on the principles of gambling. I was never a real big gambler, but they taught all the different aspects of the casino industry, down to the importance of guest loyalty. There were also industry survival courses such as one on property management, and that kind of education was exactly what my old man had meant when he'd told me I had to become as good a businessman as I was a chef if I was going to make it. The school was close-knit, and the professors were hands-on and got you internships to see different sides of the industry. My counselor, professor Vince Eade, helped me build my business degree with a hospitality specialization.

During my second year at school I started working at my girlfriend's family meatpacking company, Schulman's Meats. I started doing cleanup, then learned how to work the Hollymatic ground beef patty machine. I learned all kinds of stuff, from boxing and delivering meat to business decisions like purchases. It was a blast, and I continued there until I graduated. Working at Schulman's basically gave me a degree on "back of the house" purchasing, and it's been one of biggest influences on my restaurant career. From price negotiations to vendor responsibility to controlling costs to dealing with meat salesmen, I learned a lot.

**People think I'm wild now, but you should've seen me back then**, driving around in my big green Jeep with my long hair and Birkenstocks. The UNLV basketball team was incredible to watch, and the hotels were still old-school, like the Dunes. The Mirage hadn't been built yet, but you could feel this world was on fire. I joined a great fraternity, Alpha Tau Omega, which is not normally my style, but my brothers are such loyal friends. It was an amazing time, worthy of its own movie.

One semester I signed up for a class called 367 where everyone was organized into teams—and I ended up with my fraternity brothers as my team, not realizing how serious the class was going to be. (We were a little bit rowdy. No—real rowdy.) The entire semester was spent gearing up, from concept to execution, for an "opening" where the classroom became a small restaurant dining room and everyone in the class works for you. Our instructor was Chef Lambertz, and I was the chef for the team. When we presented my idea to do a Cajun theme for our menu, Chef Lambertz replied, "You think you can pull off Cajun? I know Cajun; you'll have a hard time impressing me with it." My teammates were not too happy, and said, "Dude, what's up with that? We should change our theme." No way. **I'd developed a fusion dish for our menu called Cajun Chicken Alfredo**: Italian pasta mixed with blackened chicken. It was a defining point for me, because I knew it was original, and therefore risky. Being the smartass I was, I was not going to back down, but I was worried.

So when our turn came to run the "restaurant," we served up blackened snapper, étouffée, and salad, but the thing that people went bananas for was the **Cajun Chicken Alfredo**. I held on to the recipe for years and made it the first menu item at my first restaurant, Johnny Garlic's.

I also had a great relationship (and still do) with a professor named John "Stef" Stefanelli. He and I were like two ends of a spectrum, but he was instrumental in helping me finish college and graduate with good grades. Stef taught me that you go big or go home. And living in Vegas, with these enormous hotels built by people who wanted to "go big," I realized that I could be anything I wanted to be. It was an insight into what life could be like if you played it on a larger level.

# Cajun Chicken Alfredo

## ⤙ SERVES 4 ⤚

Four 5-ounce boneless, skinless chicken breasts (about 1¼ pounds)

½ cup Blackening Spice Rub (page 371)

2 tablespoons olive oil

3 tablespoons minced garlic

¼ cup dry white wine

3 cups heavy cream

1 cup roughly chopped marinated sun-dried tomatoes

1 pound fettuccine

¾ cup grated Parmesan cheese

1 teaspoon fine sea salt

1 teaspoon freshly ground black pepper

¼ cup thinly sliced green onion, for garnish

*Everyone has a "first" they remember. This will always hold a special place in my repertoire—the one that saved my skin and sent me to heaven in 367. . . . Go Rebels!*

**1.** Preheat the oven to 350°F. Bring a large pot of salted water to a boil. Heat a large cast-iron skillet over very high heat.

**2.** Dredge the chicken breasts in the spice mix. Place in the cast-iron skillet. Blacken both sides of the chicken, 2 to 3 minutes per side.

**3.** Transfer the chicken to a baking sheet and place in the oven for 10 minutes or until the internal temperature of the chicken reaches 165°F on an instant-read thermometer.

**4.** Remove from the oven and slice the chicken into strips on the bias.

**5.** In a large skillet over medium heat, heat the olive oil. Add the garlic and lightly brown it, 2 to 3 minutes. Stir in the wine. Pour in the heavy cream, bring to a simmer, and cook until the sauce is reduced by half. Add the sun-dried tomatoes and chicken slices.

**6.** Meanwhile, cook the fettuccine al dente, according to the package directions. Drain.

**7.** When the sauce is at the desired consistency, stir in ½ cup of the Parmesan, the salt, pepper, and pasta.

**8.** To serve, toss the pasta with the sauce and serve on large rimmed plates. Garnish with ¼ cup green onion and the remaining ¼ cup Parmesan.

# Hong Kong Noodles

## ⮞ SERVES 4 TO 6 ⮜

6 tablespoons soy sauce

2 tablespoons minced ginger

1 tablespoon minced garlic

2 tablespoons chili-garlic paste

4 tablespoons cornstarch

2 small boneless, skinless chicken breasts, cut into ¼-inch slices

1 pound chow mein noodles (the size of spaghetti or soba noodles; I recommend Annie Chung brand)

11 tablespoons canola oil

1 cup white onion cut in ⅛-inch shreds

½ cup red bell pepper cut in ¼-inch strips

1 cup carrot cut in 3- by ¼-inch sticks

1 cup sliced celery cut on a bias, ½-inch thick

½ cup stemmed shiitake mushrooms cut in ½-inch strips

¾ cup snow peas cut in ½-inch strips

1 cup fresh bean sprouts

*(cont.)*

*When I was going to college in Vegas, I used to stop in at a $5.99 Chinese restaurant by my apartment. A man named Mr. Lee was always there, and **he'd always tell me to try the Hong Kong noodles**. But I'd get sidetracked and try all these other crazy things instead. Then one day he wasn't there and I got worried, so I asked this kid behind the counter where he was. Turned out Mr. Lee wasn't Mr. Lee—his name was Jerry—and he wasn't Chinese, he was Hispanic. And so ended my quest for authentic Hong Kong noodles. Later on, when I finally tried them, I learned that it's crispy chow mein noodles with vegetables on top. I was like, **wait a second, it tastes great—get out of my way!** Mr. Lee not required.*

**1.** In a resealable 1-gallon plastic bag, place 3 tablespoons of the soy sauce, the ginger, garlic, chili-garlic paste, and 2 tablespoons of the cornstarch and mix thoroughly. Add the chicken, seal the bag, and marinate for 1 hour in the refrigerator.

**2.** Fill a large bowl with ice and water. Bring water to a boil in a medium stockpot. Cook the noodles al dente, according to the package directions. Drain the noodles and plunge them into the ice water. Shake them dry and toss with 2 tablespoons of the canola oil to keep them from sticking.

**3.** Drain the chicken and discard the marinade. In a large skillet or wok over high heat, heat 2 tablespoons of the canola oil until almost smoking and add the chicken, separating the pieces. Stir-fry until browned on all sides and cooked through. Remove and keep warm.

**4.** In the same skillet, add 2 tablespoons more of the oil. Heat until almost smoking, then add the onion, bell pepper, carrot, and celery. Stir-fry for 2 minutes. Add the mushrooms, snow peas, and bean sprouts. Stir-fry for 1 minute. Return the chicken to the skillet and stir-fry for 1 minute. Add the hoisin, the remaining 3 tablespoons soy sauce, and the sesame oil, toss, and use a slotted spoon to transfer the mixture to a bowl and keep warm.

**5.** In a small bowl, mix the remaining 2 tablespoons cornstarch and the chicken stock. Pour the mixture into the hot skillet and simmer until reduced by one third.

**6.** Meanwhile, heat a 12-inch nonstick skillet over high heat, pour in 3 tablespoons of the oil, and heat it to almost smoking. Add the noodles, flatten into a cake and cook on one side, without stirring, until crispy and light golden brown, 6 to 8 minutes. Flip the noodles, add another 2 tablespoons oil, and cook the other side until browned, 4 to 5 minutes. Drain the noodle cake on paper towels.

**7.** To serve, place the noodle cake on a rimmed serving platter, top with the chicken and vegetables, and pour the reduced sauce on top. Garnish with the green onion.

**3 tablespoons hoisin sauce**

**¼ teaspoon sesame oil**

**1½ cups Chicken Stock (page 362 or low-sodium store-bought)**

**½ cup green onion strips (3- by ¼ inch)**

**How funky is your chicken?**

This is the culinary intersection of Crazy Tasty and Gonna Rock Your World!

# Penne with Cajun Hot Links and Chipotle Shrimp

## SERVES 4

*Chipotles in adobo can be a little too intense for some folks. That's why I made a **chipotle BBQ sauce** and turned it into **a killer pasta!** It's a huge seller at Johnny Garlic's.*

**1.** In large skillet over high heat, heat the olive oil. When hot, add the sausage. Cook the sausage until browned on both sides, 4 to 5 minutes. Add the shrimp and cook just until pink. Remove the shrimp and sausage and set aside. Lower the heat to medium and add the cream, ¾ cup of the chipotle sauce, the salt, and pepper. Add the pasta and ½ cup Parmesan and toss to combine and heat through. Reduce the liquid by about a quarter, then add the shrimp and sausage and combine.

**2.** Bring a large pot of salted water to a boil. Cook the pasta al dente, according to the package directions. Drain.

**3.** Serve in a pasta bowl and garnish with the tomato, green onion, and remaining ¼ cup grated Parmesan.

## Chipotle Sauce

**MAKES 2 CUPS**

**1.** Combine all the ingredients in blender and puree. Cover and refrigerate. Store extra sauce in a glass jar up to 2 weeks in refrigerator.

---

2 tablespoons olive oil

4 all-beef hot links, each cut on the bias into 6 pieces

20 shrimp (21-25 count), peeled, deveined, and butterflied

2 cups heavy cream

¾ to 1 cup Chipotle Sauce (recipe follows)

½ teaspoon fine sea salt

½ teaspoon freshly ground black pepper

¾ cup grated Parmesan

1 pound penne pasta

1 tablespoon diced seeded Roma tomato, for garnish

1 tablespoon diced green onion, for garnish

**CHIPOTLE SAUCE**

1 cup Kansas City–style barbecue sauce

½ cup canola oil

¼ cup fresh lemon juice

1 tablespoon Dijon mustard

¼ cup chipotle in adobo

½ teaspoon red chili flakes

¼ teaspoon cayenne pepper

¼ teaspoon freshly ground black pepper

Chicken is my number two favorite meat, behind pork. **Poultry is a star in the Tour de Fieri.** It plays in my culinary circus and is reserve grand champion in my culinary rodeo. **It's affordable and healthful,** and you can cook it in a million different ways: fry, bake, roast, boil, steam, grill. I'm blown away by the diversity offered by poultry, from the humble yet irresistible egg to the wide range of cuts, and its amazing culinary versatility.

But when I was young, I wasn't a huge fan of anything but the breast and wings. At the countless barbecues I attended, the kids were given the drumsticks, the teenagers were given the thighs, and the parents made off with the prize. The problem with the thighs is that they're the fattiest piece on the chicken, but they're often cooked at the same temperature and time frame as the wings and breast, and there was never enough time to render the fat or crisp the skin. The meat was chewy and stringy, and I hated it. When I'd go to a Chinese restaurant, I'd ask, "For two dollars more, can I get all breast meat?" But **I turned the corner when I realized it was all about cooking thighs right.**

Finally, in the last twenty years, I've become able to afford duck. It's funny how we find our simple pleasures in food, and to me duck confit should get its own chapter in the story of poultry. So . . . regardless of what you call it, cook it, or serve it, I love to partake of the poultry. Quack-gobble-doodle-do.

# POULTRY GUY'D

## How to Part a Chicken

Remove the backbone.

Slice through the center of the breast.

Separate the leg and thigh from the breast.

Cut through the joint between the leg and thigh.

Slice each side of the breast meat in half.

Cut the wings off through the joint.

Ready for Happy Birthday Stacey Fried Chicken (page 200).

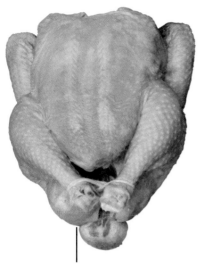

**Chicken Wings:**
Firecracker Wings
(page 57)

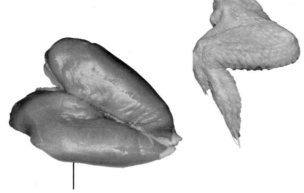

**Chicken Thighs:** "Holla 4 Chicken Marsala" (page 195), Yakitori Chicken (page 196), Oak Town Garlic Vinegar Chicken (page 202), Chicken and Seafood Paella (page 198), Buffalo Balls (page 62), Chicken Lettuce Cups (page 80), Grilled Chicken Tortilla Soup (page 108), Green Papaya Salad with Lemongrass Chicken (page 120), Jambalaya Sandwich (page 148), Pork-Outlet (page 222)

**Whole Chicken:** Big Bud's Beer Can Chicken (page 190), Brick in the Wall Bird (page 192), Happy Birthday Stacey Fried Chicken (page 200), Chicken Pozole (page 104), Grilled Chicken Tortellini Soup (page 103)

**Chicken Breast:** Chicken Dijon (page 188), Red Rocker Margarita Chicken (page 129), Dirty Bird Sketti (page 168), Cajun Chicken Alfredo (page 178), Chicken-Avocado Egg Rolls (page 86), No Can Beato This Taquito (page 94), Shrimp and Chicken Tom Kai Gai (page 106), Hong Kong Noodles (page 180)

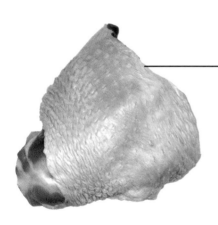

**Duck Breast:** BBQ Duck Fried Rice (page 204)

**Turkey Breast:**
Tequila Turkey Fettuccine (page 173)

**Duck Legs and Thighs:**
Duck Confit (page 203)

**Ground Turkey:**
Roasted Acorn Squash with
Turkey Sausage (page 206)

# Chicken Dijon

⟿ SERVES 6 TO 8 ⟾

¼ cup plus 1 teaspoon kosher salt

3 tablespoons sugar

1 quart cool water

4 boneless, skinless 1-inch-thick chicken breast halves (about 2¼ pounds)

4 tablespoons (½ stick) unsalted butter

3 tablespoons olive oil

¾ cup sliced shallots

1 tablespoon minced garlic

¾ cup all-purpose flour

2 teaspoons freshly cracked black pepper

½ teaspoon granulated garlic

½ cup dry white wine

½ cup Dijon mustard

2 tablespoons whole-grain mustard

½ cup Chicken Stock (page 362, or low-sodium store-bought)

¾ cup heavy cream

4 cups loosely packed baby spinach, shredded

8 slices Emmenthaler or Swiss cheese (about ¼ pound)

*Almost every time I cook with mustard it reminds me of being an exchange student in France. Especially when I make a dish like this one, with wine and cheese.*

**1.** In a resealable 1-gallon plastic bag, dissolve the ¼ cup kosher salt and sugar in the water. Add the chicken, seal tightly, and refrigerate for 1 hour or up to 8 hours.

**2.** Preheat the oven to 275°F.

**3.** In a large oven-safe skillet over medium-high heat, melt 1 tablespoon of the butter in 1 tablespoon of the oil. Add the shallots and cook until golden, stirring occasionally, about 3 minutes. Add the minced garlic and cook for 30 seconds more. Remove from the pan. Do not rinse the pan.

**4.** Remove the chicken from the brine, rinse, and pat dry. Slice the breasts in half horizontally, so that each piece is about ½-inch thick. Trim any fat. Season the flour with the remaining 1 teaspoon salt, pepper, and granulated garlic and combine well. Dredge the chicken breasts in the seasoned flour.

**5.** Combine the remaining 2 tablespoons oil and 3 tablespoons butter in the skillet and turn the heat to medium-high. Working in batches, add the chicken (do not crowd) and cook for 3 to 5 minutes, until browned on one side. Turn the chicken over and cook for 2 to 3 minutes to brown the other side. As the chicken finishes cooking, place it on a baking sheet in the oven to keep warm. Repeat with the rest of the chicken.

**6.** Pour the wine into the pan and cook until the pan juices are reduced to 2 tablespoons, about 3 minutes, scraping the browned bits off the bottom of the pan. Stir in the mustards and stock until smooth. Stir in the cream.

Bring the sauce to a simmer, stirring frequently. Return the chicken breasts to the pan, turning to coat them evenly in the sauce and incorporate the coating into the sauce (this helps to thicken the sauce).

**7.** Increase the oven temperature to a low broil if you have it and make sure there's an oven rack in the top third of your oven, or to 500°F if not. Evenly sprinkle the spinach on top of the chicken, evenly distribute the shallots and garlic on top of the spinach, and top with the cheese. Broil or bake in the oven until the cheese is melted and just starts to brown in some spots. Remove the pan from the oven and let it rest on a heatproof surface for 5 minutes before serving.

# Big Bud's Beer Can Chicken

### ❧ SERVES 4 ❧

One 2- to 3-pound chicken, organic and free-range if possible

1 teaspoon dried oregano

1 teaspoon garlic powder

1 tablespoon onion powder

1 teaspoon paprika

1 teaspoon ground ginger

1 teaspoon ground sage

1 teaspoon fine sea salt

1 tablespoon freshly ground black pepper

One 12-ounce can beer

2 garlic cloves, smashed

½ pound bacon (7 to 9 slices)

*This recipe began with a good ol' American Budweiser—**one for the bird, one for me**. So the name just stuck!*

**1.** Preheat the oven to 450°F. Rinse the chicken with cold water and pat dry with paper towels.

**2.** Combine the oregano, garlic and onion powders, paprika, ginger, sage, salt, and pepper in a small bowl. Rub half of the spice mix inside the cavity of the chicken. Gently separate the skin from the chicken breast and rub the rest of the mixture onto the meat, under the skin.

**3.** Open the beer and pour out about ½ cup. Drop the garlic into the can. Place the chicken cavity over the beer can and set the chicken, can side down, in large oven-safe skillet. Place 2 or 3 bacon slices in the top neck cavity of the chicken and drape the remaining 5 or 6 bacon slices around the outside of the chicken.

**4.** Roast the chicken for 10 minutes. Lower the temperature to 325°F and roast for 1 hour or until the internal temperature in the thickest part of the thigh registers 165°F on an instant-read thermometer.

**5.** Let rest for 5 to 10 minutes. Remove bacon and serve the chicken whole, shredded, or cut into portions. (Me, I like my whole bird on a stick!)

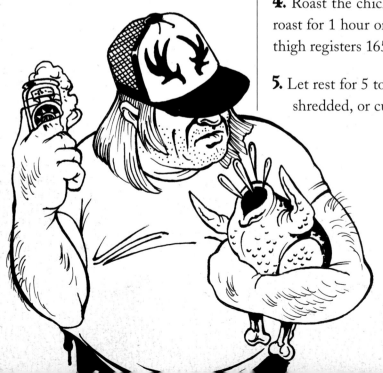

First, meditate. I have no idea what I'm doing here.

*Mise en place* and "de-bling."

Rub half of the spice mixture in the inside cavity of the chicken.

Gently separate the skin from the breast and rub in the rest of the spice mix.

Place chicken over beer can. (PBR had to do a cameo.)

Drape bacon slices over the chicken.

You can make a wicked gravy out of those pan drippings.

# Brick in the Wall Bird with Salsa Verde

⤙ SERVES 4 ⤚

One 3- to 4-pound chicken, organic and free-range if possible

1 teaspoon dried rosemary, minced

1 teaspoon ground white pepper

1 teaspoon paprika

1 teaspoon fine sea salt

1 teaspoon granulated garlic

½ teaspoon dried oregano

½ teaspoon dried basil

¼ cup extra virgin olive oil

Salsa Verde (recipe follows)

*Special Equipment:* A heavy cast-iron pan, or 4 bricks covered in aluminum foil, if you've got 'em!

**SALSA VERDE**

½ cup basil leaves

½ cup flat-leaf parsley leaves

½ teaspoon red chili flakes

1 tablespoon chopped garlic

½ teaspoon drained capers

1 teaspoon anchovy paste

*(cont.)*

**I've always been a big fan of naming my food the way an artist would choose a name for a song.** *A good name is meaningful, illustrating what intrigued me about the dish. Here I take an Italian technique—removing the backbone of the chicken and adding pressure (a brick) on the bird while it cooks—so that whole thing cooks evenly and a nice crust forms. If you've only eaten roasted or rotisserie chickens, you'll appreciate how the compression makes the meat really tender as well. I've adapted this technique to cooking chicken wings at Johnny Garlic's, and they've been a big hit. The presentation is great, and the salsa verde just makes a great thing that much better. P.S. Oh, I got sidetracked. Brick in the Wall Bird . . . as in "Another Brick in the Wall" from Pink Floyd. (Love that band and song.)*

Seasoning: rosemary, white pepper, paprika, salt, garlic, oregano, and basil

Bird beauty! Rinse the chicken and pat it dry.

Use kitchen shears or a chef's knife to remove the backbone of the chicken.

Split the breast plate and press down on the chicken on all joints to flatten it.

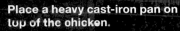

Combine the spices and rub under the skin of the chicken and on the flesh side.

Place a heavy cast-iron pan on top of the chicken.

**2 tablespoons chopped roasted red bell pepper**

**1 tablespoon chopped onion**

**2 tablespoons fresh lemon juice**

**⅓ cup extra virgin olive oil**

**Kosher salt**

Brick in da wall bird!

**1.** Use kitchen shears or a chef's knife to remove the backbone of the chicken. Rinse the chicken with cold water and pat it dry. Split the breast plate and press down on the chicken on all joints to flatten it.

**2.** In a small bowl, combine the rosemary, pepper, paprika, salt, garlic, oregano, and basil. Rub the mixture under the skin of the chicken and on the flesh side of the cavity.

**3.** Heat the oil in a very large skillet over medium-high heat and place the chicken skin side down. Place a heavy cast-iron pan on top of the chicken (if using bricks, place another large skillet on top of the chicken and put the 4 bricks in the top pan). Cook about 6 minutes or until well browned. Remove the top pan, flip the chicken, replace the pan (and/or bricks), and cook the other side for 20 to 25 minutes, or until the internal temperature of the meat reaches 165°F on an instant-read thermometer.

**4.** Transfer the chicken to a cutting board and let rest 5 minutes before carving. Serve with salsa verde.

## Salsa Verde

**MAKES ¾ CUP**

**1.** In a food processor, puree the basil, parsley, chili flakes, garlic, capers, anchovy paste, roasted pepper, onion, and lemon juice until smooth. With the machine running, slowly add the oil and process until well combined. Season with salt to taste.

**2.** Refrigerate unused portion, covered, for up to 2 weeks.

# "Holla 4 Chicken Marsala"

*You gotta love the great flavor of the thighs in this dish.* **Trim 'em and pound 'em** *the right way and everyone will be thrilled about how moist they are.*

**1.** Preheat the oven to 200°F.

**2.** On a cutting board, pound out the chicken thighs between sheets of plastic wrap to ¼-inch thickness. Trim any excess fat or membrane. Season with the salt, pepper, and 2 teaspoons of the thyme and dredge lightly in the flour.

**3.** Heat a large, heavy-bottomed skillet over medium-high heat and add 2 tablespoons of the oil. Working in batches so as not to crowd the pan, cook the chicken for 4 to 5 minutes, until lightly browned on one side. Turn the chicken over and brown the other side. Transfer the chicken to a baking sheet as it's cooked and keep warm in the oven while cooking the remaining chicken.

**4.** When all the chicken is cooked, melt 4 tablespoons of the butter in the pan drippings, still over medium-high heat, and add the garlic and remaining teaspoon of thyme. Cook about 30 seconds to 1 minute. Add the mushrooms. Cook until the mushrooms just start to soften and brown, 6 to 8 minutes. Stir in the tomato paste and cook for 1 to 2 minutes, stirring constantly to avoid burning. Stir in the Marsala wine, scraping any bits off the bottom. Add the chicken stock and increase the heat to high. Return the chicken to the pan and simmer for 4 to 5 minutes, allowing the sauce to reduce slightly.

**5.** Add the remaining 2 tablespoons butter and simmer for 3 to 4 minutes. Salt and pepper to taste. Garnish with the parsley and serve immediately.

3 pounds boneless, skinless chicken thighs (about 9 thighs)

1½ teaspoons kosher salt, plus more to taste

1 teaspoon freshly cracked black pepper, plus more to taste

3 teaspoons chopped thyme

1½ cups gravy flour (I recommend Wondra)

4 tablespoons grapeseed oil

6 tablespoons (¾ stick) unsalted butter

1 tablespoon minced garlic

1½ pounds cremini mushrooms, sliced ½-inch thick (about 8 cups)

1½ tablespoons best-quality tomato paste

1½ cups Marsala wine

¾ cup Chicken Stock (page 362, or low-sodium store-bought)

1 tablespoon chopped flat-leaf parsley

# Yakitori Chicken

1½ pounds boneless, skinless chicken thighs, cut into 1-inch pieces

3 large eggs

1 tablespoon roughly chopped garlic

2-inch piece ginger, plus 2 tablespoons peeled, roughly chopped ginger

2 green onions, roughly chopped, plus more for garnish

1 teaspoon fine sea salt

1 tablespoon all-purpose flour

1 tablespoon cornstarch

½ cup panko bread crumbs

2 quarts water

Yakitori Sauce (recipe follows)

Cilantro leaves, for garnish

Sesame seeds, for garnish

Cayenne pepper, for garnish

Sweet Chili Dipping Sauce (recipe follows)

*Special Equipment:* Twenty 6-inch bamboo skewers, soaked in water

*Shoulda been called smack-itori. . . . This is so tasty and unique it'll make ya* **smack yourself for not tryin' it sooner.**

**1.** In a food processor, pulse together the chicken, eggs, garlic, the chopped ginger, green onion, salt, flour, cornstarch, and panko until well combined. Form the chicken mixture into 1½-inch balls. To keep the mixture from sticking to your fingers, wet your hands with water between rolling the balls. Place balls on a plate, leaving space between them.

**2.** Meanwhile, bring the water to a boil over high heat, then adjust the heat so that the water is at a simmer. Roughly chop the 2-inch piece of ginger and add it to the pot. Add 8 to 10 balls at a time into the water. Cook for about 6 minutes or until cooked through. (The balls will float to the top and change color; make sure there's no pink on the outside.) Remove from the water using a slotted spoon and drain on paper towels. Repeat until all the balls are cooked. When the balls are cool enough to handle, thread 3 per skewer, leaving ¼-inch space between each ball.

**3.** Lightly oil a grill and preheat the grill to medium. Grill the skewers for 7 to 10 minutes, turning gently as they brown lightly. When the chicken is browned, lightly baste the balls with the yakitori sauce. Place the skewers on a serving plate and drizzle with additional yakitori sauce. Sprinkle with cilantro, green onion, sesame seeds, and cayenne pepper and serve immediately with the sweet chili dipping sauce.

# Yakitori Sauce

**MAKES ABOUT 1½ CUPS**

**1.** Whisk together all the ingredients in a small saucepan. Bring to a boil over medium-high heat, reduce the heat to medium, and simmer, stirring occasionally, until thickened, about 2 minutes.

# Sweet Chili Dipping Sauce

**MAKES ABOUT 3/4 CUP**

**1.** In a small bowl, whisk together all the ingredients.

**YAKITORI SAUCE**

½ cup sake

½ cup soy sauce

¼ cup mirin

2 tablespoons honey

2 teaspoons cornstarch

**SWEET CHILI
DIPPING SAUCE**

¾ cup sweet chili sauce
(I recommend Mae Ploy)

1 tablespoon chopped cilantro

1 tablespoon minced green
onion

1½ teaspoons toasted
sesame seeds

⅛ teaspoon cayenne pepper

Now that you can see these, you'll wanna call 'em "attack-itori." Go get 'em!

# Chicken and Seafood Paella

## SERVES 6

1 tablespoon saffron threads

1 cup warm water

2 cups seafood stock

4 tablespoons canola oil

6 bone-in, skinless chicken thighs (about 1 pound)

2 ham hocks

2 cups diced onion

1 cup roughly chopped celery

1 cup roughly chopped carrots

3 tablespoons minced garlic

1 cup dry white wine

1 pound Mexican-style chorizo, cut into ¼-inch slices

1 cup diced red bell pepper

3 cups Arborio rice

1 tablespoon fine salt

1 tablespoon freshly ground black pepper

6 sea scallops, muscle tabs removed

6 mussels, scrubbed and debearded

6 small clams (littleneck, cherrystone, or similar), scrubbed

*(cont.)*

*Ya know what time it is? Yep . . .* **time to buy a paella pan**, *'cause it'll make a difference and you need one anyway. (Shameless plug: call Myers Restaurant Supply.)*

**1.** Soak the saffron in 1 cup warm water for 3 minutes. Add the seafood stock, saffron, and 2 quarts water to the stockpot and bring to a simmer. Cook gently over medium-low heat for 2 hours or until reduced by half. Strain the broth (discard the solids) and keep it warm over low heat.

**2.** In a large stockpot over medium-high heat, heat 2 tablespoons of the oil. Add the chicken thighs and ham hocks and brown the thighs on both sides, 6 to 8 minutes per side.

**3.** Transfer the chicken to a plate, leaving the ham hocks in the pot. Add 1 cup of the onion, the celery, carrots, and garlic and cook for 5 to 7 minutes, until the onion is translucent.

**4.** Add the wine and simmer until the liquid is reduced by half, 6 to 8 minutes, scraping any browned bits from the bottom of the pan.

**5.** In a large straight-sided skillet or paella pan over medium-high heat, heat the remaining 2 tablespoons oil. Add the remaining 1 cup onion, the chorizo, and the red pepper and cook until the onion is translucent, 6 to 8 minutes. (Do not brown.) Add the rice, salt, and pepper and cook, stirring, until all the grains of rice are coated with oil. Reduce

the heat to medium. Spread the rice around the pan so that it is level and add 1 cup of broth at a time, without stirring. When each cup is absorbed, add the next cup. Continue adding broth until rice is al dente, then add chicken, scallops, mussels, and clams. Bury the seafood in the rice.

**6.** Add 1 final cup of broth and cover the pan tightly with a lid or foil. Simmer over low heat for 8 to 10 minutes or until seafood is cooked.

**7.** Serve in the pan, family style, garnished with the green onion and tomatoes.

**½ cup diced green onion, for garnish**

**¼ cup diced Roma tomatoes, for garnish**

# Happy Birthday Stacey Fried Chicken

**CHICKEN AND BRINE**

2 tablespoons olive oil

1 cup chopped yellow onion

½ cup chopped red bell pepper

½ cup chopped green bell pepper

12 garlic cloves

1 gallon water

½ cup sugar

⅔ cup kosher salt

1 cup white wine

½ cup honey

¼ cup black peppercorns

2 quarts ice

2 fryer chickens (4 to 5 pounds each) cut into 10 pieces each (see page 186)

**SEASONING AND FRYING**

6 cups all-purpose flour

¼ cup dried marjoram

1 tablespoon dried tarragon

*(cont.)*

*I made this dish for my great childhood friend Stacey's birthday.* **Some chefs would bake you a cake.** *Me, I make ya fried chicken. (No candles, though.)*

**1. To make the brine:** In a large stockpot over medium-high heat, heat the oil and cook the onion, peppers, and garlic until just softened, 4 to 5 minutes. Add the water, sugar, salt, wine, honey, and peppercorns and bring to a boil. Remove from heat and set aside to cool for 15 minutes. Add the ice to cool completely. Submerge the chicken pieces in the brine and refrigerate for 4 to 12 hours.

**2.** Remove the chicken from the brine, rinse, and pat dry. (Discard the brine.) In a shallow bowl, combine the flour, marjoram, tarragon, thyme, pepper, garlic, and onion powder. Place half of the flour mixture in a second shallow bowl. Pour the buttermilk into a third shallow bowl. Dredge the chicken pieces in the first bowl of flour, then the buttermilk; then dredge again in the second bowl of flour. Set the pieces on a baking sheet fitted with a wire rack and let the chicken rest 15 minutes.

**3.** Meanwhile, heat the oil in a large, deep skillet to 350°F. Add the chicken carefully, cooking in batches, if necessary. Do not overcrowd the pan. Cook the chicken until golden brown and cooked through, about 20 minutes, gently turning the pieces as they brown. Transfer to a paper-towel-lined plate and immediately season with a little seasoned salt. Keep the finished chicken in a warm oven (175°F) while you fry the remaining batches.

1 tablespoon dried thyme

2 tablespoons freshly cracked black pepper

2 tablespoons granulated garlic

2 tablespoons onion powder

6 cups buttermilk

1 quart peanut or canola oil

Seasoned salt

*Special Equipment:* A large, deep cast-iron or heavy skillet, for frying

That's scary . . .

# Oak Town Garlic Vinegar Chicken

8 tablespoons olive oil

2 medium yellow onions, cut in half and sliced thin

2 Anaheim chiles, seeded and cut into very thin strips

6 boneless, skinless chicken thighs (about ¾ pound)

¾ cup minced garlic (about 2 heads)

1 cup beer (I recommend a light pilsner)

1 cup Chicken Stock (page 362, or low-sodium store-bought)

2 tablespoons all-purpose flour

1 teaspoon kosher salt

1 teaspoon freshly ground black pepper

1 teaspoon dried oregano

1 teaspoon paprika

½ teaspoon chili powder

½ cup red wine vinegar

3 tablespoons sliced green onions

*Some of my favorite dishes came from **football tailgate parties**. This is a great one from an Oakland Raiders game. (Get it? Oak town!)*

**1.** In a large Dutch oven over medium heat, heat 2 tablespoons of the oil. Add the onions and chiles and cook for 3 to 4 minutes, until the onions are translucent. Push the vegetables to the outside edge of the pan and lay the chicken thighs skin side down in the center of the pan in one layer. Cook undisturbed for 5 to 7 minutes, until lightly browned. Add ¼ cup of the garlic and cook until fragrant, about 2 minutes. Add the beer and chicken stock and cook for 10 to 15 minutes. Transfer the chicken to a plate and let cool. Pour the juices and vegetables into a small saucepan.

**2.** Heat ¼ cup of the oil in the Dutch oven over medium heat. Add the remaining ½ cup garlic and cook, stirring occasionally, until lightly browned. Remove from the heat and let cool.

**3.** In a medium bowl, combine the flour, salt, pepper, oregano, paprika, and chili powder. Mix thoroughly, add the cooked garlic, and blend into a paste.

**4.** Press the paste onto both sides of the chicken pieces. Heat the remaining 2 tablespoons olive oil in the Dutch oven over medium-high heat and gently place the chicken in the pan. Lightly brown the chicken on both sides, 4 to 6 minutes total.

**5.** Meanwhile, simmer the reserved juices over medium-high heat for 3 to 5 minutes, until warmed through. Stir in the vinegar. When chicken is cooked on both sides, pour the vinegar broth on top and simmer for 3 to 5 minutes.

**6.** Garnish with green onions.

# Duck Confit

**If you're as into duck confit as I am**, *see page 133 for my DLT sandwich. I also like it in taquitos with caramelized red onion, on potato skins instead of bacon, and in ravioli with Asiago cheese . . . you name it.*

4 or 5 duck legs with thighs attached (about 3½ pounds)

2 tablespoons kosher salt

4 garlic cloves, smashed

4 thyme sprigs

2 tablespoons freshly cracked black pepper

3 to 4 cups duck fat, depending on size of legs, melted (your butcher may have this; otherwise you can easily buy it online)

**1.** Sprinkle the duck legs evenly with the kosher salt, cover, and refrigerate for 3 hours.

**2.** Preheat the oven to 225°F.

**3.** Shake off the excess salt and place the duck pieces in a large baking pan. Add the garlic, thyme, and pepper and pour the duck fat over to cover.

**4.** Roast the duck, uncovered, for 4½ to 5 hours, or until the duck meat pulls away from the bone.

**5.** Cool the duck in the fat until you can comfortably handle the legs. Pull the meat from the bones, shredding as you go and discarding the skin and bones. Use immediately, or strain the fat and store the duck meat submerged in the fat in an airtight container in the refrigcrator for up to 3 weeks.

# BBO Duck Fried Rice

## MARINADE

¼ cup soy sauce

¼ cup oyster sauce

1 tablespoon minced ginger

1 tablespoon minced garlic

½ teaspoon sesame oil

½ teaspoon red chili flakes

2 tablespoons honey

**Four 6- to 7-ounce boneless, skinless duck breast halves**

## DUCK FRIED RICE

2 cups brown rice

1 quart water

¼ cup soy sauce

¼ cup oyster sauce

½ teaspoon sesame oil

4 tablespoons canola oil

¾ cup ¼-inch-diced red bell pepper

1 cup ¼-inch-diced yellow bell pepper

1 cup ¼-inch-diced red onion

½ cup thinly sliced green cabbage

*(cont.)*

*Now this one's gonna **take some friends to do some choppin'.** But don't worry, it's so worth it! This fried rice eats like a meal.*

**1. To make the marinade,** in a medium bowl, combine the soy sauce, oyster sauce, ginger, garlic, sesame oil, chili flakes, and honey. Add the duck, cover, and marinate in the refrigerator for 1 to 4 hours.

**2.** Cook the brown rice in the water according to the package directions. Set aside to cool.

**3.** Heat a grill to medium-high, leaving the middle burner off, or if using a charcoal grill, bank the coals on the sides to create indirect heat. Remove the duck from the marinade and pat it dry. Pour the marinade into a small saucepan and bring to a boil for 3 to 4 minutes to (safely!) use as a basting sauce. Grill the duck over indirect heat for 10 to 12 minutes per side, basting with the marinade, until an instant-read thermometer registers 135°F. Transfer the duck to a plate, lightly cover with foil, and cool. Discard the remaining marinade.

**4. To make the fried rice,** combine the soy sauce, oyster sauce, and sesame oil in a small bowl. Dice the duck into ¼-inch pieces.

**5.** Heat 2 tablespoons of the canola oil in a wok or skillet over high heat until the oil almost begins to smoke. Add the ginger, peppers, red onion, cabbage, carrot, and celery and stir-fry for 7 minutes, until the vegetables are softened. Add the snap peas, bok choy, and garlic and cook for 1 minute. Transfer the vegetables to a plate. Heat 1 tablespoon more oil in the wok, then add the rice and cook for 6 minutes to allow it to crisp. (Do this in batches if your pan will not hold all the rice without crowding.)

**6.** Add the eggs and mix rapidly so that the eggs do not stick to the sides of the wok. When the eggs are cooked, add the soy sauce mixture. Mix thoroughly, then add the reserved vegetables and duck. Stir to combine and warm thoroughly.

**7.** Garnish with the green onion and sesame seeds and serve.

½ cup ¼-inch-diced carrot

½ cup ¼-inch-diced celery

1 tablespoon minced ginger

½ cup thinly sliced sugar snap peas

½ cup thinly sliced bok choy

1 tablespoon minced garlic

3 eggs, beaten

½ cup chopped green onion

1 tablespoon white sesame seeds, toasted

1 tablespoon black sesame seeds, toasted

# Roasted Acorn Squash with Turkey Sausage, Peppers, and Goat Cheese

SERVES 6

## TURKEY SAUSAGE

2 teaspoons thyme leaves

2 teaspoons rubbed sage

2 teaspoons kosher salt, plus
more to taste

1 teaspoon freshly cracked
black pepper, plus more to taste

¼ teaspoon cayenne pepper

1 pound lean ground turkey

## ACORN SQUASH AND
VEGETABLES

3 acorn squash, cut in half

3 tablespoons olive oil

1½ teaspoons fine sea salt,
plus more for seasoning

1 teaspoon freshly cracked
black pepper, plus more for
seasoning

2 tablespoons unsalted butter

2 cups 1-inch-sliced green
cabbage

1 red bell pepper, seeded and
cut in ¼-inch-wide strips

1 yellow bell pepper, seeded
and cut in ¼-inch-wide strips

*(cont.)*

*I very seldom shop with a list* when I'm hittin' the market or grocery store. And for this recipe, one day the acorn squash looked amazing and turkey sausage sounded healthy . . . so **this is what came out**. Oh yeahhhh.

**1. To make the turkey sausage,** in a medium bowl, combine the thyme, sage, salt, pepper, and cayenne. Add the turkey and mix well. Cover and refrigerate for 8 to 24 hours.

**2. To prepare the squash,** preheat the oven to 375°F. Trim the ends off the squash so that it will sit flat. Scrape the seeds and membranes from inside the squash halves (if you go through the end, don't worry). Separate the seeds from the membranes and rinse well. Dry the seeds with a paper towel. Place the squash halves cut side up on a baking sheet, drizzle with 2 tablespoons of the olive oil, and sprinkle with 1 teaspoon of the salt and the pepper.

**3.** Place the seeds on a separate baking sheet or prepare a separate foil sheet for them to roast on.

**4.** Place the squash and the squash seeds in the oven. Roast the squash for 30 to 35 minutes, or until golden around the edges and a knife can be inserted easily into the flesh. Remove from the oven but leave the squash on the baking sheet.

**5.** Stir the seeds every 5 minutes and check them for doneness after 15 to 20 minutes; you want them to be crisp and golden brown. Remove from the oven and sprinkle the seeds with the remaining ½ teaspoon salt. Watch out—this is when Hunter and Ryder cruise through and steal the seeds.

**6.** Heat a large skillet over medium-high heat and pour in the remaining 1 tablespoon olive oil. When hot, add the turkey, making sure to leave large chunks, about 1 inch across. Let the chunks brown, then turn and cook through, 8 to 10 minutes. Transfer to a plate and keep warm.

**7.** In the same pan, melt the butter over medium-high heat. Add the cabbage and cook until it starts to color and wilt, about 4 minutes. Add the peppers and onion and cook for 6 to 8 minutes, until the onions are soft and the peppers are still a little al dente. Add the turkey and the garlic. Cook for 2 to 4 minutes more to blend the flavors. Adjust the seasoning with salt and pepper if necessary.

**8.** Turn the oven to a low broil.

**9.** Divide the turkey mixture among the squash halves. Crumble the goat cheese over the tops, sprinkle with the roasted squash seeds, and place under the broiler just until the cheese is warm. Garnish with a bit of parsley and serve immediately.

½ large sweet onion, cut into ¼-inch slices

1 tablespoon minced garlic

4 ounces soft goat cheese (about ½ cup)

2 tablespoons chopped flat-leaf parsley, for garnish

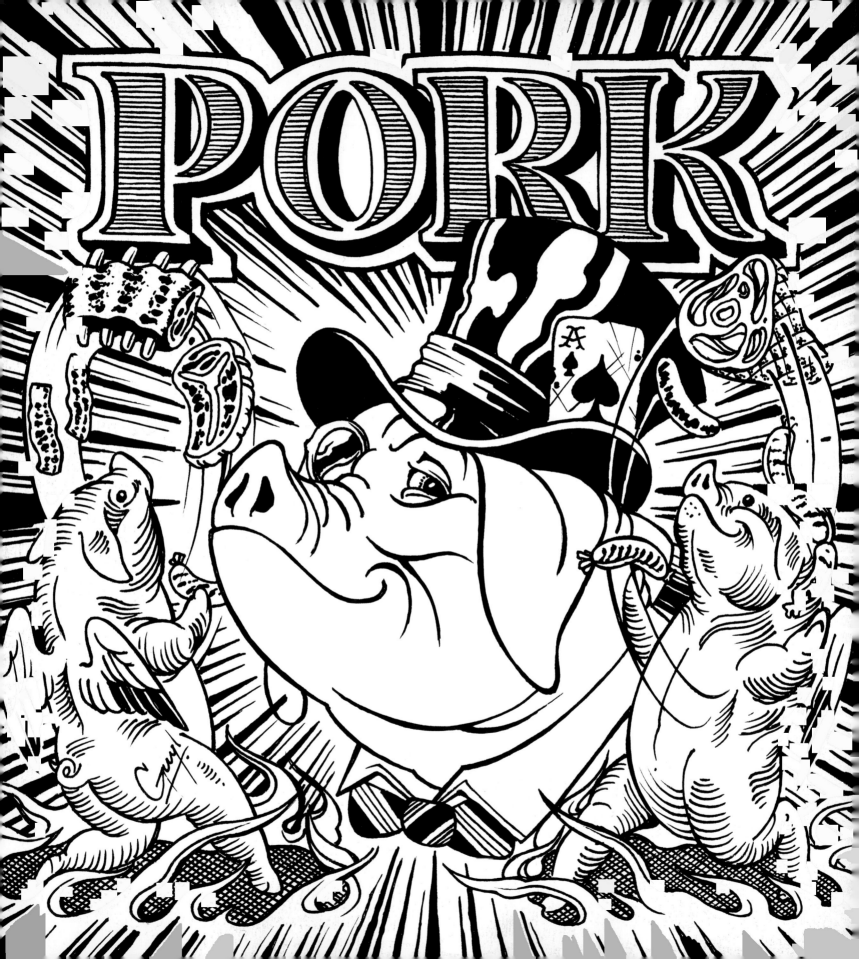

Our family raised pigs when I was a kid, and given how many battles I had with the finer swiner, it's ironic that I actually like them so much today. Those were some rough-and-tumble days. **One of my chores** as a ten-year-old **was to pick up two buckets of slop** for the pigs (yes, *slop,* in two five-gallon buckets with no lids) that came from scraped plates at the lunch counter at the gazebo in downtown Ferndale.

To accomplish this transit, **I'd hang the buckets off the handlebars of my BMX bike** and slowly, gingerly ride home. It was a good mile trek down a country road to my house on Rose Avenue. As I peddled out of town I was a free target to all who saw me, and **one little bump and it was a slopomatic slopfest**. With water at eight pounds a gallon, the slop must've been eleven pounds, so I was carrying two close-to-fifty-pound buckets of everything from soup to protein to vegetables and bread. Needless to say, **I had many a disastrous middle-of-the-road full-blown wipeout.** And if that happened, I had to rush home carrying the remaining slop, just to rush back to the scene of the crime with buckets of water (because if Dad found slop in the road on his way home, Guido was in trouble).

The pigs always knew when five o'clock came around. They'd start going nuts, crowding the entry in such a frenzy that I couldn't open the door. So I'd get pushed and inevitably splashed with slop by the time I'd fed them. There's no dog going for a bone that is more tenacious than a pig going for slop. They're 100 percent muscle. When one of the pigs got out, there was only one way to capture it: **grab it by the hind legs and walk it back to the pen like a wheelbarrow.** I'll never forget the times when my aunt, cousin, and I had to wrangle eight pigs by tackling and pushing. And that's just the beginning—be on the lookout for the "See-squeal," *Pigs Gone Wild: The Guy Fieri Story.*

Nevertheless, I was always a fan of the pork, and in recent years, it's been my honor to work with the National Pork Board. Through them **I coined the phrase POP, "Pal of Pork,"** because it's probably the most versatile protein you'll find at the market. From curing to smoking to serving for breakfast, lunch, and dinner, pork works across almost all ethnicities, whether you're cooking à la minute to fifteen hours, low and slow. What other item can you use as a condiment or an entrée, cook with its rendered fat, use to make everything from dog snacks to people snacks (smoked pig ears to pork crackling), and even make sausage casing from? Everything in the pig is usable. When something is being universally enjoyed from hoof to snout, you've got to know it's the protein that reigns supreme.

Unfortunately, in the last thirty or forty years we've been focusing on making pork less fatty, so we started breeding it to be lean. Pork was bred to be so lean that it started to look white, and it got the moniker "The Other White Meat." We ended up eating lean protein and then layering extra cheese and bacon and mayonnaise on top. Listen: **good, top-of-the-line Berkshire pork is marbled with fat—so you never have that dry meat problem.** The fat represents flavor and moisture. I'm excited to support the National Pork Board's work to show the diversity, health benefits, and value of pork. Breeders are starting to go back to the roots, and artisanal pork movements are springing up. I believe in quality over quantity; practice moderation but have the best.

This is where I grew up. Rose Avenue, Femdels, California.

# PORK GUY'D

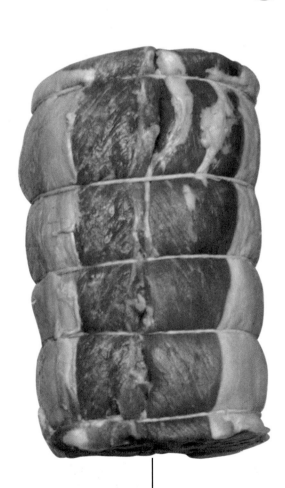

**Pork Loin:** "Chico's Puerto Rican Pork Roast" (page 216), Pulled Pork Hash con Huevos (page 225)

**Pork Spareribs:** Braised Pork Ribs and Italian Sausage (page 230)

**Bacon:** Pork-Oulet (page 222), Bacon-Jalapeño Duck Nuggets (page 68), Bacon-Wrapped Shrimp (page 76), Big Bud's Beer Can Chicken (page 190), DLT 44 (page 133), Texas Hold'em (page 136), and many, many more!

**Pork Butt:** Nor Cal Carnitas (page 228), Saigon Sub (page 150), Chico's Puerto Rican Roast Pork (page 216), Pulled Pork Hash con Huevos (page 225)

**Pork Blade Steak:** Pork Blade Steak Piccata (page 224)

**Pork Tenderloin:** Watermelon Pork Tacos (page 220)

**Ground Pork:** Petaluma Paté (page 58), Ginger Pork Potstickers (page 90), Sloppy Joes (page 134), Pepperoni Burger (page 138), Jambalaya Sandwich (page 148)

**Boneless Pork Chop:** Summer Grilled Pork (page 218)

# Pesto-Crusted Pork Roast

### ❧ SERVES 4 TO 6 ❧

**BRINE**

¼ cup smashed garlic cloves

½ teaspoon red chili flakes

1 tablespoon black
peppercorns

⅓ cup kosher salt

**PORK**

One 3- to 4-pound bone-in
pork loin

½ cup prepared basil pesto

2 teaspoons red chili flakes

2 tablespoons minced garlic

1 teaspoon kosher salt,
plus more for seasoning

1 tablespoon freshly cracked
black pepper, plus more for
seasoning

1 onion, roughly chopped

1 cup roughly chopped carrots

½ cup smashed garlic cloves

2 tablespoons olive oil

*Special Equipment:*
**Kitchen twine**

**1.** Combine the brine ingredients in a resealable 1-gallon plastic bag filled one-third with water. (You can also use a large bowl or pot.) Add the pork and brine in the refrigerator for 2 to 3 hours and up to 8 hours.

**2.** Drain the pork, rinse it under cool water, and pat it dry with paper towels.

**3.** Preheat the oven to 350°F.

**4.** Stand the roast upside down on the cutting board (see the photo, opposite). With a sharp thin knife, slice carefully between eye of the loin and the bottom of the bone. Slowly cut as you roll out the loin from the bone (leaving it attached at the end).

**5.** In a small bowl, combine the pesto, chili flakes, minced garlic, salt, and pepper. Mix well and spread the mixture evenly on the inside of the rolled-out loin. Carefully roll the loin back up and tie up with kitchen twine.

**6.** In a large roasting pan, sprinkle the onion, carrot, and smashed garlic. Drizzle with the olive oil, and season with salt and pepper. Place the pork roast on top of the vegetables, tent the pan with heavy-duty aluminum foil, and roast for 2½ to 3 hours, until an instant-read thermometer in the middle of the meat registers 145° to 150°F.

**7.** Let the meat sit, tented, for 15 to 20 minutes to rest.

**8.** Remove the kitchen twine, remove the meat from the bone, and cut into 1½-inch-thick slices.

**9.** Drizzle the pan juices over the top and serve immediately with the cooked vegetables.

Pour the brine seasonings into a resealable l-gallon plastic bag filled one-third with water.

Place the pork in the bag and seal. Refrigerate for 2 to 3 hours.

Remove the meat from the brine, pat dry, and slice between the eye of the loin and the bone . . .

slowly rolling out the loin from the bone . . .

but leaving it attached at the end.

Spread the pesto on rolled-out loin.

Carefully roll the loin back up.

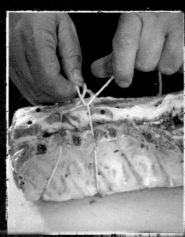

Tie up with kitchen twine.

Place the tied pork on top of the vegetables in the roasting pan.

# Chico's Puerto Rican Pork Roast

### ⤖ SERVES 10 ⤖

2 large onions, peeled and quartered

1 red bell pepper, seeded and quartered

1 tablespoon dried Mexican oregano

1 cup Spanish green olives with pimentos

1 tablespoon Spanish paprika (pimentón)

1 teaspoon granulated garlic

1 teaspoon dried basil, crushed

1 teaspoon Saizón Seasoning (recipe follows)

1 tablespoon Sofrito (recipe follows)

¼ cup drained capers

¼ cup distilled white vinegar

One 8- to 10-pound boneless pork shoulder roast, with fat cap, rind trimmed off (Boston butt)

*One of the greatest cameramen I've worked with is director of photography* **Anthony "Chico" Rodriguez** *of* **Diners, Drive-ins and Dives**. *He's proudly Puerto Rican, and this is named for him!*

**1.** In a food processor, combine the onions, bell pepper, oregano, olives, paprika, granulated garlic, basil, saizón seasoning, sofrito, capers, and vinegar and pulse until well blended.

**2.** Place the pork on a large platter. Slide a sharp knife between the fat cap and meat, creating a pocket. Fill with ½ cup of the seasoning mixture, then pour the remaining mixture over the roast. Cover tightly with plastic wrap and refrigerate overnight, or at least 8 hours.

**3.** Transfer the pork to a roasting pan, cover with foil, and place in a cold oven. Turn on the oven to 325°F.

**4.** Bake, covered, for 5 to 6 hours, or until an instant-read thermometer in the middle of the meat registers 190°F and the meat is beginning to fall apart. Remove foil and brown for 30 minutes. (If the pork looks as if it is getting too dark, tent with foil for the remainder of the cooking time.) Remove from the oven and allow the meat to rest for 20 minutes. Shred or chop the meat as desired, removing the fat cap, bones, and any ligaments.

## Saizón Seasoning

**MAKES ½ CUP**

**1.** Toast and grind the coriander and cumin seeds. Allow to cool completely. Combine with the other ingredients and store in a dry, dark place in an airtight container for 3 months, or freeze for up to 6 months.

## Sofrito

**MAKES 4 CUPS**

**1.** In the bowl of a food processor, fitted with the metal blade, add all the ingredients and pulse until well combined, scraping sides of the bowl if needed. Adjust seasoning to taste. Place in a glass jar and refrigerate for up to 6 weeks or freeze into portioned amounts and use as needed.

**SAIZÓN SEASONING**

2 tablespoons coriander seeds

2 tablespoons cumin seeds

2 tablespoons Spanish paprika (pimentón)

2 tablespoons granulated garlic

1 tablespoon kosher salt

1 tablespoon freshly ground black pepper

**SOFRITO**

1½ cups cilantro (stems okay)

1 red bell pepper, seeded and quartered

1 green bell pepper, seeded and quartered

1 orange or yellow bell pepper, seeded and quartered

1 medium white onion, quartered

¾ cup seeded and diced tomato

⅓ cup apple cider vinegar

¼ cup olive or grapeseed oil

¼ cup Mexican oregano

1 tablespoon kosher salt

1 tablespoon freshly ground black pepper

1 teaspoon cayenne pepper

**With Chico and The Big Bunny.**

# Summer Grilled Pork

Four 1-inch-thick boneless pork chops

1 teaspoon kosher salt

1 teaspoon freshly cracked pepper

10 thick-cut applewood-smoked or regular bacon slices (about 12 ounces)

3 tablespoons cream cheese, at room temperature

2 tablespoons panko bread crumbs

¼ cup thin strips roasted red bell pepper

¼ cup chopped drained artichoke hearts (jarred, in water)

2 tablespoons sliced pickled jalapeños

1 tablespoon balsamic vinegar

¼ cup honey

¼ cup Dijon mustard

½ cup beer (IPA-style preferred)

*It's summertime, or not, and you're cooking pork on the grill. Check this one out. It's **pork on pork**—can't go wrong there—and it's **stuffed with all kinds of big flavors** and basted with some rockin' honey, beer, and mustard glaze.*

**1.** Pound out each pork chop between two pieces of plastic wrap until ¼ inch thick. Season both sides with salt and pepper.

**2.** Preheat a grill to medium.

**3.** On a large sheet of heavy-duty aluminum foil, lay out the bacon strips vertically, overlapping them by ¼ inch. Arrange the pork chops in one layer over the bacon. Spread a thin 2-inch-wide layer of cream cheese horizontally across the portion of the pork closest to you. On top of the cream cheese, evenly distribute the bread crumbs, roasted pepper, artichokes, and jalapeños. Starting with the edge closest to you, carefully roll the pork into a cylinder, lifting the foil to keep it outside the roll. Drizzle the vinegar over the bacon and close the foil tightly to keep the cylindrical shape.

**4.** In a small skillet over medium heat, combine the honey, mustard, and beer. Simmer for 4 to 5 minutes, until reduced by one-third and thickened. Set aside half of the sauce for serving and the other half for basting.

**5.** Place the foil-covered cylinder on the grill and cook for 7 to 8 minutes on each of the four sides. Remove the foil and crisp the bacon on the grill, turning four times and basting with the honey-mustard sauce at each turn. Remove from grill after basting for 5 to 6 minutes, or when an instant-read thermometer in the middle of the meat registers 140°F.

**6.** Let rest for 5 minutes, then cut into ¾-inch slices. Serve with the remaining honey-mustard sauce.

# Watermelon Pork Tacos

## PORK

1 pork tenderloin, silverskin removed, cut into 1-inch-thick slices

1 tablespoon onion powder

1 teaspoon red chili flakes

1 teaspoon freshly ground black pepper

2 tablespoons chopped ginger

1 tablespoon seeded, minced serrano chile

2 tablespoons minced garlic

3 tablespoons soy sauce

2 tablespoons oyster sauce

½ teaspoon sesame oil

## VINAIGRETTE

2 tablespoons rice vinegar

¼ cup olive oil

1½ tablespoons soy sauce

¼ teaspoon sesame oil

*(cont.)*

*It doesn't get much more tender than the pork tenderloin. And* **whoa, does it ever host the flavor party.** *This is one mean, lean, healthy lettuce taco machine.*

**1. To make the pork,** combine all the ingredients in a resealable 1-gallon plastic bag and marinate for 30 minutes.

**2.** While the pork is marinating, whisk together all the ingredients for the vinaigrette. In a medium bowl, combine all the ingredients for the salsa. Very gently fold in the vinaigrette. Chill.

**3.** Trim off the soft dark green end of the romaine. Cut off the root end and separate the leaves to create 4-inch-long lettuce "shells." Rinse, dry, and chill the leaves.

**4.** Preheat a grill to medium. Discard the marinade. Grill the pork for 3 minutes on each side. Remove from the heat, let rest 3 minutes, and roughly chop into ½-inch pieces.

**5.** Fill the lettuce shells with the pork, top with the salsa, and devour!

## SALSA

**1 cup watermelon cut into ¼-inch cubes**

**1 cup seeded English cucumber cut into ¼-inch cubes**

**1 Hass avocado, pitted, peeled, and cut into ¼-inch cubes**

## LETTUCE "SHELLS"

**1 romaine lettuce head**

Oh, they will flock-o to this taco!

# Pork-Oulet

¼ pound thick-cut bacon, cut into ½-inch pieces

3 pounds pork butt, cut into 2 by 3-inch pieces

4 bone-in, skinless chicken thighs (about ½ pound)

2 teaspoons kosher salt

1 tablespoon freshly cracked black pepper

1 cup peeled and quartered cipollini onions (about ¼ pound)

1 cup ¼-inch-diced carrots

½ cup ¼-inch-diced celery

¼ cup roughly chopped garlic

3 tablespoons all-purpose flour

3 cups Chicken Stock (page 362 or low-sodium store-bought)

2 bay leaves

1 teaspoon dried thyme

½ teaspoon dried sage

Four 15-ounce cans cannellini beans, drained

¼ cup sherry vinegar

¼ cup chopped flat-leaf parsley, for garnish

*If it's sunny out, get ready to put on sunscreen. And if it's cloudy in Nor Cal, get out the pork-oulet ingredients—**this dish cures the gray day blues.** This is hands-down one of our family favorites.*

**1.** In a cast-iron Dutch oven over medium-high heat, cook the bacon until just crisp. Transfer with a slotted spoon to a paper-towel-lined plate.

**2.** Season the pork and the chicken with salt and pepper. Add the pork pieces to the bacon fat and brown on all sides over medium-high heat, about 10 minutes. Set the pork aside on a large plate.

**3.** Add the chicken thighs to the fat and brown evenly on all sides, 8 to 10 minutes. Remove and add to the plate with the pork.

**4.** Add the onions, carrots, and celery to the fat and cook for 3 to 5 minutes or until lightly caramelized. Stir in the garlic and cook for 1 minute more. Whisk in the flour and cook for 2 minutes or until golden brown, then add in the stock, bay leaves, thyme, and sage, stirring to combine.

**5.** Put the pork pieces into the sauce and cover. Reduce the heat to medium-low and simmer until the meat is fork-tender, about 2 hours. Add the chicken and beans, cover, and simmer for 25 minutes, stirring occasionally.

**6.** Transfer to a serving platter and remove the bay leaves. Serve hot with a drizzle of the sherry vinegar and a sprinkle of the parsley.

# Pork Blade Steak Piccata

## ❧ SERVES 4 TO 6 ❧

### MARINADE

¼ cup garlic cloves, smashed (about 12 cloves)

3 tablespoons drained capers

½ cup white wine

1½ tablespoons Dijon mustard

1 teaspoon kosher salt

2 teaspoons freshly cracked black pepper

1½ tablespoons grated lemon zest

3 tablespoons fresh lemon juice

### PORK

Four 1-pound pork blade steaks

½ teaspoon fine sea salt

½ teaspoon freshly cracked black pepper

1 tablespoon fresh lemon juice

1 tablespoon drained capers

1 tablespoon chopped flat-leaf parsley, for garnish

*If you haven't tried the blade steak, then **today is your lucky day**. Yes, a bit more work to eat than a loin chop, but wow, it's worth it for the flavor. Check out that rad knife!*

**1.** In a medium bowl, combine all the marinade ingredients and stir until fully incorporated. Add the blade steaks, cover, and marinate for 30 minutes (up to 3 hours) at room temperature.

**2.** Preheat a grill to high. Remove the steaks from the marinade, brushing off any large pieces. (Reserve the marinade, bring to a boil in a saucepan for 3 to 4 minutes, and set aside to baste while you grill.)

**3.** Cook for 3 to 5 minutes per side, basting with the reserved marinade. When well marked on both sides, remove from the grill. Let rest 5 minutes. Slice and season with the salt, pepper, lemon juice, capers, and parsley.

# Pulled Pork Hash Con Huevos

## Pulled Pork

**MAKES 6 TO 8 CUPS**

*It's pulled pork time and you don't have a smoker or the boyz from Motley Que to cook for ya?* **Here's a righteous way to go Big Pork indoors.**

**1.** Rinse and dry the pork shoulder. Combine all the spices and rub the mixture all over the pork. Cover and refrigerate for 1 hour or up to 24 hours.

**2.** Make the mop mixture by combining all the ingredients in a bowl.

**3.** Let the pork come to room temperature. Heat a large cast-iron Dutch oven over high heat. Sear the pork on all sides, about 8 minutes per side. Reduce the heat to medium-low and add ½ cup of the mop. Cover and cook gently in the Dutch oven, continuing to pour a couple of tablespoons of the mop over the pork every 45 minutes to 1 hour, until cooked through, 3 to 4 hours (when the internal temperature reaches 190°F on a digital thermometer). The pork releases a lot of fat, creating its own juices, but you can add a bit of water if needed.

**4.** Preheat the oven to 225°F.

**5.** Remove the pork from the Dutch oven and wrap tightly in plastic wrap, then in aluminum foil. (Note: Plastic wrap is heat tolerant to about 375°F; this method keeps the moisture in and allows the pork to steam.) Place the pork on a baking sheet and roast for 1 to 2 hours, until the bone slides out easily and the pork doesn't resist when pulled with 2 forks. Let the pork rest at room temperature until cool enough to pull. Then shred or chop meat, discarding ligaments or tough pieces.

### PORK AND SPICES

8 pounds bone-in pork shoulder (Boston butt)

⅓ cup ground black pepper

3 tablespoons paprika

2 tablespoons granulated garlic

2 tablespoons onion powder

¼ cup fine salt

¼ cup chili powder

¼ cup ground cumin

¼ cup firmly packed dark brown sugar

¼ cup dry hot mustard

### MOP

1 cup apple cider vinegar

2 tablespoons Worcestershire sauce

1 tablespoon freshly cracked black pepper

2 tablespoons cayenne pepper

1 tablespoon kosher salt

2 tablespoons canola oil

½ cup water

*(cont.)*

1 quart 1-inch-diced skin-on red potatoes (about 1 pound)

1½ teaspoons kosher salt, plus more for seasoning

1 chayote squash

2 tablespoons olive oil

2 pasilla or poblano chiles

1 Anaheim chile

½ cup ¼-inch-diced Spanish chorizo

1 cup ¼-inch-diced yellow onion

1½ cups ¼-inch-diced red bell pepper

2 tablespoons minced garlic

Freshly ground black pepper

4 cups Pulled Pork (page 225)

8 eggs

1 cup grated pepper Jack cheese

Tomatillo Sauce (recipe follows)

2 Hass avocados, pitted, peeled, and sliced

⅓ cup grated cotija cheese

2 tablespoons chopped cilantro

# Hash

**When in doubt, hash it out!** *That's what I say to great meat leftovers. Make a tasty hash! (And add some eggs to make the breakfast purists happy.)*

**1.** In a stockpot, cover the potatoes with cold water by 3 inches. Add the kosher salt and place over high heat. Bring to a boil. Boil for 5 minutes, or just before fork tender, then drain in a colander and cool.

**2.** Preheat a grill to high.

**3.** Cut the squash into 1-inch slices lengthwise, discarding the large center seed. Brush with 1 tablespoon of the olive oil and grill until marked on both sides. When cool, cut the squash into ½-inch dice.

**4.** Add the pasilla and Anaheim chiles to the grill and turn until skin is charred and blackened. Transfer to a bowl. Cover and let sit for about 10 minutes, until they have cooled and the skins peel away easily. Peel the chiles and remove the seeds. Cut into ¼-inch dice.

**5.** In a medium skillet over medium-high heat, cook the chorizo for about 3 minutes, until starting to crisp. Drain on paper towels. Set the pan aside with the drippings for cooking the eggs.

**6.** In a large cast-iron skillet over medium-high heat, heat the remaining 1 tablespoon olive oil. Add the onion and cook gently for 2 minutes, until translucent. Add the red bell pepper and cook for 2 minutes more. Add the potatoes, squash, and chiles. Season with salt and pepper to taste. Cook for 4 to 5 minutes, until the potatoes begin to brown. Add the pork and three-quarters of the chorizo. Combine well and increase the heat to high. Allow the mixture to cook for a few minutes before stirring to encourage "bark" on the pork and a nice crust on the potatoes. After 4 to 5 minutes, adjust the heat to medium, add the garlic, and cook for 1 minute. Stir only occasionally to keep achieving the crust. Cook 10 to 12 minutes more, until the potatoes are golden brown.

**7.** Over medium heat, fry the eggs sunny side up in the reserved chorizo drippings. Season with salt and black pepper.

**8.** To serve, layer each plate with hash, an egg, and a sprinkle of the pepper Jack on top of the egg. Top with the tomatillo sauce and add a couple of slices of avocado per egg, a bit of the reserved chorizo, some grated cotija cheese, and a sprinkle of cilantro.

## Tomatillo Sauce

**MAKES 4 CUPS**

**1.** In a medium nonreactive saucepan over medium heat, heat the olive oil. Add the yellow onion and red pepper and cook until almost soft, about 6 minutes. Add the green onion, garlic, and jalapeño and cook for 2 minutes more. Add the tomatillos and any juices that accumulated on the cutting board. Simmer for 8 to 10 minutes. Puree in the saucepan with a stick blender or in a blender (in batches, if necessary). Stir in the cilantro and keep warm. Garnish with additional cilantro.

**2.** Store in a covered container in the refrigerator for up to 1 week.

**TOMATILLO SAUCE**

1 tablespoon olive oil

½ cup small-diced yellow onion

1½ cups small-diced red bell pepper

⅓ cup sliced green onion

2 tablespoons minced garlic

1 tablespoon finely minced jalapeño

One 28-ounce can tomatillos (or freshly roasted), drained and roughly chopped

1 tablespoon chopped cilantro, plus additional for garnish

# Nor Cal Carnitas

One 5-pound pork butt, cut into 4 pieces (bone left intact)

3 pounds refined lard or suet (or oil of choice—but lard is key)

2 red onions, roughly chopped

1 garlic bulb, peeled and roughly chopped

3 tablespoons kosher salt

Corn tortillas, warmed, for serving

Pico de Gallo (page 365)

Salsa, for serving (your favorite brand)

Lime wedges, for serving

Radish slices, for serving

Guacamole Sauce (page 95), for serving

*I'm a big proponent of promoting from within. The original version of this recipe was taught to me by a young cook named César who had started out as a dishwasher at Johnny Garlic's. We would play this game where he'd teach me a traditional Mexican dish and I'd teach him something Italian or Asian. Every other week one of us would cook and the other would learn. One Sunday he asked me if I was free to come over to his place. I show up and there I am, the only gringo, with about twenty-five Latino guys cooking traditional Mexican food. It's always interesting to see what can happen—what doors can open—when you take yourself out of your comfort zone and explore new foods.*

**1.** Remove the pork from the refrigerator 1 hour before cooking.

**2.** Heat enough lard to submerge the meat in a large thick-walled pot over high heat to 250°F. (The pot needs to be large enough to fit all the pieces of pork side by side, not on top of each other, and preferably not touching each other.) Add the onion and garlic and cook 5 to 6 minutes, or until golden brown, but do not burn. Remove the onion and garlic with a slotted spoon and discard.

**3.** Carefully add the pork pieces to the lard and allow the oil to reach 250°F again. Do not let the pork stick to the bottom or sides of the pot. Stir every 30 minutes to ensure even coloring. Cook for 1 to 1½ hours, until the pork is caramel-colored and registers an internal temperature of 170° to 180°F on an instant-read thermometer.

**4.** Once the meat has reached 170°F, sprinkle the kosher salt into the fat. Cook the pork for 5 minutes more, or until thermometer reaches 180°F, then transfer the pork to a platter. Cover and let rest for 15 minutes. Discard the fat.

**5.** Shred the meat and serve with tortillas, pico de gallo, salsa, limes, radish slices, and guacamole.

Twinkle, twinkle little pig.

# Braised Pork Ribs and Italian Sausage

## SERVES 6

2 tablespoons olive oil

¼ pound pancetta, diced

3 pounds pork spareribs, silverskin removed, cut into individual ribs

Kosher salt and freshly ground black pepper

1 pound hot Italian sausage, cut into 1-inch pieces

1 pound sweet Italian sausages cut into 1-inch pieces

2 cups 1-inch-diced red bell pepper

2 cups diced yellow onion

¼ cup diced garlic

½ cup white wine

Two 28-ounce cans whole San Marzano tomatoes, coarsly chopped

3 tablespoons chopped flat-leaf parsley

3 tablespoons chopped basil

1 teaspoon red chili flakes

1 pound radiatori pasta, cooked al dente

1 bunch green onions, sliced

½ cup finely grated Parmesan cheese

*Here's one of the big old-school pasta dishes that I love! Pork three ways, San Marzano spicy tomato sauce, and* **one of the coolest pastas: radiatori, "little radiators."** *Mangia!*

**1.** Preheat the oven to 300°F.

**2.** In a large Dutch oven over medium heat, heat 1 tablespoon of the olive oil and cook the pancetta until crispy and golden. Transfer to a paper-towel-lined plate. Season the spareribs with salt and pepper, then add them to the fat and brown well on both sides. Place the pot in the oven, uncovered and bake until tender, about 1½ hours.

**3.** In a large skillet, heat 1 tablespoon of olive oil over medium-high heat. Add the sausages and brown on all sides. Add the red bell pepper, yellow onion, and garlic and cook until the onion is translucent. Add the wine and scrape up any browned bits. Add the tomatoes. Bring back to a simmer and add the ribs, parsley, basil, chili flakes, and salt and pepper to taste.

**4.** Move the Dutch oven to the stovetop and add the sausage mixture. Cover and simmer over medium-low heat for another 1½ hours or until the meat is tender to the point of falling off the bone.

**5.** Serve the ribs and sausage over the pasta and garnish with the pancetta, green onions, and Parmesan.

I could sit here and write a book of beef stories alone. I've tried my hand at it all, from raising and butchering a few steers to spending time on a ranch to castrating and roping and bulldoggin' and riding steers. But one of my favorite stories starts way back in the day, when I was a little kid in a booster seat. If a restaurant served prime rib, **my parents would ask for a rib bone for me**, to my delight. I must've looked like **Bamm-Bamm on *The Flintstones*, sitting there with my bone.**

One night at a fine dining restaurant when I was about three, I had my big beef rib, and my Gramps (Mom's dad) was sitting to my right. My grandfather was a great cook, a big influence on my mother in cooking, and a really slow eater. As the story goes, I noticed he still hadn't finished his prime rib, so I leaned over to him and said, **"If you ask them real nice, Gramps, they won't make you eat it all."** (I've heard this story my whole life. It must've been a riot because each time they repeated it my "Mamee" would just laugh and laugh.)

As I grew up I continued along the carnivorous vein. The butcher at Valley Grocery, John Miceli, knew me well. I'd go in there after school and buy beef jerky, salami, and mortadella and sign our charge account. I always had to watch the expenditure and be cool about the amount, but **I was a fanatic and always had some jerky in my pockets**. (To this day, salty, cured, smoked meat is the number one thing they put in my dressing room when I'm shooting a show.)

**When I was a kid, it was always about what was for lunch and especially what was for dinner.** Appropriately enough, the first meal I ever made featured steak. At ten years old, I was confident I could make dinner, and after a famous discussion one day with my mother, she gave me the green light. So off I went to the Valley Grocery to make John Miceli my coconspirator. I walked up to the counter and told him, "I get to cook tonight, and I want to make meat." So he gave me two really thick rib-eyes (I think) and sent me on my way. I set about preparing the meal. I knew about seasoning and soy sauce, because with tofu and steamed fish being served at my house I'd learned to doctor things up. I already knew how to make a salad because I was always on salad detail anyway. The spaghetti was less successful . . . I cooked the pasta and sauce and water all together, with very mushy results.

When my father came home, we all sat down and started to eat. Then my father set down his fork and knife. I thought, *Oh boy, I am going to get it.* But **he looked at me and said, "You know what? This might be the best steak I ever had."**

That early victory made me want to understand about beef, all the way to the basics. In the sixth grade I worked at the Ferndale meat market. I've cut steaks, smoked and wrapped beef, and I've even butchered a few steers. The differences among cuts and grades are amazing, and it's just as important to pay attention to how it was raised. As with all proteins, getting back to grass-fed, hormone-free, open range beef rewards you with healthy meat and incredible taste. You get what you pay for, and you don't have to eat a huge 22-ounce porterhouse; try a flavorful 10-ounce New York strip. **Enjoying premium meat in moderation is the key.** (You might find that funny coming from a guy who people think eats his way across America, but if I ate until I was full every time, we'd have a different book on our hands here.)

**Bottom line: we built a country on beef**—it provided everything from gunpowder horns to boots, saddles, and chaps to baseball gloves. You can smoke, grill, cure it, cook it hot and fast or low and slow. It's beautiful.

Now, on the topic of lamb, I never understood why some people didn't seem to like it, because from a young age I was always served properly cooked young lamb. But when I got to college, I had just one taste of **improperly cooked old mutton and realized why people feel the need to smear mint jelly all over it.** You'll find none of that tomfoolery in these pages.

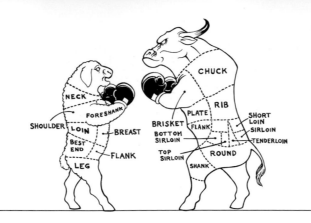

# BEEF AND LAMB GUY'D

**Beef Chuck:** Guid's Goulash for Zlotowitz (page 250), Good Pho You (page 98)

**Ground Beef:** Weird Spaghetti (page 174), Guy-talian Nachos (page 350), Hot Wieners, Rhode Island Style (page 354), Hunter's Hero (page 358), Sloppy Joes (page 134), Fieri Spaghetti and Meatballs (page 166)

**Skirt Steak:** Gaucho Steak (page 252)

**Filet Mignon:** Steak Diane (page 249)

**Chateaubriand:** My Super Thai Beef Salad (page 118)

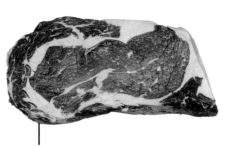

**Rib-Eye Steak:** Beef BourGuid-on (page 242), Guido's Lomo Saltado (page 254)

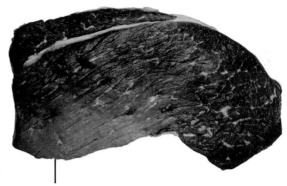

**Brisket:** "Bring it On" Beef Brisket (page 240), Texas Hold'em (page 136), St. Pat's Pasta (page 175), Irish Nachos (page 55)

**Tri-Tip:** Johnny Garlic's Grilled Peppered Tri-Tip with Cabernet-Balsamic Reduction (page 251)

**Top Round:** Chicago Italian Beef Sandwich (page 140), Baltimore Beef Bad Boy (page 142), Chicago Beef Pizza (page 164)

**Flank Steak:** Bloody Mary Flank Steak (page 239), Queen Korina's Salad (page 122)

**Beef Marrow and Neck Bones:** Good Pho You (page 98)

**Sirloin:** Good Pho You (page 98)

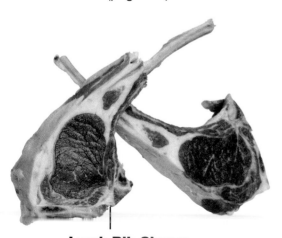

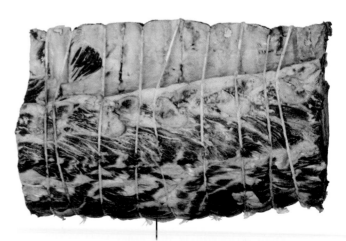

**Lamb Rib Chops:** Lamb Chops with Marsala-Blackberry Sauce (page 259)

**Lamb Loin Chop:** Lamb Loin Chops with Mint Pesto (page 260)

**Boneless Rib or Loin Roast:** Birthday Prime Rib (page 247), Dry-Aged Rib-Eyes (page 256)

# Bloody Mary Flank Steak

### ❧ SERVES 4 TO 8 ❧

Along the lines of my mojito chicken and Red Rocker margarita chicken recipes, I went on a quest to discover new ways to cook with alcohol, exploring its properties and its effects on different combinations of ingredients. As I created this recipe, I realized that tomato sauce, horseradish, and garlic all go beautifully with beef, and a Bloody Mary was something I'd be very happy to drink alongside a beefy main dish. **The flavors made a natural marriage**. I first made this dish with a tri-tip cut, which is easier to find out here on the West Coast, but flank steak works nicely too. The vodka has a tenderizing effect. The vegetable juice keeps it juicy, and the salt gives it a nice brine. Plus, **how many times in life do you have the chance to name something Bloody Mary?**

**1 cup vegetable juice (I recommend V8)**

**½ cup vodka**

**1 teaspoon fine sea salt, plus more for seasoning**

**1 teaspoon freshly ground black pepper, plus more for seasoning**

**1 teaspoon hot sauce (I recommend Tabasco)**

**1 tablespoon fresh lemon juice**

**1 tablespoon Worcestershire sauce**

**2 garlic cloves, crushed**

**1 teaspoon onion powder**

**1 teaspoon ground celery seed**

**1 tablespoon prepared horseradish**

**¼ cup olive oil**

**1 pound flank steak**

**Small celery stalks and leaves, and grilled tomatoes, for garnish (optional)**

**1.** In a large bowl, thoroughly mix all the ingredients except for the flank steak and the garnish. Pour half the marinade into a resealable 1-gallon plastic bag and add the flank steak. Marinate in the refrigerator for at least 8 and up to 24 hours.

**2.** Pour the remaining marinade into a saucepan over medium-high and simmer until it is reduced by half, 10 to 15 minutes. Season to taste.

**3.** Preheat a grill to high or heat a skillet over high heat. Remove the flank steak from the marinade and wipe off the excess liquid with paper towels. (Discard the meat's marinade.) Grill or pan-sear both sides, then lower the heat to medium and cook to medium rare (135°F), 8 to 10 minutes.

**4.** Let the flank steak rest, covered with foil, for 5 to 10 minutes. Cut the steak on the bias across the grain and serve with the reduced marinade. If desired, garnish with celery and tomatoes.

# "Bring It On" Beef Brisket

### SERVES 6

4 ½ to 5 pounds beef brisket

1 tablespoon kosher salt

2 tablespoons freshly cracked black pepper

2 tablespoons canola oil

2 yellow onions, cut into 1-inch rings

2 leeks, white and light green parts only, cleaned and cut into thirds

2 shallots, quartered

1 carrot, cut in half lengthwise, then into 1-inch chunks

4 celery stalks, cut into thirds

¾ cup Chili Sauce (page 368)

½ cup low-sodium beef stock (I recommend Kitchen Basics)

1 12-ounce beer, at room temperature (I recommend pale ale)

*Brisket has such incredible flavor* that it doesn't have to have a ton of extra added to it. This is a great recipe—it's super simple but delivers big flavor.

**1.** Preheat the oven to 350°F.

**2.** Rinse the brisket and pat it dry. Season each side with the salt and pepper, pressing them into the beef. In a large cast-iron Dutch oven over high heat, heat the canola oil to the smoking point. Add the beef, fat side down, and sear until well browned. Repeat on the other side, 3 to 4 minutes per side.

**3.** Top with the onions, leeks, shallots, carrot, and celery. Combine the chili sauce and beef stock and pour over the brisket. Cover and roast in the oven for 2 hours, basting every 30 minutes.

**4.** Add the pale ale, cover, and cook for 1½ hours more, basting every 30 minutes.

**5.** Remove from the oven and let the brisket rest at room temperature for 1 hour.

**6.** Remove the brisket from the Dutch oven and set it on a cutting board. Carefully remove the fat cap with the edge of a fork and discard. Remove the vegetables and run them through a food mill or puree in a food processor. Skim the fat from the pan juices or use a gravy separator. Add the pureed vegetables back to the Dutch oven with the pan juices. Adjust the seasonings if necessary and heat the sauce over low heat.

**7.** Slice the beef on the diagonal, across the grain, and serve with the sauce.

# Beef BourGuid-on

1½ cups dry red wine

Kosher salt and freshly ground black pepper

4 tablespoons Worcestershire sauce

2 pounds boneless rib-eye steak, trimmed and cut into ¾-inch cubes

Canola oil

¼ cup all-purpose flour, plus more for dredging

1 medium red onion, cut into ¼-inch-thick rings

¼ pound bacon, diced

3 tablespoons olive oil

¾ cup diced carrot

¾ cup diced parsnip

1 cup frozen pearl onions

¼ cup flour

2 tablespoons minced garlic

3 cups low-sodium beef stock (I recommend Kitchen Basics)

2 teaspoons chopped thyme

½ cup chopped flat-leaf parsley

2 teaspoons chopped oregano

1 pound egg noodles, cooked, for serving

¼ cup grated Parmesan cheese

*This is **old-school goes Guy–style**. Any chance I get to add some veggies in for the kids, I do! Big, full flavor, veggies, noodles—what else do ya need? (Some righteous red wine!)*

**1.** In a large nonmetallic bowl, combine ¾ cup of the red wine, 1 teaspoon salt, 2 teaspoons pepper, 2 tablespoons of the Worcestershire sauce, and the rib-eye steak. Marinate for 30 minutes to 1 hour at room temperature.

**2.** Heat 2 inches of canola oil in a large pot or Dutch oven over high heat to 350°F.

**3.** Dredge the red onion rings in flour. Working in batches, drop them into the hot oil and fry until golden brown. Remove the onion rings with a slotted spoon and drain on a paper-towel-lined plate.

**4.** In a large skillet over high heat, cook the bacon until crisp. Transfer the bacon to a paper-towel-lined plate with a slotted spoon, reserving the fat in the pan.

**5.** Remove the beef from the marinade, pat dry, and add in batches to the bacon fat in the skillet. Cook over medium-high heat, browning the meat on all sides. Add olive oil to the pan if necessary (you'll need a total of 2 to 3 tablespoons of fat). Transfer the meat to a plate. Add the carrots, parsnips, and pearl onions and cook until the onions are light brown, 8 to 10 minutes.

**6.** Lower the heat to medium and add the flour to the vegetables, stirring to combine. When the flour begins to brown, add the garlic and cook for 2 minutes. Whisk in the remaining ¾ cup red wine. Stir in the beef stock and remaining 2 tablespoons Worcestershire. Simmer over medium heat for 10 minutes until thickened.

**7.** Return the beef to the skillet along with the bacon, thyme, most of the parsley, and oregano and heat through. Adjust the seasonings to taste with salt and pepper.

**8.** Serve immediately on a bed of egg noodles garnished with the Parmesan and a  bit more parsley.

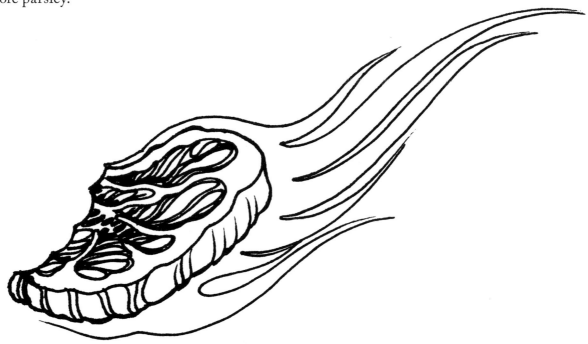

# From France to Flambé Captain

While I was growing up, my parents hosted foreign exchange students for many years, from Sweden, Japan, and Norway. So when I turned fifteen I decided I wanted to go to France as an exchange student. As a sophomore in high school, I enrolled in French class at College of the Redwoods to get the basics, and then I was off for ten months to learn about French food and become fluent. I ate some incredible food in France. I'd send my dad and mom letters telling him I'd eaten something or other and then one day I wrote, "This is amazing, I really think I know what I want to do. I want to be a chef and own restaurants."

In action at the flambé cart, a polyester wunderkind

He responded, "Well, then you need to get a job in the restaurant business. Where do you want to work?"

I'd been around fancy food in France, so I said I'd do fine dining. So my dad went round to the two fine dining places in Eureka, the Red Lion Inn and the Eureka Inn, got me job applications, and mailed them to me in France. I filled them out and wrote letters to both saying where I was and what I was doing, and that I'd like to work with them next summer. Upon returning I confidently headed over to claim my job. John Porter, the general manager at the Eureka Inn, didn't understand what I'd been asking, and his positions were all filled. But the Red Lion had a job for me busing tables. So there I was at sixteen, busing tables—not exactly the rock star kitchen position I thought I would get.

Then I started watching the guys cooking tableside with flambé carts. Flambé culture is a throwback to how people defined old-school elegance, and all about the theater of it all. The two flambé captains, Dan and Don, had the market down and were making tons of money. And it was a cool position because you could talk to people but you didn't wait on them, and you received side tips from guests plus part of the server's tips. I told the manager he should hire me as a flambé captain, and he said you have to be eighteen. So I told them I was eighteen. But then it was that I wasn't experienced. . . .

I was thinking, *Wait a minute, how can I get any experience if they don't let me try?* So I took the pan, some tongs, the little dishes, a pepper mill, and the Grey Poupon home to practice the recipes and the moves—like how to toss the brandy bottle in the air and twirl the pepper grinder behind your back. I studied until I could perform the flambé captain meal without cooking any of it!

Then I started cooking the actual meals at home. I got the racket fully down and waited for my chance. One day Dan wasn't able to make it to work, it was just Don, so Mark Milligan, the dining room manager, was filling in cooking at the tables. When something had to be done, I jumped in and said, "I can do it!"

So he said, "Okay, all you have to do is a Caesar salad, no cooking." I did it and the people at the table were wowed, so then he told me to make the Steak Diane, and he watched me make the steak. By the end of the night I'd graduated not to flambé captain but to a fill-in guy, which was good enough for the time being.

I was so happy—even with the delicious polyester outfit I had to wear. It had the dickies with the ruffles you had to tuck into the shirt and the vest under the jacket. It was such a cheesy outfit that I wore a sweatsuit over it when I drove to work, just in case I had to get out to pump gas.

I've got all kinds of stories, but the greatest was cooking for a couple who were celebrating their forty-fifth wedding anniversary. The Red Lion has three restaurants: the lounge, the coffee shop, and the fine dining restaurant. This was the fine dining section, outfitted with high-back leather booths. So there I was, coming up to the table, with the lady sitting close to the end of the table while the guy sat in the middle of the booth. They weren't speaking to each other. She had a beehive hairdo that would put Marge Simpson to shame. She was clapping her hands at everything, so happy, and it's very obvious to me that she hadn't been out to eat since they got married. He'd had about six scotch and sodas and was eating French onion soup. I came out to make Steak Diane, and she asked a question every time I did something.

"What are you putting in now?"

"Ma'am, I'm putting in the butter."

She continued to ask me questions as I cooked, and meanwhile her husband didn't say a thing to me. She was drinking a little Chardonnay, and every time she sipped she talked about how she was getting tipsy.

Now, to fully understand the rest of the story you've got to know a little of the choreography and the cart set-up. The key to being a great flambé captain was the ability to flip the pepper grinder, arc the stream of brandy from the bottle, and open the jar of Grey Poupon with one hand. The key to the Grey Poupon move is to grab it in one hand, open the lid with two fingers, and with the other hand take a tablespoon of it and put it into the pan, while closing the lid on the Dijon with the same hand that's holding the jar. The lid never goes back on that tightly. And flambé captains set up their carts with a variety of pieces. It's a rolling cart with two burners and a metal ring securing a tablecloth. You're supposed to place the tablecloth over the edge of this cart to a certain level so that it doesn't drag, but I never liked that because it looked as if your cart was wearing high waters, so I would hang mine down a bit further.

I finished the Steak Diane and presented it to her, and sat there and answered every question under the sun. But it clearly wasn't their habit for her to have

Practice, practice, practice.

My first night as maitre d'
at the Red Lion.

My flambé technique has evolved over the years . . .

money, I'm sure, and the guy had barely looked up, so I started wheeling the cart away with no tip.

But as I began to roll away, the tablecloth got caught in the wheels. I didn't look down—I just pulled the cart, and it yanked the tablecloth, and the Grey Poupon began to tip off the cart. Everything started happening in slow motion, like I was rounding third base with a dog chasing me in a bad dream, and I was thinking that the yellow mustard would hit the brown carpet and cause a stain. Oh my God, I could tell I was going straight back to busing tables.

But what happened next was one of the defining moments of my young culinary career. That mustard jar hit precisely on the corner of the cart, and the lid was just loose enough to open, and a mustard globule arced through the air. NASA couldn't re-create this action in a thousand tries. The husband was well into his ninth scotch and soda and his wife was taking another sip of her wine as I was trying to hurdle over the cart. There was no chance I could catch the mustard. The monster glob hit the foot of her glass and splattered over her eyebrows. From her eyebrows up to her hairdo, she was covered in mustard. She looked at me, totally confused. Her husband fell over in the booth, kicking his feet back and forth, dying of laughter. And she still had no idea what had happened. She moved her head and there was a silhouette of her hairdo on the back of the booth. While she stared at me with this questioning look, her hair came down like a matted Berlin wall, right into her face, covered in mustard. I about died!

The dude tipped me forty-five bucks. He said it was the best anniversary ever!

# Festivus Maximus Prime Rib

### ~ SERVES 15 TO 18 ~

*So it's my birthday and I'm going big . . . prime rib is just the ticket!*
*Great friends, slow-cooked prime rib, and lots of laughs—the recipe for a great*
*birthday!*

**1.** Preheat the oven to 300°F. Remove the roast from the refrigerator at least 1 hour before cooking. Pull back the fat cap, using a thin boning knife, but do not remove it completely. (Cut between fat cap and the meat.)

**2.** In a medium bowl, combine the garlic, rosemary, salt, pepper, celery salt, and beef base. Evenly spread this mixture under the fat cap, directly on the meat. Replace the fat cap and tie the roast with kitchen twine every 2 inches.

**3.** Place the onion and carrots in the bottom of a heavy roasting pan. Place the meat, fat cap up, on the vegetables. Add the water and ¼ cup of the wine to the pan and roast for 2½ to 3 hours, until an instant-read thermometer in the middle of the meat registers 130°F.

**4.** Transfer the meat from the roasting pan to a cutting board and tent it lightly with aluminum foil to rest for 20 minutes. Discard the vegetables.

**5.** Place the roasting pan over high heat and pour in the remaining 1¾ cups wine. Scrape up browned, roasted bits from the bottom of the pan, stirring frequently. Cook until the liquid is reduced by two-thirds, about 15 minutes. Strain into a saucepan and skim off any fat. Whisk in the butter and season with salt and pepper to taste for the au jus.

**6.** Slice the roast and serve with the au jus and horseradish.

16 pounds boneless prime rib roast

¼ cup chopped garlic

3 tablespoons chopped rosemary

2 tablespoons kosher salt, plus more for seasoning

2 tablespoons freshly cracked black pepper, plus more for seasoning

1 tablespoon celery salt

1 tablespoon beef base

3 onions, cut into 2-inch rings

4 carrots, quartered

¾ cup water

2 cups dry red wine, such as cabernet sauvignon

¼ pound (1 stick) unsalted butter, cut into cubes

Prepared horseradish, for serving

*Special Equipment:*
**Kitchen twine**

# Steak Diane

**Filet is the key steak for this**, *but you can rock it with your favorite cut or even grill it and serve it with the sauce.*

**1.** Season the steaks on both sides with the salt and pepper. In a large skillet over medium-high heat, heat the olive oil. When it shimmers, add the steaks. Brown the steaks on both sides, 3 minutes per side. Transfer the steaks to a plate and set aside, lightly covered with foil.

**2.** Add the shallot and mushrooms to the oil and cook for 2 minutes, stirring frequently. Add the garlic. When the garlic is lightly colored, add the brandy (be careful; it can ignite). Add the mustard, Worcestershire, and wine and simmer for 2 minutes to reduce slightly. Add the demi-glace and simmer for 2 to 3 minutes more. Return the steaks to the pan and finish cooking them to the desired temperature, 2 to 4 minutes, depending upon the size of the filets and desired temperature. For medium-rare, cook to 135°F on an instant-read thermometer.

**3.** To serve, place a steak on each plate. Whisk the butter into the sauce to finish it, and pour the sauce over the steak. Season with freshly cracked black pepper.

Four 6- to 8-ounce filet mignons

1 teaspoon kosher salt

1 teaspoon freshly cracked black pepper, plus more for seasoning

¼ cup extra virgin olive oil

1 shallot, minced

3 cups thinly sliced cremini mushrooms

4 garlic cloves, minced

½ cup brandy

2 tablespoons Dijon mustard

2 tablespoons Worcestershire sauce

½ cup dry red wine

¾ cup demi-glace (available at your butcher or through Amazon)

1 tablespoon unsalted butter

# Zlotowitz Goulash

### ⤙ SERVES 8 ⤚

4 pounds beef chuck, trimmed, cut into 2-inch cubes

Kosher salt and freshly ground black pepper

¼ cup olive oil

2½ cups finely diced onions

2 cups diced carrots

¾ cup seeded, finely diced Anaheim chiles

1 tablespoon seeded, minced serrano chile

1 cup finely diced shallots

2 tablespoons caraway seeds, toasted and ground*

1 tablespoon sweet Hungarian paprika

2 tablespoons hot Spanish paprika

1 teaspoon red chili flakes

2 tablespoons minced marjoram

2 teaspoons minced thyme

¼ cup balsamic vinegar

¼ cup tomato paste

1 quart Chicken Stock (page 362)

2 bay leaves

Grilled Polenta (page 314)

*Toast caraway seeds over high heat, stirring constantly for 1 to 2 minutes until lightly browned. Then grind.*

When a friend says, "Hey Guy, do you have a great goulash recipe?" and I don't. . . . You know I gotta bust one out the next day. So now, when asked, I can respond, **"Ohhhh yeah . . . of course! And I named it after you!"**

**1.** Preheat the oven to 325°F.

**2.** Season the chuck with 1 tablespoon each salt and pepper. In a large Dutch oven (preferably enamel-coated cast iron) over medium-high heat, heat the olive oil until just smoking. Working in batches, brown the beef on all sides, taking care not to crowd, about 8 to 10 minutes per batch. Set the meat aside on a plate or rimmed baking sheet to catch the juices.

**3.** Add the onions, carrots, and Anaheim chiles to the Dutch oven and cook for 5 to 6 minutes, stirring often to loosen the browned bits in the pan. Add the serrano chile and shallots and cook until the shallots are browned and all the liquid is evaporated, about 15 minutes. Add the toasted and ground caraway, paprikas, chili flakes, marjoram, and thyme and cook for 1 minute. Stir in the vinegar and cook 2 minutes to reduce slightly. Stir in the tomato paste and cook for 3 minutes more. Slowly stir in the stock. Add back the beef and any collected juices. Add the bay leaves and stir gently to combine. Cover and cook in the oven for 2 hours, stirring occasionally.

**4.** Adjust the seasoning with salt and pepper, remove the bay leaves, and serve with polenta.

# Johnny Garlic's Grilled Peppered Tri-Tip with Cabernet-Balsamic Reduction

### SERVES 4

*Cajun Chicken Alfredo was the first thing on the Johnny Garlic's menu . . . and pepper tri-tip* **had to have been the second.**

**1.** Tenderize the steaks with a mallet to ½-inch thickness. Rub with 1 tablespoon olive oil, then season evenly with pepper and salt. Cover and refrigerate for 4 to 8 hours.

**2.** In a medium saucepan over medium-high heat, heat remaining olive oil. Add the onion and cook until lightly browned, 5 to 8 minutes. Add the garlic and cook until garlic begins to brown. Add the wine and vinegar and scrape up any browned bits from the pan. Add sugar and simmer the mixture over medium-low heat for 20 to 30 minutes, stirring occasionally, until reduced to ¾ cup. Strain well and return to high heat until syrupy, about 5 minutes.

**3.** Preheat a grill to medium-high. Add the steaks and grill them on one side for 4 to 5 minutes. Flip the steaks and grill 3 to 4 minutes more, or until the steaks are done (135°F for medium rare).

**4. For the fried baby spinach:** In a heavy-bottomed skillet over high heat, heat the oil to 350°F. Add the spinach in batches and fry very briefly until crisped, about 30 seconds. Immediately remove to a paper-towel-lined plate. Season with salt and pepper.

**5.** Serve steak drizzled with reduction and topped with Fried Baby Spinach.

2 pounds tri-tip or flank steak, cut into 4 pieces on the bias

2 tablespoons extra virgin olive oil

¼ cup black peppercorns, lightly cracked

2 tablespoons kosher salt

¼ cup minced red onion

1 tablespoon minced garlic

1 cup cabernet sauvignon or similar dry red wine

½ cup balsamic vinegar

2 tablespoons dark brown sugar, packed

*Special Equipment:*
**Meat mallet**

**FRIED BABY SPINACH**

1 quart canola oil

4 cups baby spinach

Fine sea salt and ground black pepper

# Gaucho Steak with Four-Herb Chimichurri

### ⌘ SERVES 4 TO 6 ⌘

## FOR THE STEAK

1 teaspoon minced garlic

1 teaspoon chopped cilantro

2 tablespoons olive oil

3 tablespoons white or silver tequila

1 tablespoon fresh lemon juice

1 tablespoon fresh lime juice

½ teaspoon kosher salt

1 teaspoon freshly cracked black pepper

1½ pounds skirt steak, trimmed

**(cont.)**

*Skirt steak has gotta be one of my favorite cuts of meat, with great texture, fat, and flavor. And **it all gets rocked to another level** with this chimichurri!*

**1.** Combine all the steak ingredients in a large bowl, cover, and marinate in the refrigerator for 1 to 3 hours.

**2. To make the chimichurri sauce,** pulse all the ingredients lightly in a food processor until a coarse sauce forms. Cover and set aside for 2 hours in the refrigerator.

**3.** Preheat a grill to high or heat a large skillet over high heat. Drain the marinade and cook the steak to medium-rare, 4 to 6 minutes on each side. Let sit for 5 to 10 minutes, then cut against the grain in ¼-inch slices and top with chimichurri sauce.

## FOR THE FOUR-HERB CHIMICHURRI

2 tablespoons chopped cilantro

2 tablespoons chopped flat-leaf parsley

1 tablespoon chopped basil

1 tablespoon chopped oregano

3 tablespoons rough-chopped white onion

3 tablespoons rough-chopped red bell pepper

4 large garlic cloves, smashed

1 teaspoon kosher salt

1 tablespoon freshly cracked black pepper

½ teaspoon ground cumin

2 tablespoons red wine vinegar

1 tablespoon crushed dried pasilla chile

2 tablespoons extra virgin olive oil

# Guido's Lomo Saltado

## SERVES 4 TO 6

Double-Fried French Fries
(page 324)

One 1-pound boneless rib-eye,
trimmed of excess fat and cut
into ½ by 2-inch pieces

1 tablespoon freshly cracked
black pepper

¼ cup balsamic vinegar

½ cup soy sauce

1 tablespoon fish sauce

2 teaspoons cornstarch

2 tablespoons Worcestershire
sauce

2 tablespoons minced garlic

2 teaspoons minced ginger

2 tablespoons canola oil

1 red onion, cut into ½ by
2-inch strips (about 2 cups)

1 red bell pepper, cut into ½ by
2-inch strips (about 1 cup)

1 yellow bell pepper, cut into ½
by 2-inch strips (about 1 cup)

5 Roma tomatoes, cut into
1-inch wedges

½ cup Pilsner-style beer

1 tablespoon Key lime juice

*(cont.)*

*Lemme get this straight—**rib-eye, french fries, garlic, and beer.** This is a dish? Sign me up for some of this Peruvian favorite.*

**1.** Fry the french fries at 325°F until golden brown.

**2.** Season the meat with the pepper, tossing to coat.

**3.** In a medium bowl, combine the vinegar, soy sauce, fish sauce, cornstarch, and Worcestershire. Whisk with a fork to blend well. Add the garlic and ginger and stir to combine.

**4.** Place the wok over high heat. Heat the canola oil until it just begins to smoke. Add the onions, red and yellow peppers, and tomatoes. Stir-fry for 5 to 6 minutes, until the onions begin to soften. At this point, drop the prepared french fries into the oil for a final fry.

**5.** Push the vegetables to the sides to create a space in the center of the wok and add the beef. Stir-fry for 2 minutes, then add the beer and the vinegar-soy mixture. Stir frequently for 1 to 2 minutes. Add the lime juice and toss to combine. Taste for seasoning.

**6.** Remove the french fries from the oil, drain briefly, add them to the stir-fried mixture, and toss.

**7.** Serve on warm plates with the rice. Garnish with the parsley and serve immediately. I like a little aji pepper sauce! Give it a shot.

2 cups cooked white rice, for serving

¼ cup chopped flat-leaf parsley

Hot sauce, for serving (I recommend aji or Peruvian)

*Special Equipment:*
Large wok

# Dry-Aged Rib-Eyes with Horseradish Gremolata

### ⮞ SERVES 6 ⮜

6-pound boneless beef rib or loin roast

Kosher salt and freshly cracked black pepper

Horseradish Gremolata (recipe follows)

**HORSERADISH GREMOLATA**

12 tablespoons (1½ sticks) unsalted butter, at room temperature

2 teaspoons minced garlic

¼ cup grated fresh horseradish

1 tablespoon distilled white vinegar

1 teaspoon minced lemon zest

½ teaspoon kosher salt

1 tablespoon finely chopped flat-leaf parsley

*Special Equipment:*
1 package cheesecloth (about 2 yards), rimmed baking sheet with a rack to fit

**1.** Make space in the back of a refrigerator at a steady temperature of 32° to 38°F, and humidity range of 50 to 60 percent (see page 258).

**2.** Rinse the roast well and pat it completely dry. Wrap it in three layers of cheesecloth and place it fat side up on a rack fitted inside a rimmed baking sheet. Put the roast in the back of the refrigerator.

**3.** After 24 hours, remove, unwrap, discard the cheesecloth, and wrap the roast with fresh cheesecloth. Return to the refrigerator for 6 to 10 days. Check occasionally to assure the roast is dry and nothing has been piled on top of it.

**4.** When the roast has finished aging, remove the cheesecloth, cut away the fat, and trim the ends and any discolored parts of the roast.

**5. To make the horseradish gremolata:** In a medium bowl, whisk the butter with the garlic, horseradish, vinegar, lemon zest, and salt. Stir in the parsley; set aside.

**6.** Preheat a grill to medium-high. Slice the roast into six 1½-inch-thick steaks. Season with salt and freshly cracked pepper. Cook the steaks for 4 minutes, then flip and cook 3 minutes more. Let rest for 5 minutes, then transfer to a serving platter. Top with horse-radish gremolata.

## Tips for Dry-Aging in Your Fridge

While your meat is dry-aging, your refrigerator's temperature should stay constant between 32°F and 38°F, and its humidity should range between 50 and 60 percent. Refrigerator thermometers should be used to measure both conditions. A sling psychrometer, available at HVAC supply shops or online, is a relatively inexpensive (around $20 to $40) yet accurate tool for measuring relative humidity. Considering that dry-aged beef sells for about twenty-seven bucks a pound, this onetime investment will pay for itself immediately!

# How to Dry-Age a Steak

*I first experienced dry-aged meat while working at Schulman's Meats in Vegas. It looked funky—all dried out—took a long time, and made the meat lose weight, and I asked, "Is it really that much better?"* **One bite and you'll know for yourself.**

Wrap the steak in three layers of cheesecloth, fat side up.

Place on a pan fitted with a wire rack and place in refrigerator.

After 24 hours, unwrap and rewrap and return to refrigerator for 6 to 9 days.

After the aging process is over, unwrap.

Trim the ends.

Trim away any discoloration.

Trim the fat, then slice into six steaks, or leave whole to roast!

# Lamb Chops with Marsala-Blackberry Sauce

### SERVES 4

*Little lamb chops—ya can't beat 'em, and they so easily take on great flavors. The brine of the tapenade, the sweetness of the Marsala, a little tang from the jam, and crunch from the panko make this dish funky, eclectic, and delicious!*

**1.** In a shallow baking dish or resealable 1-gallon plastic bag, combine the olive tapenade, 2 tablespoons of the olive oil, and the pepper. Add the lamb chops and turn them to coat. Cover or seal and marinate for 1 hour at room temperature.

**2.** Preheat the oven to 250°F. Place a rack on a baking sheet to hold the cooked lamb chops.

**3.** In a large skillet over medium-high heat, heat the canola oil. Coat each chop in the egg, then dredge in the panko, pressing it to adhere. Place in the skillet, working in batches if necessary so as not to crowd. Cook for about 3 minutes on each side, until lightly browned. Transfer the chops to the rack and keep warm in the oven.

**4.** When all the chops have been cooked and are in the oven, wipe out the skillet with a paper towel. Heat the remaining 1 tablespoon olive oil over medium-high heat. Add the diced onion, and cook until translucent. Add the garlic and cook for 1 minute more. Stir in the Marsala and cook to reduce the liquid by half. Whisk in the blackberry jam and stock, bring to a low simmer, and cook until reduced to 1 cup, 7 to 8 minutes.

**5.** Remove the lamb from the oven, allow to rest, lightly tented with foil, for 5 minutes, and serve with the sauce.

½ cup prepared green olive tapenade

3 tablespoons olive oil

2 teaspoons freshly cracked black pepper

Sixteen 3- to 3½-ounce lamb rib chops

½ cup canola oil

2 eggs, beaten

2 cups panko breadcrumbs

¼ cup small-diced onion

2 tablespoons minced garlic

1 cup Marsala wine

¼ cup blackberry jam

2 cups Chicken Stock (page 362 or low-sodium store-bought)

# Lamb Loin Chops with Mint Pesto

## SERVES 4

2 pounds lamb loin chops (8 to 10 chops), cut individually

1 tablespoon olive oil

1 teaspoon dried oregano

½ teaspoon dried thyme

1 teaspoon dried rosemary

1 teaspoon freshly ground black pepper

½ teaspoon fine sea salt

Mint Pesto (recipe follows)

**MINT PESTO**

2 garlic cloves

¼ cup pine nuts

¾ cup loosely packed basil leaves

1½ cups loosely packed mint leaves

¾ cup loosed packed flat-leaf parsley leaves

½ cup grated Parmesan cheese

½ teaspoon fine sea salt

½ teaspoon freshly ground black pepper

¼ cup extra virgin olive oil

*This is gonna be your go-to lamb recipe* **when someone says, "I don't like lamb!" Those are always fighting words to me.** *You say you don't like something, I'll hook up a recipe that will make you a believer.*

**1.** Preheat a grill to high.

**2.** Rub the lamb chops with the olive oil. In a small bowl, combine the oregano, thyme, rosemary, pepper, and salt. Rub the mixture all over the chops. Let them marinate for 30 minutes or up to 2 hours at room temperature.

**3.** Grill the lamb chops for 2 to 3 minutes per side for medium-rare. Serve with mint pesto.

## Mint Pesto

**MAKES ¾ CUP**

**1.** Pulse the garlic in a food processor until chopped. Add the pine nuts and pulse to chop. Add half the herbs and process for 30 seconds, then add the rest and chop for 15 seconds or until well combined. Add the Parmesan, salt, and pepper and pulse briefly until combined. With the machine running, slowly add the oil in a steady stream and process to the desired thickness. Use immediately.

I was completely spoiled by the abundance of fresh seafood available to me while growing up in Northern California. Eating fresh-off-the-boat Pacific salmon twice a week and Dungeness crab all through the winter was the norm for me, and I figured that's just how everyone experienced seafood the world over. **My parents would trade pants and boots from their Western clothing store for salmon and crab from the fishermen**. We ate so much seafood that I'd often request more meat at mealtimes.

I've always been a fan of the versatility of salmon, as it can be served raw, cooked, or smoked. The list is long and wide of ethnic cuisines that use salmon, and **Dungeness crab is most definitely the king of crabs**. Needless to say, due to my upbringing I always had a palate that was trained to expect pristinely fresh fish. Well, welcome to the real world, Guido, it isn't always—but it's definitely worth the extra mile to get the good stuff, **even if you have to trade the shirt off your back (or the pants from your parents' store).**

But the meal that indicated my future as a seafood junkie was a particularly epic dinner at my cousin Tom Ramsay's house. I was seventeen, newly back from my time in France, and Tom had flown in four-pound Maine lobsters. (They seemed like 400 pounds to me; I'd never seen them that big in my life!) I remember eating this lobster and being totally out of my mind. I could not believe how this much great flavor and texture was possible. I ate until I couldn't eat another bite. For a seventeen-year-old kid, that's stuffed.

Today I enjoy seafood for its health benefits and the variety of ways you can serve it. We often get into a pattern of cooking fish one or two ways, but it's probably the protein on the menu with the greatest potential for diverse recipes. Here I've included some of my favorite plays on seafood. Experiment, stretch your palates, and get creative—just make it fresh.

A Fieri home-cooked sushi dinner, circa 1987!

The lobster-fest, courtesy of cousin Tom.
See . . . I was always this way!

# SEAFOOD GUY'D

*Here's the lowdown on some of my favorite types of seafood. These are not only great on the plate, but can be harvested in a sustainable manner.*

## Salmon

Salmon is the number one selling seafood these days. The mighty king salmon weighs in at thirty pounds plus, and the name pretty much says it all. You're not going to get a better flavor than a wild-caught king salmon. If you can get wild, always go for it. They're better because they're eating things that they're supposed to, like sardines and anchovies, and they're more muscular because they have to chase their food. (It's common sense. Farmed salmon are fed pellets and end up looking like fat footballs.)

Californians will say they have the best king salmon in the world (sorry, Alaska) because of the long tributaries that the salmon have to run to get upriver. The oil content and flesh of the fish are more robust.

The stepsister to the king is coho or silver salmon. They're smaller, about six to ten pounds, a bit drier, and less buttery and fatty.

Sockeye or red salmon are often sold as fillets. They're about four to eight pounds with a bright red color and a good flavor profile.

Chum salmon is the cheapest of the lot and is generally found in canned products. It doesn't have the flavor profile that the others do, but it provides a decent protein that's good for you.

## Pacific Sole

One of the most undervalued fish out there is Pacific sole. It's got excellent flavor, firm flesh, and a good price point, plus it's good stuffed, fried, broiled, or steamed. Atlantic sole has been overfished, so make sure you're getting the West Coast version. True Dover sole is imported from Europe, and while it's got great texture and flavor, it can get pricey.

### Tilapia

Most commonly farmed, tilapia is a budget-friendly low-mercury option. They're quick-cooking, mild in flavor, and easy to work with whether you're sautéing, grilling, or frying. Look for tilapia farmed in the United States, as there have been water quality issues with tilapia farmed in China and Taiwan. As you can imagine, there's a big difference between fish grown in still green water and water with a river running through it.

### Catfish

Catfish gets a bad rap. People think of it as a muddy groundfeeder that tastes as bad as that sounds. But when raised in a river or a farmed environment with flowing water, they're clean tasting, with a delicate flavor that's not mucky in the least.

### Cod

Cod wins the prize as an all-around good fish. Due to its massive popularity, Atlantic cod has been severely overfished. Long line, jig, or trap-caught cod from Alaska is the most sustainable choice. Most important, avoid trawl-caught cod, which scrapes and disrupts life on the ocean floor. There are about eighty different species, and some rock cod or rock fish get sold as Pacific red snapper. They're all good sautéed, fried, broiled, grilled, or barbecued.

### Oysters

Ever wonder why oysters have funky names like Malpeque, Hog Island, and Fanny Bay? Oysters are named after the place where they're harvested, and the names can help clue you into what you're about to dig into. The salinity and brininess of the oyster's flavor, as well as how large or small and plump it is, will vary based on its being from the East or West Coast, what the current and tidal activity is, and what time of year it's being harvested. For example, if oysters grow in places with more current, you can expect a more muscular oyster that's not as soft as one with less current. Much like wine, the only way to discover what you like is to taste them. You'll find each locale has subtleties of its own. When buying oysters, whatever the variety, look for ones with a deep "cup," not too big but deep enough to hold a plump little oyster and a little briny juice. When eating them freshly shucked, you want that salty-sweet flavor with a nutty, clean, metallic finish. They shouldn't be fishy tasting. And you can feel good eating oysters, because these little mollusks are good for the environment—they help clean the water.

It's a matter of taste, but generally the smaller oysters are the best on the half shell. The larger oysters are sometimes referred to as "barbecue oysters" because they don't fall apart as easily and can take on some heat while still staying moist and tender.

### Clams

The king of clams is the geoduck (pronounced "gooey duck"). In Japanese they call it the mirugai, and it's served raw as sushi or steamed. It's as big as a football and very expensive. The hokkigai is an Atlantic surf clam that's also served in sushi. Both have a chewy texture and sweet, slightly salty, firm meat.

Out of Alaska, Canada, and Washington, you'll find razor clams. Their flavor profile is similar to abalone, and their distinctive shape makes them great for fish chowders or stews. Thin-shelled steamer clams are found on the East Coast, as are littlenecks (also called cherrystone or quahogs), which have a thicker shell and a heartier shelf life. West Coast Manila clams have the perfect meat-to-shell ratio, are sweet and tender, and steam and open up easily. They're also great for pastas. And the Ipswich clam is the best steamer clam in the world. They're even good fried, and you get a mouthful, not a little tiny clam strip. When you buy chopped clams for chowder, they're generally commercially harvested Atlantic surf clams.

## Abalone

You'll find farm-raised abalone because in recent years there's been overharvesting of West Coast red abalone. But the New Zealand blue are pretty darn good, too, and you can eat the whole thing. You don't have to trim and pound it—it's pretty tender already!

# Mike the Fisherman

When it's good, seafood is really good for you, but when it's bad it can be a scary, mercury-ridden, unsustainable ride. Information about what we're eating or buying is slowly getting easier to come by across the country, and I applaud the companies that are getting behind the cause. Mike Lucas, owner of North Coast Fisheries right here in Santa Rosa, is first in line when it comes to safe and sustainable practices for his company, and he's joined the Clean-Fish Alliance to help promote complete transparency for the consumer about where the fish comes from, how it's produced and caught, and whether it's wild or farmed.

*Keep it simple, stupid* applies to all seafood, according to Mike. He's a third-generation fisherman, and fishing families know how to cook fish. Just like beef-producing families I've met, they serve it up with no sauces on top to disguise the flavors. For example, following his purist method, Mike recommends boiling Mexican shrimp in salty water for two to three minutes, just until they float and turn orange. And his favorite way to cook live lobster or crab is to get a big pot of hot water boiling, then salt it just like the ocean. Boil them until done (for a 2-pound lobster, no more than 16 to 18 minutes, and 19 to 22 minutes for Dungeness crabs). Serve.

## Mussels

Mussels are a cost-effective protein and can be steamed, smoked, boiled, or fried. On the Atlantic coast, you'll usually find cultured blue mussels with orange or tan meat inside. They are grown on ropes and then detached. Prince Edward Island mussels from the east coast of Canada are the most popular black mussels across the country, but if you're willing to spend a little more you'll find that Mediterranean mussels produced on the West Coast are even better. Salt Spring Island, a variety of Mediterranean mussels, might cost a little more, but they're all fat and plump, perfect and tender. Green lip mussels from New Zealand are a good mouthful; they're farm-raised and most commonly come into the country already on the half shell, cooked and frozen. Some do come in live, but their shelf life is short as they like to leave their mouths open and the air kills them.

## Shrimp

For the last several years, the black tiger out of Thailand, Vietnam, Bangladesh, and India has been the most popular farm-raised shrimp on the market. But the *vannamei* species of white farmed shrimp is now taking over because of its superior growth rate and a heartiness that resists disease—you'll notice fewer spots on the shells. You do give up a little bit on the flavor with the *vannamei*, as the tiger is firmer and has more snap. But the "wild Mexican prawn"—whether brown or white—is the most flavorful shrimp you can get, along with the Mexican white shrimp, which has a grayish-white shell. We have a domestic shrimp of the same species called the wild white shrimp.

Rock shrimp out of the Gulf of Mexico are good for a pasta or a casserole. They don't have the full flavor profile of larger shrimp, but they can stand on their own when battered and fried.

Pink shrimp (*Pandalus jordani* or *borealis*) are very small shrimp from the West Coast, Maine, and Canada that are sold already cooked. These are extremely flavorful and great for shrimp cocktails and salads.

Shopping tip: When shrimp are sold, they're sized by count per pound; jumbo shrimp are 16/20 per pound. (In other words it takes sixteen to twenty of them to weigh one pound.) Sometimes you'll see that ratio in a recipe, and it'll help you buy the right size shrimp for your dish.

## Lobster

The East Coast has its classic tail-and-claws lobsters, and let's face it—a fresh-steamed hardshell right off the lobster boat is so tender that it doesn't even need butter. But there are a lot of species out there and choices when it comes to buying lobster tails. California lobster is spiny and has a bigger tail than East Coast lobster, but no claws. Australian cold-water tails are fantastic—firm and sweet. You can just broil them and they're ready to go. But warm-water Aussie tails are softer and not as good. Chefs often use them because they're about $8 a pound less but still "Aussies." Honduran and Nicaraguan tails are also good . . . but not as good as the cold-water

Aussie. So if you can, go for fresh East Coast lobsters, but the farther you are from the lobster pound, the more cold-water Aussies may be the way to go.

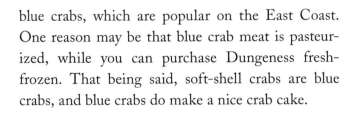

## Crab

This may be my West Coast roots talking, but I prefer Dungeness crab over king crab. Dungeness is a colossal swimming crab, which means a big body and more meat. I think they're better eating. Don't bother with snow crabs; you can starve to death trying to eat them, and spider crabs . . . well, there's just nothing in there. Tanner crabs are even weaker on the meat front. Dungeness also have more flavor than blue crabs, which are popular on the East Coast. One reason may be that blue crab meat is pasteurized, while you can purchase Dungeness fresh-frozen. That being said, soft-shell crabs are blue crabs, and blue crabs do make a nice crab cake.

## Calamari

Bought frozen or fresh, calamari is a great product. East Coast *loligo* or Boston squid are the best to cook with, with their plump tubes and tentacles. Their larger size means they're more tender and forgiving. Less forgiving are the smaller California calamari, as they're easy to overcook and turn into a plate full of rubber bands. But when cooked right—sautéed, grilled, or fried—this is one seafood that does it all.

# Blackened Sesame Salmon with Cellophane Noodle Salad

4 teaspoons chili powder

2 teaspoons wasabi powder

2 teaspoons ground ginger

2 tablespoons black sesame seeds

2 tablespoons sesame seeds

1 teaspoon fine sea salt

2 tablespoons fresh lime juice

2 tablespoons chili-garlic paste

Four 6-ounce center-cut salmon fillets, skin and pin bones removed

2 tablespoons canola oil

Cellophane Noodle Salad (recipe follows)

2 tablespoons finely chopped cilantro

*This has it all*—*the spice, the richness of the salmon, nutty sesame seeds, veggies, fruity sweetness. I mean, the list goes on! This will be one of your faves.*

## Salmon

**1.** In a small bowl, mix the chili powder, wasabi powder, ginger, sesame seeds, and salt.

**2.** In a shallow bowl, combine the lime juice and chili-garlic paste. Dredge the salmon through the mixture and then coat with the spice and seed mixture.

**3.** In a heavy skillet over medium heat, heat the oil. Add the salmon and cook for 3 to 4 minutes, then flip and cook for 2 to 3 minutes on the other side for medium-rare.

**4.** Place a mound of the noodle salad in the bottom of a wide bowl, then place the salmon on top. Garnish with the cilantro.

## Cellophane Noodle Salad

MAKES 6 CUPS

**1.** Bring a large stockpot of water to a boil. Add salt and the noodles. Cook for 1 to 2 minutes, or until tender. Pour the noodles into a colander and rinse under cold water. Shake the colander to remove the excess water, place the noodles in a large bowl, and toss them gently with the canola oil.

**2.** In a small bowl, combine all the dressing ingredients and mix well.

**3.** Add the carrots, mango, apples, cilantro, and green onions to the noodles and toss until combined. Pour the dressing onto the salad and toss to combine. Serve immediately.

## CELLOPHANE NOODLE SALAD

1 tablespoon kosher salt

½ package (4 ounces) cellophane noodles

1 tablespoon canola oil

1 cup shredded carrots

1 cup diced mango

½ cup green apple matchsticks (¼ by 1-inch)

¼ cup chopped cilantro

½ cup thinly sliced green onion, cut on the bias

## DRESSING

2 tablespoons fresh lime juice

1 tablespoon mirin

1 tablespoon rice vinegar

1 teaspoon agave nectar

1 teaspoon fine sea salt

½ teaspoon minced garlic

½ teaspoon minced ginger

# Abalone

1 abalone
(about 4 by 6 inches
in the shell)

1 egg

2 tablespoons milk

¼ cup all-purpose flour

1 cup panko bread crumbs

2 teaspoons chopped flat-leaf
parsley

1 teaspoon fine sea salt

1 teaspoon freshly ground
black pepper

2½ tablespoons olive oil

3 tablespoons butter

**Special Equipment: Boning
knife or paring knife, mallet or
meat tenderizer**

*In Italy they say a father can pass along a barrel of aged balsamic vinegar to his son as an inheritance, in France it's some primo wine or truffles, and in Nor Cal it's all about the abalone.* **This is seafood gold! Treat it with respect!**

*Some abalone facts:*

**The meat can be white, green, or even blue.**

*You're allowed three abalone a day during the season, with a limit of 24 per season.*

*We called this one huge 10½-incher Abzilla.*

**1.** Abalone meat is likely to be too firm when it comes to you. When you get the abalone, you can put it in the fridge for a day, clean it, then put in the fridge for another day. This will loosen it up pretty nicely. If you leave it in a cooler for a couple of days, it will loosen up as well.

**2.** Using a thin, sturdy wooden spatula, pry the front of the abalone free from the shell. Trim off everything that isn't white; be very careful not to overtrim. For the tougher places to reach, you can use a scouring pad and scrub some of the black off. The trimmings can be saved and used in chowder, if desired.

**3.** The part that is attached to the shell is called the foot. Trim off the outer layer of the foot. It's good to have a boning knife or paring knife to get the outer layer of the foot off in the crevice (curved area).

**4.** If you're going to eat the abalone right away, you need to tenderize the meat. Wrap it in a towel and smack it lightly several times with a mallet or a large flat-sided tenderizer (or even a two-by-four!). The towel keeps the abalone from slipping.

**5.** Once the abalone has softened up, cut it into ½-inch slices. It helps to pound it after you slice it as well. Then you can use a meat tenderizer to pound it until you feel it start to soften up.

**6.** Using the flat side of the mallet, pound the meat to the thickness of a boneless chicken breast, about ¾ to 1 inch. Make sure to put in an extra effort around the edges and the foot side, as they will be tougher.

**7.** Whisk the egg and the milk together in a small bowl. Prepare another bowl with the flour. Combine the panko, parsley, salt, and pepper in a third bowl. Dip the meat in flour, then in the egg wash, and then in the panko mixture.

**8.** When you're ready to cook, in a large skillet, heat the olive oil and butter over medium-high heat. Too much butter and it can burn, and it's too overpowering. Too much oil and you lose the sweetness.

**9.** When the oil-butter mixture starts to sizzle, place the abalone slices in the pan and cook, turning once, until golden brown, 5 to 7 minutes in all.

# Matthew's Malibu Oysters

4 large oysters (BBQ size)

⅓ cup mayonnaise

1 tablespoon white wine vinegar

2 tablespoons grated Parmesan cheese

1 teaspoon freshly cracked black pepper

¼ teaspoon cayenne pepper

¼ teaspoon ground white pepper

2 teaspoons olive oil

2 tablespoons finely diced red bell pepper

2 tablespoons finely diced red onion

1 teaspoon minced garlic

½ cup shredded baby spinach, firmly packed

1 cup PicNik dried potato sticks (found in the snack aisle)

½ cup shredded Havarti cheese

Rock salt (if cooking in oven)

*It's the classic old story of showing up at a buddy's house with the fresh oysters and using what's in the cabinet to make oysters Rockefeller . . . you know what happens . . . yep, things get outta control. At least, that's what happened at McConaughey's.*

**1.** Preheat a grill to high or the oven to 500°F. Shuck the oysters and set aside in their shells in the refrigerator or on ice.

**2.** In a small bowl, combine the mayonnaise, vinegar, Parmesan, black pepper, cayenne, and white pepper.

**3.** In a small skillet, heat the olive oil over medium-high heat. Add the bell pepper and onion and cook for 3 minutes. Add the garlic and spinach, turn the heat to low, cover, and allow the spinach to wilt, about 1 minute.

**4.** Gently combine the vegetables and the mayonnaise mixture. Stir in the potato sticks. Adjust the seasoning to taste.

**5.** Divide evenly into four portions and top each oyster with the mixture. Sprinkle with the Havarti and place on the hot grill or on a baking sheet in the oven for 5 to 6 minutes, until bubbly and cooked through. (I like to put them on a bed of rock salt if I'm doing them in the oven.) Watch them carefully!

**6.** Let sit for 5 minutes and serve. (Caution: they're still hot!)

Mise en place.

Get ready to shuck!

Insert an oyster knife into the hinge. Find the rear hinge point of the oyster.

Gently but firmly twist and turn at the hinge, securing with a towel. Apply mild to medium pressure, lightly pushing and twisting the shucking tool.

Remove the top shell, taking care not to spill the oyster's "liquor."

Gently scrape the oyster to release from shell. Carefully disconnect the oyster from the bottom shell.

Balance topped oysters on rock salt so they don't spill.

Serve 'em up.

# The Kulinary Kollision

When we came up with the idea to do a Southern-style barbecue *and* sushi restaurant, we were met with some strange looks. So let me explain my creative process. First of all, my wife, Lori, doesn't like sushi, so by the time sushi-loving Hunter was six she began to stop coming with us to get our fix because she got sick of eating the tempura and teriyaki options on the menu. She had no other choices. In the meantime, following my passions, I'd done a barbecue course down in Houston and taken sushi training in L.A. I got to thinking that barbecue restaurants in general do not always have great ambiance. You've got picnic tables, BBQ sauce down your shirt, and to-go containers. And sushi restaurants can sometimes seem intimidating when you walk in the door. Why not serve them both in a rock 'n' roll kinda place?

My business partner thought it was crazy, and everyone I talked to thought it was too wild. But one day we took all our managers and friends down to the city and brought them to a variety of sushi and barbecue joints in succession. It was agreed that you could eat them both in the same day or meal period, and the creative process kicked into gear. Our first restaurant location for Johnny Garlic's had burned down, and we had some idle time to launch the new idea while the reconstruction was going on.

# of Tex Wasabi's

We were looking for a name, and things like Rodeo Godzilla came up, but I like restaurants with a character attached. So, we conjured up an old guy whose dad was Texan and his mother was Japanese . . . and he goes by Tex Wasabi. The logo is a cowboy riding a koi fish like it's a bucking bronco. Graphic designers kept coming up with cartoon-like characters when I wanted a classic cowboy silhouette, so it was my tattoo artist Joe Leonard who came to the rescue and met my vision. For the menu we pulled together items like the Waka Waka Salad (page 117) and pork sliders and something called gringo sushi, which had no raw fish in it at all. We took seasoned sushi rice and stuffed it with blackened chicken and avocado or french fries and wrapped it in Western food items like tortillas.

That caused a lot of controversy, and we got a lot of comments like, "Come on, this is crazy!", but I kept saying, This is going to work. We fired up a real-deal BBQ smoker with hickory and cherry wood and built the sushi bar right in the middle of everything. We staffed the off-the-hook thirty-foot cocktail bar with an over-the-top team of bartenders and loaded the kitchen with a top-notch crew of cooks and chefs. Add a little rock 'n' roll and a super service staff and the guests went bananas . . . and bananas is good.

# Chorizo Clams

## ~ SERVES 2 ~

1 tablespoon canola oil

¾ cup diced dried Spanish chorizo, casing removed

½ cup diced onion

½ cup diced red bell pepper

½ teaspoon salt

3 garlic cloves, smashed

¼ teaspoon red chili flakes

1 tablespoon seeded, finely diced jalapeño

¼ cup tequila, white preferred

¼ cup Chicken Stock (page 362 or low-sodium store-bought)

2 pounds littleneck clams, scrubbed

½ cup chopped cilantro

¼ lemon

4 slices rustic sourdough bread

2 tablespoons olive oil

Cilantro sprigs, for garnish

*It's **spicy, bread-dipping, clam-broth-a-licious.** This isn't just a dish, it's a full-blown event. (The recipe calls for 2 pounds of clams—**do yourself a favor and double it.**) Rocked this one at the demo for the International Home and Housewares show in Chicago.*

**1.** In a heavy stockpot over medium-high heat, add the canola oil and cook the chorizo for 3 to 5 minutes, or until lightly browned. Add the onion, peppers, salt, and garlic and cook for 4 to 5 minutes, until the onion has softened. Add the chili flakes and jalapeño and cook for 2 minutes more. Then add the tequila and chicken stock. Bring to a boil and add the clams and chopped cilantro. Cover tightly and cook until all the clams open, 8 to 10 minutes, stirring once. Discard any unopened clams.

**2.** While the clams are steaming, drizzle the bread with olive oil and broil or grill until just crisp, about 45 seconds each side.

**3.** Divide the clams into 2 shallow serving bowls and ladle the cooking liquid on top. Squeeze the lemon over the clams. Garnish with the bread and a cilantro sprig.

This is what the clams look like in the ocean near Flavortown!

# Spicy Steamed Mussels

## SERVES 4

*Oh, oh, oh . . . yeah, yeah, yeah!* **These rock!** *I recommend two loaves of* **crusty bread, some big towels, and your favorite vino.** *This may change what you think mussels were all about. . . .*

**1.** Pick through the mussels, making sure they are all tightly closed and all the beards have been removed.

**2.** Heat a large Dutch oven over medium heat and pour in the vegetable oil. When the oil is hot, add the onion, and cook until translucent but not brown, about 5 minutes. Add the garlic, ginger, and serrano and cook 1 to 2 minutes, then add the curry powder, coriander, wine, and water and bring to a boil.

**3.** Add the mussels and cover. Steam the mussels for 6 to 8 minutes, stirring occasionally, until they have all opened.

**4.** Preheat a grill pan over medium-high heat. Drizzle the bread with olive oil and grill 1 minute per side.

**5.** Remove the mussels from the heat and discard any that are still closed. Place the mussels on a large serving platter and cover to keep warm. Return the pan to the heat, add the cream, season with pepper to taste, and bring to a simmer. Add the cilantro, green onions, and lime zest and juice. Pour the liquid over the top of the mussels. Serve the bread with the mussels.

2 pounds mussels, scrubbed and debearded

¼ cup vegetable oil

1 large onion, diced

4 garlic cloves, minced

One 2-inch piece ginger, minced

2 serrano chiles, seeded and diced

1 teaspoon curry powder

2 teaspoons ground coriander

½ cup white wine

¼ cup water

1 large ciabatta loaf, cut into ½-inch-thick diagonal slices

2 tablespoons olive oil

3 tablespoons heavy cream

Freshly ground black pepper

½ bunch cilantro, chopped

3 green onions, sliced

Grated zest and juice of 1 lime

# Tex Wasabi's Koi Fish Tacos

Juice of 1 lime

1 tablespoon white tequila

1 teaspoon ground cumin

1 teaspoon fine sea salt

1 teaspoon freshly ground black pepper

¾ pound cod or firm white fish, cut in 1-inch pieces

Sixteen 8-inch corn tortillas

Canola oil, for frying

½ cup tempura flour

1 cup prepared tempura batter made with very cold water

¾ cup panko bread crumbs

1 cup shredded white cabbage

½ cup shredded red cabbage

3 tablespoons chopped cilantro leaves

¼ cup very thinly sliced red onion

Pico de Gallo (page 365)

Tequila Lime Aïoli (recipe follows)

*I have a thing for making food from scratch that breaks away from traditional styles and methods. So in making fish tacos **I wanted to go beyond the usual grilled method and do them in my own funky way**. I pushed it to another level by frying the fish in a tempura batter and panko crust.*

*No, I don't actually use koi in this recipe, but koi fish are reminiscent of Asia and tattoo art, and you know I gotta have fun with the name. Yee-haw!*

**1.** In medium bowl, combine the lime juice, tequila, cumin, salt, and pepper and mix thoroughly. Add the fish and toss to coat. Marinate for 10 minutes (up to 1 hour) in the refrigerator.

**2.** Warm the tortillas on a grill or in a pan. Cover with a kitchen towel to keep warm.

**3.** In a medium Dutch oven, heat the canola oil to 350°F. Put the tempura flour, tempura batter, and panko in 3 separate shallow bowls.

**4.** Remove the fish from the marinade and shake off the excess. Dredge the fish in the flour, dunk in the cold tempura batter, and roll in panko, pressing it onto the fish. One piece

**TEQUILA LIME AÏOLI**

3 tablespoons premium white tequila

Juice of 1 lime

1 cup sour cream

¼ cup milk

2 teaspoons minced garlic

¼ teaspoon ground cumin

2 tablespoons minced cilantro

Kosher salt and freshly cracked black pepper

at a time, add the fish to the oil, making sure to keep the fish pieces separated. Fry for 4 to 5 minutes, until light golden brown, turning as needed. Remove with a slotted spoon and drain on paper towels.

**5.** In a medium bowl, mix the cabbages, cilantro, and onion. Stack 2 tortillas for each taco. Divide the fish on top and add the cabbage mixture, pico de gallo, and tequila lime aïoli. Serve immediately.

## Tequila Lime Aïoli

**MAKES 1¼ CUPS**

**1.** In a medium bowl, mix all the ingredients. Chill for 1 hour, then season with salt and pepper, to taste.

# Johnny Garlic's Cedar Plank Salmon

2 tablespoons canola oil

2 jalapeños, seeded and cut into rings

1 tablespoon minced garlic

½ cup white wine

3 tablespoons whole-grain mustard

1 cup apricot preserves

Four 6-ounce boneless, skinless salmon fillets

2 teaspoons fine sea salt

1 teaspoon freshly ground black pepper

Four 3-inch rosemary sprigs

Grated zest of 1 lemon

*Special Equipment:*
4 food service-quality cedar planks

*With the same intensity that some people contemplate how things were invented, I think about food and where it came from. Everything from beef jerky to salt cod to pasta has its own story.* **So when I first heard about cooking on cedar planks, I was intrigued.** *It amazed me that this readily available material could be put on the center of the fire to act like natural cookware while imparting flavor. The first time we threw a piece of salmon down on a cedar plank with some different glazes and sauces on top, our team and our guests were blown away at the restaurant. That was about fourteen years ago, and general awareness has evolved since then—but* **if you haven't tried it yet, you're in for some wild cookin' and big flavor.**

**1.** Cut four 4-inch squares of parchment paper.

# Grilling Method for Cedar Plank Salmon*

If using a grill, soak the food grade cedar planks in salted water for at least an hour. Place the salmon directly on the planks. Prepare grill for indirect grilling on medium-high heat. Grill over direct heat for 3 to 4 minutes, then transfer to indirect heat, covered, until medium-rare. Serve right off the plank!

Skinning the salmon fillet.

Soak the cedar planks in water for at least an hour.

Place the salmon directly on the plank over indirect heat on the grill.

Grill, covered, for 20 to 30 minutes, until medium-rare.

\* This is cooked on my killer Vidalia grill. One of the best!

**2.** In a small skillet over medium heat, heat the oil. Add the jalapeños and cook until soft and lightly browned, 3 to 4 minutes. Add the garlic, and before it begins to brown, stir in the wine. Add the mustard and apricot preserves and bring to a simmer. Turn the heat to low and simmer for 20 minutes or until thickened. Cool completely.

**3.** Meanwhile, preheat the oven to 400°F.

**4.** Lightly salt and pepper each fillet and place a rosemary sprig on top. Liberally spread the apricot mixture on the salmon.

**5.** Place each cedar plank on a gas burner. (Do not leave unattended!) When the planks have begun to smoke, place them in the oven.

**6.** Roast the salmon until medium-rare, 8 to 10 minutes. Let the salmon sit for 2 to 3 minutes before serving. Garnish with the lemon zest. Serve off the plank.

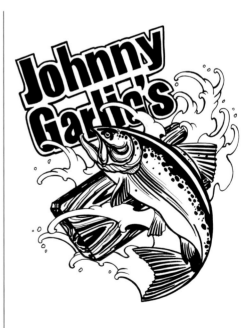

# Southern Shrimp Boil

### ⇌ SERVES 6 ⇋

3 tablespoons vegetable oil

10 ounces andouille sausage, cut into 1-inch rounds

1½ cups peeled and halved cippolini onions (about ¼ pound)

6 garlic cloves

1 jalapeño, diced

1 pound baby artichokes (about 8 small), trimmed and halved

3 quarts water

1 pound small red-skin potatoes

3 tablespoons shrimp boil spice (I recommend Zatarain's)

1 tablespoon kosher salt

3 bay leaves

1 teaspoon hot sauce (I recommend Crystal)

1 teaspoon freshly ground black pepper

2 ears of corn (about 1 pound), shucked and cut into thirds

1 pound shell-on shrimp (16/20 count), deveined

3 green onions, sliced, for garnish

Garlic Bread (recipe follows)

*A cold PBR, jammin' some Lynyrd Skynyrd, and gettin' down with some spicy corn, potatoes, and peelin' shrimp!* **That's what I'm talking about!**

**1.** In a medium stockpot, heat the oil over medium heat. Cook the sausage, cippolini onions, garlic, jalapeño, and artichokes until lightly colored, about 5 minutes. Add the water, potatoes, shrimp boil spice, salt, bay leaves, hot sauce, and black pepper. Cover the pot and bring to a boil. Reduce the heat to low, add the corn, and cover. Cook until the corn is tender, about 15 minutes.

**2.** Add the shrimp and cook until pink and firm, about 5 minutes. Remove the bay leaves.

**3.** Serve immediately in a large serving bowl. Garnish with the green onions. Serve with garlic bread.

# Garlic Bread

### SERVES 6 TO 8

**1.** In a small bowl, combine the butter, garlic, green onion, Parmesan, and parsley, and add hot sauce and salt and pepper to taste.

**2.** Preheat the broiler, with the rack 4 inches from the heat.

**3.** Split the baguette. Spread the butter mixture on both halves. Place the bread on a sheet pan and toast under the broiler until golden brown and bubbly, about 2 minutes.

## GARLIC BREAD

½ pound (2 sticks) butter, at room temperature

2 garlic cloves, minced

1 green onion, minced

2 tablespoons grated Parmesan cheese

1 tablespoon finely chopped flat-leaf parsley

Hot sauce
(I recommend Crystal)

Salt and freshly cracked black pepper

One 24-inch French baguette

# Nor Cal Cioppino

### ➤ SERVES 8 TO 10 ➤

¼ cup olive oil

4 cups diced yellow onions (about 4 medium onions)

1½ cups thinly sliced fennel

1 cup chopped red bell pepper

½ cup minced garlic

½ cup tomato paste

1½ cups dry red wine

6 cups tomato sauce (I recommend San Marzano)

½ cup clam juice

¼ cup lemon juice

1 quart water

2 bay leaves

2 tablespoons red chili flakes

1 tablespoon dried oregano

1 tablespoon dried basil

2 tablespoons fine sea salt

1 tablespoon freshly cracked black pepper

2 tablespoons sambuca liqueur

4 pounds cooked whole Dungeness crabs, each one broken into 4 pieces, with the pieces cracked to let the sauce in

2 pounds littleneck clams, cleaned and scrubbed

(cont.)

*One of my all-time faves, I mean all-time.* **I'll eat this until I pass out**. *If you're ever in Nor Cal in January, check out the huge cioppino feed in Cloverdale. If you can't get there, then keep this recipe on hand at all times.*

**1.** In a large stockpot over medium heat, heat the oil and cook the onion, fennel, red pepper, and garlic until lightly browned. Add the tomato paste and cook until it browns, stirring often. Add the wine, tomato sauce, clam juice, lemon juice, water, bay leaves, chili flakes, oregano, basil, salt, pepper, and sambuca and simmer for 1 hour.

**2.** Add the crabs to the sauce and simmer for 25 minutes.

**3.** Add the clams and simmer for 5 minutes.

**4.** Add the fish and shrimp and cook 4 to 5 minutes or until the shrimp turn pink. *Do not stir.*

**5.** Remove the bay leaves, stir in the parsley, and serve immediately with bread.

2 pounds firm white fish, such as cod or halibut, cut into 2-inch pieces

2 pounds shrimp (16/20 count), shell-on, deveined

1 cup coarsely chopped flat-leaf parsley

Sourdough bread, for serving

# AND SIDES

When I was growing up, my family was into macrobiotic cooking, and **in my second-grade world that meant veggie torture**. To be honest, I just got by with vegetables and really didn't appreciate them until I started to cook. That's when I realized the symbiotic relationships vegetables have with protein and starch, because otherwise it's like an orchestra with only an electric guitar. That's a big mistake. Vegetables play a key role in nutrition and also in the eating experience. **Where would we be without the lettuce on a burger**, or the peppers on a pizza, or the carrots in a stew? You dig?!

Similarly, **sides are important**. If the sides are done right, then three sides can make a dinner, kind of like three stars on a basketball team versus one star and a bunch of fans. And **I would rather not make a side at all than make a boring side**. It doesn't have to be so over-the-top full of flavor that it blasts everything else off the plate, but seldom will you see me make plain white rice or pasta and butter. The other night the boys wanted pasta but didn't want red sauce. I didn't have the ingredients to make pesto, but I had some nice butter, great extra virgin olive oil, and a hunk of Parmigiano-Reggiano. I put that together, hit it with sea salt and cracked pepper, and it sang. Those were simple but premium ingredients combined with good technique. Do that and you're several steps beyond serving up boxed mac-n-cheese. **It may sound funny coming from me, but less can be more**—just treat it with respect and do it right.

# VEGETABLE GUY'D

## "Thrill it, Don't Kill it"

I grew up and live in Northern California, where the variety of vegetables is endless year-round. My parents were always steaming this and that and experimenting with everything from vegetarianism to macrobiotic cooking, and my sister was a developing vegetarian. So some of my childhood vegetable immersion was involuntary, and I admit that I led a revolt in the name of meat protein. From my perspective, the (over) abundance of vegetables in my life was a big part of what motivated me to get into the kitchen in the first place.

But today I enjoy all veggies with the exception of just a few. Essentially any broccoli you put in front of me is still kind of my nemesis, but I have a method and a theory that I've put in practice to conquer my foes.

It all comes down to execution. I believe that if there's a vegetable you don't like, there's a good chance you've never eaten it when it's been handled and cooked properly. Proper nurturing changes how you experience vegetables by improving their flavor and texture, ultimately broadening the variety of vegetables that you like to eat. No two vegetables are alike. You've got to give them individualized respect and care. They're as essential to cooking as clay is to a potter. A potter will never let his clay dry out or fire it at the wrong temperature. Remember, vegetables are living plants that need to be stored correctly and never, ever overcooked.

If there's an item I've got locked in my mind as something I don't like, the guru technique that I use to get myself ready is to try it when I'm really hungry.

To get you started, here are my vegetable basics.

## Artichoke

***(Ryder's favorite . . . and he's five!)***

**Freshest and cheapest: spring**
**Guy's go-to method: steamed**

These funny flowers with hairy chokes are a big thing where I come from, and once you've got them down you'll discover they're very versatile. They can be served steamed, marinated, sautéed, or fried. Steaming is the best way to get them to a neutral point, where you're able to work with them in a variety of dishes.

To prepare fresh artichokes for steaming, cut them in half lengthwise, remove the choke inside with a spoon, and immediately rub lemon juice onto the exposed flesh or heart to prevent it from turning brown—which can happen really fast.

When shopping, look for artichokes with plump leaves that are held tightly together and not discolored. If you're using them in a cold form, such as in salads, marinated artichokes are great, and canned or jarred work well if you're sautéing or frying them.

## Asparagus

**Freshest and cheapest: spring**
**Guy's go-to method: steam lightly, then stir-fry**

Asparagus always reminded me of this particular type of grass, weed-like and thick, that grew around my town when I was growing up. It being so popular, it was one vegetable I knew I had to conquer even though as a kid I didn't really like it. So I waited until I was really hungry, insisted on froufrou pencil-thin asparagus, then tried some wrapped in prosciutto. You can wrap a shoe in prosciutto and it'll taste good. I now realize the reason I like the pencil-thin the best—not to say that finger-size asparagus was or is bad, but I had often eaten them when they'd been overcooked.

Here's a tip: if you give the larger asparagus a little steam ahead of time and then an ice bath (50 percent water to ice) they'll take on a stir-fry so much easier because you won't end up killing the exterior of the vegetable before the middle has had a chance to cook.

Now I will eat them in a tree with a bee, with a goat in a boat, or a mouse in a house, barbecued, sautéed, in a risotto, in a soup—you name it. The simple pleasure of properly cooked asparagus is its tender-crisp texture and subtle but distinguishable flavor. It can be eaten cold to hot and plays in a number of different arenas and almost all ethnicities of food.

# Avocado

**Freshest and cheapest: spring and summer**
**Guy's go-to method: right out of the skin**

What a gift from the vegetable god. Avocado is nature's fast food, so willing and ready to help. All you need to do is get it open and it'll serve your sandwich, fish, salad, tortilla chip, or even a piece of bread as natural mayonnaise. It is creamy, deeply flavorful, and rich, and can play the leading role as well as be the supporting cast member. I buy them when I don't need them and let them ripen in the bowl. It's like having your own farmers' market at home for inspiration. I'll look at a newly ripened one and think, *I've gotta use that bad boy or it's on its way out,* then find a way to fit it into my meal. For example, when making a pasta salad with vegetables, some briny olives, and cheese, tossed with lemon

## The Way We Were: An Avocado Story

When I moved to Long Beach after college I rented a house with a tree in the backyard that started to bear fruit one day. I figured it was a walnut tree, but lo and behold it was avocado. Suddenly I had hundreds of them. I came rolling to work with fat double-paper grocery bags full of them, and we ate them until the cows came home. We'd simply crack them open, smear them on bread with a little lemon off the lemon tree, top with some fresh cracked pepper and salt, and it was the absolute, pure best. Then I took one of my avocado pits and did what everybody says to do—I stuck three toothpicks into it and it sprouted and grew in a pot on the windowsill. To my surprise the plant grew 1½ feet tall, so I bought some organic soil and transferred it to a bigger pot. I was careful to bring my tree inside on cold winter days, and it continued to grow big and strong, until it had a thick, two-inch base. I was so proud. My avocado tree, nurtured from a pit, was going to bear fruit some day. So when I moved to Northern California I was like the kid from *A Christmas Story* in my enthusiasm. Then my Rottweiler lifted his leg on it . . . I brought my shriveled tree to a plant doctor and he said, "The acid went through to the root. This thing is dead." Oh, the grief I felt! It remained in the pot with no leaves on it, a dead stick, for two years. I just couldn't bring myself to throw it out.

juice or a vinaigrette dressing, I'll drop a few cubes of avocado in, and when its creamy texture comes through, that salad is taken to another level.

## Beans

**Freshest and cheapest: year-round**
**Guy's go-to method: soaked, then simmered**

Dried versus canned, you ask? I appreciate the convenience of canned when you need the beans and don't have an afternoon to cook them. But when you can, go for the dried. Pick through the beans for rocks and bad beans, soak them overnight, then fortify their flavor with seasonings while they simmer in water.

No matter how tough the variety of bean, I think they have a firmer texture every time when they haven't been sitting in a can of water. Serve them

Root vegetables

hot or cold, mash them, fry them—they can do it all. Take garbanzo beans—a must-have in my book. If you're not a fan of them, look to your source. Dried out in a deli buffet, they're chalky and horrible. But freshly cooked garbanzo beans, just out of the water, are tender, have a smooth texture, and are very versatile. They hold up to sautéing, they mash, they take on marinade—in general, they play well with others. One of my favorite things to do is season them, then toast them in the oven to create a garbanzo bean crouton. It's a nice snack food.

## Beets

**Freshest and cheapest: year-round**
**Guy's go-to method: roasted**

Ladies and gentleman, if you tell me you don't like beets, just try them my way one time. I was at my friend (and one of the best chefs I know) Gerard's house, and he was serving up a dark red and yellow beet over a salad of mixed greens, pickled onions, and blue cheese. Typically for dinners he has a crudité platter to start me off, but this time he didn't, so by the time the beets were in front of me I was hungry. I dove in and was blown away. I'd had beets in the can, candied, all the wrong ways. But give me roasted beets that are cooled and hit with a vinaigrette and I am in the heaven of the beet. The next day I called Gerard to find out what those beets were and went to four different grocery stores looking for the Chioggia. Now I eat them four ways to Sunday. As with other foods, my theory is the intensity of flavor is bigger for small varieties and a little milder for larger, so yeah, I'm a baby beet fan.

## Bell Peppers

**Freshest and cheapest: summer**
**Guy's go-to method: they play in all styles**

When it comes to bell peppers, a lot of people think first of the green ones, which have a unique, fresh, vibrant flavor that some don't like. But as the green pepper matures it turns red, and the flavor transforms into something sweeter. I like green bell peppers with beef, but the red I will use just about anywhere. Other than tomatoes and maybe radishes, so few vegetables lend that rich, bright red color. And all the bell peppers—yellow, orange, green, or red—can be roasted, sautéed, stir-fried, served raw, or cooked into casseroles. Look for firm peppers that aren't soggy or wrinkled, and the key to making them work well in your recipe is to take the membranes out as well as the seeds. (For a range of spicy peppers, see Pepper Guy'd on page 50.)

## Broccoli

**Freshest and cheapest: fall**
**Guy's go-to method: whatever you do, don't overcook**

I've conquered eggplant, Brussels sprouts, and squash, but to this day, no matter the situation or recipe, I seem to be defeated by broccoli. However, I will admit that it's versatile. Broccoli can be served raw or cooked and it stands up well from the sauté pan to the grill to the deep-fry to cold deli platters. It carries a lot of

weight in the world of cooking. Don't overcook the florets—treat it and eat it the right way and you've got my blessing.

## Brussels Sprouts

**Freshest and cheapest: fall and winter**
**Guy's go-to method: sliced thin and sautéed**

When I was on *The Next Food Network Star*, at the point in the competition when there were five people left we were all called to the table. They told us, "We're not happy with the food we're seeing from you guys. If you don't start stepping up your culinary style, a lot of people will start going home. The next dish has to be your best." Of course, this is a complete setup, but we all had a powwow and started calling out the names of food to get our favorite ingredients, determined to wow them! Just seconds before we were about to start cooking, the host, Marc Summers, came in at that moment and said, "We have a technological issue here. Move from the cutting board in front of you, one over, to the left." So Nate went over to Reggie's, and I got Nate's cutting board. He tells us to cook with the food in front of us. I look down and mine was full of Brussels sprouts. I thought, *I'm dead. I'm going home.* I'd never really been a fan of them, had never successfully cooked one in my life or paid attention to what others were doing with them. They were simply not in my wheelhouse. So I cut one in half and tasted it. It was like cabbage. I'd never put that similarity together before, and I like cabbage. So I salted some water, parboiled them, hit them in an ice bath, and sliced them thin. Next I tossed them with caramelized carrots, onion, garlic, pancetta,

# It's Not Easy Being Green: Broccoli's Final Stand

As a kid I was never into a lot of trouble, and I believe it was partially because we had to report to our family's dinner table at five-thirty every night. Life was dissected and real conversations were had at that table, and there was no room for not showing up. The meal was an event, and my parents didn't hold back with the cooking, either. They explored a macrobiotic way of eating for a time, and there'd be two or three layers of bamboo steamers and pots of water going. They would trade cowboy boots and jeans to fishermen bringing in their morning catch. My friends had Mrs. Paul's fish sticks and I had line-caught salmon. I can appreciate it now, but back then I found it gnarly! A typical night might be brown rice or bulgur, steamed fish, and vegetables . . . and my parents loved broccoli florets and stalks. But I felt like I was eating a little tree, and I could not handle it. So if I saw broccoli on the menu, I'd go and grab myself some carrots and sauté them instead.

One night, my dad and I went to the carpet on eating the broccoli florets in lemon butter sauce; it was to be the final stand. He said, "Eat the broccoli." I said, "I can't eat the broccoli." So knowing I'd do anything for some greenbacks, he bet me five bucks to eat it, but no way was I choking it down for him. So he offered ten bucks, then thirty bucks, but I didn't budge. Finally, $40 sat on the table for me to eat this plate of broccoli. This was in 1978. What's that in today's world, $150? Eight pieces of broccoli sat on that salad plate, so I pulled myself together and started shoveling lemon butter–coated broccoli. I was chomping down to money town, and Dad looked at me and said, "You swallow that. Don't you spit it out!" But the broccoli had other plans. Those florets suddenly started coming out with the milk I had tried to choke them down with. I was cupping my mouth, but it all just came out of my nose like a firehose of veggie matter. Of course I was crying at that point, and my mother came over to comfort me. I was never required to eat broccoli again, but I never got the forty bucks.

To this day, I'm not a fan. I can tempura broccoli and it'll be fine, or I can get through it blackened, but I've just never gotten over that lemon butter broccoli.

and Parmesan cheese and threw it all into a dish to make a gratin. Bobby Flay said it was one of the best dishes he'd had in the competition.

Now I eat them raw in salads, particularly baby Brussels, which have a great texture. Or I'll slice them thin and sauté or steam or roast them.

## Cabbage

**Freshest and cheapest: year-round**
**Guy's go-to method: any and all possible ways**

I am a savage of the cabbage. Give it to me raw in the taco, pickled, boiled, in a slaw, or in a salad. But keep it fresh, crisp, bright, and cool. Just the other night I was making a salad with beautiful hearts of romaine, pickled pepperoncini, heirloom tomatoes, and avocado and it needed the tang and bitterness of cabbage. So I thinly sliced some red cabbage and made a zingy, zangy French vinaigrette with some balsamic and red wine vinegar and fresh garlic. Wow! Nothing complements corned beef better than cabbage, or a pulled pork sandwich better than a cabbage slaw. I like them all—napa, savoy, green, red, and anything associated with "the family".

## Carrots

**Freshest and cheapest: fall and winter**
**Guy's go-to method: scrub and do not overcook**

I have a thing for foods with versatility, those that can be cooked and served in all fashions from raw to fried. To have an item that can play all the roles is a beautiful thing when you don't have a lot of ingredients on hand, yet you want to create really good food. In my world carrots fall into the top three of universal vegetables for their nutrient value, roughage, vibrant color, sweet taste, and tender and great texture. Unfortunately a lot of people just eat the "baby carrots" sold in bags at the grocery store. These are not typically actual baby carrots but larger carrots that have been cut and rubbed down to the smaller size (notice the package says "baby-cut.") I believe this creates a bitter, flavorless product because the sweet flavor and nutrients are found near the skin of the carrot. So my best recommendation—which goes for many vegetables—is to wash them thoroughly with a bristle brush but do not peel them. Organically grown carrots, the smaller the better, are my go-to choice. If you're careful not to overcook them, they'll keep their form and still have some bite and texture. Get away from mushy vegetables—if a carrot has some crunch in a stir-fry, I'm down with it.

## Cauliflower

**Freshest and cheapest: fall and early winter**
**Guy's go-to method: mashed**

I've already given my true confession on broccoli, and cauliflower was also once a problem. Not wanting my kids to grow up to have my aversion to it, I decided to create something for them that they would like. So I cooked the cauliflower florets in milk, hit them with nutmeg, salt, and pepper, and mashed them with a little butter to make what they thought were mashed potatoes. It was a great way to introduce a new vegetable, and I've found that roasting it also works well, lending a nuttiness and slight creaminess.

When buying, look for nice firm heads. Cauliflower has a creamy white color that you can usually only achieve with smashed potatoes or the porcelain of the plate itself. Stud it with some green beans or whatever you like—it's beautiful.

## Celery

**Freshest and cheapest: fall**
**Guy's go-to method: raw baby leaves or stir-fried**

If there's one thing in this world that I cannot resist when I'm working a stalk of celery, it's to cut into it and grab the three or four pale yellow, tender, super phenomenal stems from the center of the head. I will reach over onto somebody's plate if I see one—I really cannot stop myself. (Shhhhh—don't tell anybody that doesn't know about it, there'll be a run on internal celery stalks.) Celery is a fantastic natural sweetener, falling into the range of carrot and onion, which is why mirepoix (a mix of the three that's used as a flavor base) is so popular. The texture, sweetness, and depth of flavor, from cooked to raw, make celery really versatile. But it gets a bad rap because most people buy *big*, gigantic celery heads and actually try to cook with the two layers of inedible "I am green but I am cardboard, I am green wood" outer stalks. We think because we washed it it's ready to go, but put peanut butter on that stuff and any kid will tell you, "Whoa, that's awful!" That celery needs to be chopped to a pulverized level and used for stocks and soups—that's it. After those are taken care of, use the inner pale green stalks for stir-fry, as they're not too stringy or fibrous. I use the leaves and all when I juice it. I can gauge the quality of a bloody Mary by the celery put in the glass. (And set aside the center of the stalk to send to me.)

## Celery Root

**Freshest and cheapest: fall and winter**
**Guy's go-to method: thinly sliced, raw in a slaw**

This gnarled root looks so horrible, but get a knife out and look to its inner beauty. Once you're past the beast of the outer root, I promise that the incredible sweet flavor and snow white color of celery root will win you over. It's another universal player—great cooked in stews or served raw, thinly sliced, in salads. Tell me you like coleslaw and I'll tell you to make it with celery root instead of cabbage and you'll never look back. Mix it with lemon juice, garlic, capers, and mayonnaise and don't tell anybody what they're biting into, in case they've been scared off by the beast in the past.

## Corn

**Freshest and cheapest: mid- to late summer**
**Guy's go-to method: roasted**

I can remember eating sweet corn raw, right on the cob, when I was a kid. When I first saw stalks of corn growing in a field I couldn't believe it, thinking, *Corn comes in a package? Oh my gosh! It grows on some kind of vending machine!* But I still hold it in awe as a vegetable, because there are so many ways to use corn. It adds natural sweetness and crisp texture to a whole spectrum of recipes, from a cool salad to the heat of chili and stews. You can dry it and grind it to make polenta or corn bread or masa for tortillas, and you can even pop it. I like to roast it by pulling the husk back and removing the ever-so-annoying silk (they should use that stuff to torture people); then I soak it in water so that when you throw it in the oven or on the barbecue, the moisture and internal flavor are locked in. Of course boiling is fine, but if you get it a little caramelized by cooking it in the husk, the flavor is awesome. I don't mind canned corn, better than nothing, but my choice is frozen corn if I have to. (I feel the same way about frozen okra.) Frozen corn is a little mushier than fresh, but the natural sweetness is a worthwhile addition to chile con carne or for putting into a stew or pot pie, if you can't get fresh.

## Cucumbers

**Freshest and cheapest: summer**
**Guy's go-to method: raw**

I am a fan of cucumber's depth of unique flavor and its crunch. But when you need something that's fresh, crisp, and bright, cucumbers are like the vegetable version of watermelon. They hold an almost effervescent, clean flavor that's unmatched.

As I mentioned before, I prefer not to skin any of my vegetables because I hate to lose their nutrients in the process, but if peeling is the expectation in whatever you're making, make sure your cucumber is young, to avoid old, tough skin, and give the English cucumber a try. It has a mild flavor, its skin is thin, and it has fewer seeds, too. For all cucumbers, you're looking for a nice, firm vegetable. No one likes a squooshy cucumber.

## Daikon Radish

**Freshest and cheapest: fall and winter**
**Guy's go-to method: Microplaned, raw**

After a long day of work we generally don't spend the time to garnish our plates at home. But with the ingredients already in your fridge, you can make some really good things happen on the plate, and it adds so much to the experience of the meal. One of my firm beliefs is that all garnishes should be edible, and one of my favorite weapons in my garnish arsenal is the daikon radish. Most people think of the hot red radish when they hear radish, but the daikon is a whole other story. It has a little pepper to it, but nothing like the little red guy. That goes back to my theory that the smaller the variety of vegetable, the more robust the flavor. You can slice a daikon or Microplane ribbons out of it. It works in cold salads, in sushi, on a crudité platter, pickled. I don't tend to cook it, but you can find a wide range of Asian recipes that use it in everything from stir-fries to soups. Just remember: because it's very versatile, inexpensive, and unique, with a mild flavor and crunch, daikon is your garnish buddy.

# Eggplant

**Freshest and cheapest: summer**
**Guy's go-to method: sliced, floured, and sautéed**

Who was the caveman walking in the jungle who looked down at the eggplant, and said, "Me wanna eat 'em"? It must've been the cousin of the guy who spotted an oyster and said, "Mmm, look, me open and suck out of shell!" Eggplant may get a bad rap—even from me—but that's partly because of the plight of the common large eggplant. People like its meaty texture, but so often it isn't handled the right way, and the skin is bitter and tough, or if the skin's been taken off then the whole thing is mushy, and if it's fried then the healthy component is gone. People do a lot of salting and pressing to take the bitterness out of the large varieties, but I say just go to the smaller Japanese eggplants; they're easier to work with and have thin skins, small seeds, and a sweet flavor. A billion people can't be wrong—try eggplant today. Try it when you're hungry, sliced thin, lightly floured, and sautéed, then stacked up with mozzarella and tomato sauce. That's hard not to like.

# Garlic

**Freshest and cheapest: summer**
**Guy's go-to method: whatever you do, do not burn!**

To me, garlic is the Johnny Depp of vegetables. It can play so many roles, starting with the wild and crazy, harsh, snappy, hot, and aggressive raw garlic, whether chopped or pressed and pulverized and thrown in raw. But garlic can play it cool and not take over the show, such as when you slice it thin with a razor blade the way they did in *Goodfellas* and it melts into your sauce, or when you roast it low and slow in the bulb and create a sweet vegetable butter. It's how you treat it that makes the difference. It's like having a lion for a pet: treat it with respect or it will eat you.

This bodacious bulb is such a centerpoint to my cooking that I named one of my restaurants Johnny Garlic's. You'll find it in almost every ethnicity of food, raw, granulated, or roasted. But garlic is often abused and misinterpreted. Particularly in the winter months, the variety of garlic available is almost as vast a spectrum as apples. Think of the range of texture, color, flavor, and sugar content found between a Golden Delicious and a Granny Smith. The same holds true between elephant garlic and Chinese garlic, with a range of heat, acid, and flavor. The smaller the clove, the more potent it is. Buy firm bulbs, keep them in the dark so they don't sprout, and don't burn it or you'll have to start over. Never build a dish on a bad, burned garlic foundation. You can pick it up in a dish like a skunk in the room.

## Ginger

**Freshest and cheapest: fall**
**Guy's go-to method: grated (use the juice!)**

This gnarled rhizome has a strong, distinct flavor that can be used well in marinades and seasoning oils, and it's found in a huge variety of Asian dishes. But ginger has the ability to be put into play with all kinds of foods. You're adding a little bit of herbaceous spiciness with ginger instead of a hot peppery heat. Chop it into big pieces and season a warm soy-garlic or cilantro sauce (removing the chunks before serving), or shred it and squeeze the juice out for a tangy marinade. I learned from a Japanese woman long ago to buy a 99-cent grater and collect the juice, not the pulp.

## Green Beans

**Freshest and cheapest: summer**
**Guy's go-to method: blanch, then shock**

My bean theory is the smaller the better, for everything from pickled bean salad to a sauté to a tempura. Green beans handle all the culinary methods well, but small and firm are the way to roll. Past that, I believe they need a little precook boil or steam, then an immediate shock in an ice bath before you do anything else with them. Don't make them go through the arduous process of sautéing or pan-frying or what-

ever it may be until they're fully cooked. The bean's exterior will overcook before it becomes tender on the inside. My dad and I used to argue about this. You can take a raw green bean and sauté it until it's done, but to keep that optimally edible, al dente firmness, you've got to go with the blanch-and-shock treatment before tackling another method.

One of the things I like to do with green beans is to make a nice little pickling solution of salt, sugar, and vinegar. When you add one of those beans to a bloody Mary, it's off the charts. Or blanch and shock, then sauté them with a little soy sauce, ginger, and onion, cooked down until the soy sauce clings to it. Get outta here—that's good!

## Jicama

**Freshest and cheapest: year-round**
**Guy's go-to method: raw**

You look at jicama and think, what is that big, hard, brown thing? But when you skin it and slice it thin, then toss it with a little vinaigrette, that bright white color and great crunch plays very well with others. It's an inexpensive way to fortify typically cold vegetable dishes using carrots, celery, tomatoes, broccoli, or mushrooms. But make no mistake, jicama is a stand-out character—just splash a sprinkle of some chili powder on there and it's simple and fun.

## Kale

**Freshest and cheapest: summer and fall**
**Guy's go-to method: soups and stews**

Kale has so often been given the garnish position, but its texture withstands a lot of cooking processes.

It can stand up to high temperatures and still hold its vibrant color and texture. So often when you're eating a soup or stew you find you're looking for something to bite into, and kale holds strong.

## Leeks

**Freshest and cheapest: spring**
**Guy's go-to method: soups and sautés**

Leeks have a really nice mild onion flavor that's almost lemony. I like them in soups, salads, sautés—you name it. But people often don't know how to work with leeks; they're famous for the dirt they carry in between their leaves. Here's how you win at this one: Chop off the end of the leek, then cut the leek in half lengthwise. Cut into the size needed for your dish, then stir the cut leeks in a big bowl full of water just like it's a load of laundry. The dirt will fall to the bottom of the bowl. Voilà!

## Lettuce

**Freshest and cheapest: summer**
**Guy's go-to method: served up cold and crisp**

**Iceberg** I do believe we are a nation of crunch lovers. We just love anything that's crisp. I know that there's not much flavor or vitamin content in iceberg, but you gotta kick down and love it anyway. It's the super duty lettuce that can do it all. It can do time with a hot burger patty and still stay crunchy. It may have been overdone in the seventies, but you know you love it in the wedge with Maytag blue cheese, nice

heirloom tomatoes, and thick-cut bacon at the steakhouse. You're crazy if you don't. So I admit this is my go-to culinary workhorse of the lettuce world.

**Romaine** The all-powerful romaine can play ball in all categories. Problem is, people think you can't cut those outer leaves off. Take note that those four exterior leaves have been sitting there in the sun getting tough, like a dark green tongue of a shoe. So take off those outer leaves, toss them into the compost, and get to the tender, juicy, crisp hearts.

**Baby mixed lettuces** These are awesome if they're treated with respect. Don't overdo it with dressing—the lighter and thinner the better. If I can't get them loose at the store, I choose to buy them in the box over the bag.

## Mushrooms

**Freshest and cheapest: year-round**
**Guy's go-to method: do not overcook _or_ undercook**

Mushrooms are still in my like-but-don't-love category, but what I enjoy most about mushrooms is their flavor. I am a texture junkie, and I find them dry when they're raw and too mushy and slimy

when they're overcooked. But give me a portobello, cremini, or shiitake in a stir-fry and I'm good. Portobellos have a great meaty texture, and they add body to a dish. Chanterelles, porcini, and oysters have a diversity of flavor that I can respect. But button mushrooms or mushrooms that have been stuffed with something they shouldn't have been . . . not so much. That's like seeing your favorite rock band in a high school auditorium with a bad PA system.

# Okra

**Freshest and cheapest: summer**
**Guy's go-to method: fried**

I am down with anything that transforms itself into a natural thickener in recipes. I think that's right on. Why I like the shape of okra. It reminds me of a pepper. Now, I am with everybody else when it comes to not liking okra when it's prepared like the slimy cross between a jellyfish and a pepper pod. I get freaked out, too. But tell me you don't like fried cornmeal-dredged okra rounds. If you don't, you haven't tried the right ones.

# Onions

**Freshest and cheapest: summer**
**Guy's go-to method: king of the kitchen**

I can't say enough about onions. On *The Next Food Network Star*, when people were asked what their number one ingredient was, for me it was the onion—the universal superstar of all foods. Onion adds acid and sharpness when raw and sweet and savory flavors when cooked. White onion for chili; yellow for everything; red for raw; Vidalia or Maui for fried; green for salad, grill, and garnish; leek; shallot . . . must I go on? But all of them can handle almost any type of cooking, and that's what I'm looking for! In my world the onion owns the kitchen, and it's good that it makes you cry, because if it didn't you might overuse it. One of the biggest things people should learn is how to cut it correctly. Always use a sharp knife. I choose not to buy onions in bags because I like to feel their firmness and weight individually. Big onions worry me, because I wonder how long they've been out of the ground, if they've been stored well, and if they might have a dried-out center. I like them to be larger than a baseball but smaller than a softball, with a firm feel and intact skin.

## Peas

**Freshest and cheapest: spring and summer**
**Guy's go-to method: right out of the garden**

I can remember standing in the garden that was down the alley behind my parents' store in Ferndale and cracking open these sweet little pea pods with little nub tails on them. There was a brief mist created as the pod opened with a pop. The herbaceous sweetness, the crunch of the skin, and the creamy flesh of each pea was awe inspiring. I didn't have any money to buy candy and knew nothing about peas, but they definitely did the trick. Later on at the dinner table I looked down at my plate of peas and asked, "Why did you cook them? They were so good on their own." I've always liked peas, even frozen peas in fried rice at Chinese restaurants. The first time I ate at Rao's in New York I had prosciutto and peas, and I couldn't shove them in my mouth fast enough. It was like coming full circle. People around me said, "What's he doing? Check it out—he's eating the whole bowl!" That's right, no problem.

Frozen peas are better than canned, but if you can get fresh peas, I say *Amen*.

## Potatoes

**Freshest and cheapest: year-round**
**Guy's go-to method: the right potato for the right job**

The potato is one of the most misunderstood vegetables—all potatoes are not alike. It's loved in so many ways, and utilized in so many ways. The russet is high in starch and can withstand a lot, so it's great for pan-frying and french fries, and its tough skin makes it the perfect baked potato. The Yukon gold makes gently creamy whipped potatoes. Red potatoes are great for roasting, the smaller the better. Good potatoes can last a long time, but you have to store them in a cool, dark place in a bag with some aeration, such as a burlap or a plastic bag with holes. I'm not a fan of buying them in a five-pound bag. It might be convenient, but it's not really a price discount, and buyer beware in terms of what's in there. They need to feel firm, dense, and alive. Take a swing at specialty and heirloom potatoes if you see them. Peruvian ones with red onions, capers, sun-dried tomato, olive oil, and herbs will sit there and just explode with flavor.

and when it's sliced and mixed with baby greens I love the big, full flavor and texture. I am a fan of charring anything because it converts the sugars and adds another dimension.

# Shallots

**Freshest and cheapest: summer**
**Guy's go-to method: less is more**

The shallot has such a refined, clean oniony taste. It's the less-is-more vegetable, because it gently adds flavor to a sauté or dressing, adding mild onion concentration.

# Spinach

**Freshest and cheapest: spring and fall**
**Guy's go-to method: washed and stored properly**

Sautéed, baked, raw, or steamed, spinach is a super veggie. From its tender baby state to its broad, leafy state, it transcends all ethnicities. Keep your spinach wrapped in a paper towel inside a plastic bag in a crisper. Properly washed leaves need to be dry and firm, not wet and mushy. And that goes for the dressing as well.

A note on frozen spinach: Some things I'd much rather eat frozen than canned any day of the week. These include peas, spinach, and corn. They're picked at their prime and individually quick-frozen, not sitting in liquid and deteriorating. Granted, there's some mushiness involved, but frozen spinach can play a lot of great roles, such as in spanakopita or lasagna.

# Radicchio

**Freshest and cheapest: winter**
**Guy's go-to method: grilled**

I never had an aversion to radicchio; it just wasn't on my budget radar when I was in college. Working as much as I did, I ate what I could afford. But I branched out as I got older. Grilled radicchio salad is what put this vegetable on the map for me. Grilling mellows out the slightly sharp and bitter radicchio,

## Tomatillos

**Freshest and cheapest: late summer**
**Guy's go-to method: freshly roasted**

I really believe the average person cruises the grocery store, sees the tomatillo, and says, "Eeew, when did tomatoes start having skins on them?" They do look just like a tomato with a husk, after all. But these are a must-have in Mexican food. They've got a bitterness, sweetness, savoriness, and saltiness all at the same time. You can get them canned, but I like them fresh because you can roast them and round out the flavor a little bit more. Whatever you do with them—grinding them up in a salsa (see page 95) or serving them by themselves—they add a vibrance that makes anything from chicken to seafood to veggies pop.

## Squash

**Freshest and cheapest: fall**
**Guy's go-to method: the right squash for the right dish**

Acorn is probably my favorite squash—roasted, stuffed, in risotto, you name it. The key to me is having the right squash for the right dish. (I mean, there's *no* substitute for spaghetti squash.)

## Sweet Potatoes

**Freshest and cheapest: late summer and early fall**
**Guy's go-to method: fried**

When buying sweet potatoes, look for ones with firm, smooth, dry skin—and not too big. I had too many scoops of marshmallows and secret casseroles as a child, so I'm not much of a sweet potato casserole fan, but I like sweet potato fries and hash. A good sweet potato fry is twice cooked to get the most moisture out of them. Not a fry and fly—we're talking a double fry or a double bake to bring the crunch out!

# Tomatoes

**Freshest and cheapest: late summer**
**Guy's go-to method: ripe, right off the vine**

In the grocery store you'll often find tomatoes that were picked green and gas-ripened off the vine, making the tomato a mere shadow of itself. It's just not right for America's favorite fruit! You're better off buying canned San Marzano tomatoes than this type of "fresh" tomato, because the canned ones are picked and canned at their peak ripeness. Yes, I'd love to buy them straight from the farmers' market every day (and living in California as I do, this is pretty much possible), but the rest of the country is more dependent on the seasons for their local tomato feasting. When tomato season rolls around in your region, do yourself a favor and buy one from a farmer, cut into it, and make a BLT with *that*!

> To properly dress a salad, pour a little of the dressing down the edge of the serving bowl holding the lettuce. Lightly coat the side of the bowl, then toss. This way you won't weigh down the leaves and end up with an oily, globby mess, and you'll use less dressing.

# Asian Fried Quinoa "C. R. Bipim Delight"

## ⟿ SERVES 4 ⟾

1 ½ cups quinoa

3 cups water or vegetable stock

3 tablespoons grapeseed or olive oil

2 cups diced onions (about 1 ½ medium onions)

¼ cup chopped shallots

¼ cup minced garlic

½ cup minced ginger

1 cup finely chopped green onion

1 cup finely diced carrots (4 small carrots)

2 cups shredded baby bok choy

1 cup finely diced celery

2 cups shredded napa cabbage (about ¼ head)

1 cup diced sugar snap peas

3 tablespoons low-sodium soy sauce, plus more to taste

2 large eggs, lightly beaten

A lot of the healthy dishes in my repertory have stemmed from cooking for my sister, Morgan (C. R. Bipim Delight is my nickname for her). She's been vegetarian as long as I can remember, and **I'm not a fan of just handing someone some steamed broccoli while I go eat turkey and all the fixins**. So I've always made two or three unique veggie dishes that she can enjoy, and I don't just do the traditional; I put my Guy spin on it. But when my sister was diagnosed with melanoma, she was given a strict diet with an eclectic list of foods that she could eat to keep the pH of her body at the level she needed. I believe one of the greatest ways you can show love and respect for someone is to cook for them, so the first time I was to see Morgan after her diagnosis, I asked that she come to my house for dinner. I headed over to my buddy Kenny's gourmet store Pacific Market with the list of those ingredients on my BlackBerry and realized that my standard go-tos like brown rice, pasta, and garlic were not necessarily on it.

Then I noticed quinoa on the list. My first taste of quinoa had gotten a mixed review. It seemed a bit like uncooked, crunchy bulgur wheat, and I wasn't thrilled with it, even though I'm a notorious junkie for most grains and pasta. Nonetheless, I decided that quinoa would be the basis for the entrée portion of the meal. I had a few hours to mess with it before my premiere, so I cooked a little, tasted it, and had the inspiration that it could be cooked twice, just like fried rice with some vegetables.

I've had a few iconic moments at the dinner table when Mom and Dad have looked at me and said, **"You've got to put that in your cookbook."** Well, in this case, they all *turned* and said that about this dish. So alongside my Cajun Chicken Alfredo and Pork Ole, here comes my **fried quinoa**.

**1.** In a large dry heavy-bottomed skillet over high heat, toast the quinoa until lightly golden, 5 to 6 minutes, stirring frequently. Add the water and reduce the heat to medium. Cover and cook until the quinoa opens and the liquid is absorbed, about 20 minutes. Transfer to a bowl to cool.

**2.** Wipe out the skillet and heat 1½ tablespoons of the oil over medium-high heat. Add the onions and cook until well browned and soft, about 20 to 30 minutes, stirring occasionally. Stir in the shallots and cook for 2 minutes, then the garlic, ginger, and green onion and cook for 3 to 4 minutes more. Add the carrots, bok choy, celery, cabbage, and snap peas and stir until just wilted. Pour in the soy sauce and combine well. Transfer the mixture to a bowl and keep warm.

**3.** Heat the remaining 1½ tablespoons oil in the skillet over medium-high heat and add the quinoa. When it is heated through, pour the eggs over the quinoa and stir-fry until the eggs are cooked. Return the vegetables to the pan. Adjust the seasoning with additional soy sauce if necessary.

# Banana Pepper Sauerkraut

### ⤙ SERVES 4 ⤚

2 cups best-quality sauerkraut, drained

1½ cups jarred banana peppers, drained

2 to 3 tablespoons pickled jalapeño rings

¼ cup apple cider vinegar

1 teaspoon kosher salt

1 tablespoon freshly ground black pepper

½ teaspoon cayenne pepper

½ teaspoon granulated garlic

*Oh, this just turns on the water jets in my mouth.* *It's awesome on hot or cold dishes, sandwiches or salads, you name it. This is your new go-to condiment.*

**1.** In a food processor fitted with the steel blade, combine all the ingredients and pulse until finely chopped and well combined. Taste and adjust the seasoning as desired. Serve with Chico's Puerto Rican Pork Roast (page 216) and refrigerate any leftovers.

# Ridiculously Good Radicchio Bundles

*Should I have called these bundles or bombs? They're wrapped like bundles, but* **the flavor is da bomb!**

**1.** Core the radicchio and remove any wilted outer leaves. Cut the head in half and then separate the leaves into 8 double-thick "shells." Lay 1 slice of prosciutto in the hollow of each shell, then add a couple of strips of roasted pepper, 2 bocconcini halves, a few strands of the basil, a pinch of the black pepper, and a teaspoon of the pesto.

**2.** Tie the leaf bundles closed with the kitchen twine, as you would a roast, going around twice and tucking in the ends as needed. Drizzle lightly with 2 tablespoons of the olive oil.

**3.** Preheat a grill to medium-high. Lay the bundles on the grill and cover. Cook for 3 minutes, then turn over and cook another 3 minutes. Remove from the grill and cut the strings. Drizzle with the remaining 1 tablespoon olive oil and the vinegar and serve immediately.

One 10-ounce radicchio head (small and firm, about grapefruit size)

8 thin slices of prosciutto (about 3 ounces)

1 cup roasted red bell pepper strips

8 bocconcini (fresh buffalo mozzarella balls), 1 pound total, cut in half

8 fresh basil leaves, cut crosswise into thin shreds

1 teaspoon freshly cracked black pepper

¼ cup pesto

3 tablespoons olive oil

1 tablespoon balsamic vinegar

*Special Equipment:*
8 pieces kitchen twine, each about 10 inches long

# Grilled Polenta

=∞ **SERVES 6 TO 8** ∞=

1½ cups water

1½ cups Chicken Stock
(page 362 or low-sodium
store-bought)

2 teaspoons kosher salt

1½ cups medium- or coarse-
grain instant polenta

1 teaspoon chopped thyme

1 teaspoon chopped marjoram

1 teaspoon freshly ground
black pepper

3 tablespoons unsalted butter

¾ cup grated Parmesan
cheese

¼ cup olive oil, for grilling
or pan searing

*Special Equipment:*
**10-inch springform pan**

*Polenta is so versatile*, so adaptable, taking on flavors and adding great texture. This one is delicately flavored, soft on the inside, and has a nice crust on the outside.

**1.** In a medium saucepan over medium-high heat, bring the water, chicken stock, and salt to just a boil. Lower the heat and slowly whisk in the polenta. Whisk continually until the mixture starts to thicken up, 2 to 3 minutes. Add the thyme, marjoram, pepper, 2 tablespoons of the butter, and the Parmesan and stir for about 30 seconds, or until well combined and very thick. Taste and adjust the seasonings.

**2.** With the remaining 1 tablespoon of butter, liberally grease a 10-inch springform pan on the bottom and about 2 inches up the sides. Pour in the hot polenta and use a rubber spatula rubbed with butter to smooth out the top. Set aside to cool to room temperature, then cover with plastic wrap and refrigerate for 2 hours to set. This can be done up to one day before grilling or pan-frying.

**3.** Remove the sides from the pan and cut the polenta into wedges with a knife or circles with a biscuit cutter. Lightly oil a grill set to medium-high, or heat a large cast-iron skillet over high heat. Brush each side of polenta with olive oil, and grill or cook undisturbed until golden brown, about 3 minutes each side. Serve hot.

# Turning Greens

*Oh, this is a trip.* *I was sittin' in upstate New York, and this unique lookin' dish was placed in front of me. I took a few pokes with my fork to taste it . . . and* **three helpings later I had to cook up my own.**

**1.** In a large skillet over medium-high heat, cook the ham until the fat starts to render out. Add the capicola and salami and cook for 4 minutes. Stir in the olive oil, onion, bell pepper, and fennel and cook until the onion starts to brown, 6 to 10 minutes. Add the garlic and cook for 2 minutes, taking care not to burn the garlic. Add the escarole and the chicken stock. Cover and let the escarole wilt, about 5 minutes.

**2.** Uncover and stir in the vinegar and lemon juice. Add the butter, black pepper, granulated garlic, chili flakes, sugar, and salt and stir to combine. Transfer to a serving bowl and serve immediately, sprinkled with the Parmesan.

½ cup country ham matchsticks

½ cup spicy capicola matchsticks

½ cup salami matchsticks

1 tablespoon olive oil

1 cup yellow onion matchsticks

1 cup green bell pepper matchsticks

¼ cup fennel matchsticks

3 tablespoons minced garlic

3 pounds escarole, trimmed, rinsed, dried, and shredded across the leaf (avoid using the tough stems)

½ cup Chicken Stock (page 362 or low-sodium store-bought)

¼ cup red wine vinegar

1 tablespoon fresh lemon juice

2 tablespoons unsalted butter

1 teaspoon freshly cracked black pepper

½ teaspoon granulated garlic

½ teaspoon red chili flakes

½ teaspoon sugar

1 teaspoon fine sea salt

½ cup finely grated good-quality Parmesan cheese

# Szechuan Green Beans

2 cups plus 1 tablespoon canola oil

¼ cup soy sauce

2 tablespoons chili-garlic sauce (I recommended Tuong Ot Toi Viet Nam)

¼ cup rice vinegar

2 tablespoons hoisin sauce

1 tablespoon mirin or white wine

½ teaspoon sesame oil

1 teaspoon chopped cilantro

1 tablespoon minced ginger

1 tablespoon minced garlic

1 pound green beans, trimmed

2 tablespoons chopped peanuts

*This awesome mean green bean* can be served alongside some steamed brown basmati rice with a little cucumber salad for a perfect vegan meal.

**1.** Heat 2 cups of the canola oil in a medium Dutch oven to 350°F.

**2.** In a small bowl, combine the soy sauce, chili-garlic sauce, vinegar, hoisin, mirin, sesame oil, and cilantro.

**3.** In medium skillet over medium heat, heat the remaining 1 tablespoon canola oil. Add the ginger and stir-fry for 2 to 3 minutes, being careful not to let it burn. Add the garlic and cook for 1 minute or until it turns light brown.

**4.** Working quickly to prevent garlic from burning, add the soy sauce mixture. Heat through and remove from the heat.

**5.** Fry the green beans in the canola oil for about 45 seconds, or until they turn dark green. Remove the beans from the oil with a skimmer and drain off the excess oil. Add the beans to the sauce. Toss to coat and garnish with the peanuts.

Lean, mean, and green.

A fantastic *view* of the famous Guid-Moc-*Shoe*!

# Cuid-Moc-Shoe

*As I've always said, if you're gonna make a side dish,* **make it the real deal.** *This, my friends, is just that—my take on the Louisiana staple corn maque choux. Oh, you are* so *gonna love this!*

**1.** Heat a grill or grill pan to high.

**2.** Lightly oil the corn husks and roast it lightly on the grill, 5 to 6 minutes.

**3.** Meanwhile, char the bell peppers on the grill or lightly oil them and char under the broiler.

**4.** Let the corn cool. Remove the husks and silk and cut the kernels from the cob. Peel and dice the bell peppers.

**5.** In a large skillet over medium heat, cook the bacon until crispy. Transfer with a slotted spoon to a paper-towel-lined plate. Add the onions, jalapeño, and bell peppers to the bacon fat and cook for 3 minutes. Add the corn and celery and cook until the celery is al dente, 3 to 4 minutes. Add the flour and stir until lightly browned. Slowly add the wine and chicken stock. Stir until thickened, about 5 minutes. Season with the salt and pepper.

**6.** Serve garnished with the bacon and tomatoes.

2 tablespoons canola oil

3 fresh ears corn, preferably white, husks on

1 red bell pepper

1 green bell pepper

¼ pound bacon, diced

1 red onion, diced

1 yellow onion, diced

½ jalapeño, diced

3 celery stalks, diced

3 tablespoons all-purpose flour

¼ cup white wine

¾ cup Chicken Stock (page 362 or low-sodium store-bought)

1 tablespoon fine sea salt

1 tablespoon freshly ground black pepper

¼ cup Roma tomatoes, seeded and diced

# Goody Girl Championship Potatoes

≈ **SERVES 6 TO 8** ≈

One 3-ounce package dry crab boil (I recommended Zatarain's)

2 tablespoons kosher salt, plus more as needed

3 pounds red-skin potatoes

1 pound thick-cut bacon, diced

1 cup diced red onion

1 tablespoon minced garlic

¼ pound (1 stick) butter, at room temperature

1 cup finely grated cheddar cheese (about 4 ounces)

1 green onion, chopped

½ teaspoon cayenne pepper

½ teaspoon paprika

¾ cup sour cream

Freshly ground black pepper

*The Goody Girls are a champion barbecue team from Houston, Texas, that we met at the Jack Daniel's World Championship Invitational barbecue competition. We hit it off with these guys and girls, and they ended up inviting us down to the Houston Livestock Show and Rodeo, where* **the Goody Girls throw a party like no other.** *So here we come rolling in from California to cook with them, and what do we make? We rolled sushi in the barbecue area where they were cooking breakfast, lunch, and dinner for 500 people. There was some good old storytelling and recipe swapping. This style of potatoes was originally the brainchild of a good dude named RB on the team, so I did my riff on it and named it after them as a tribute. Big love goes out to the Goody Girl team.*

**1.** Fill a 6-quart pot two-thirds full of water and add the crab boil and 2 tablespoons salt. Stir until blended. Cut the potatoes in half, then into half-moon slices ¼-inch thick. Add the potatoes to the pot. Bring the water to a boil and cook the potatoes until fork-tender. Drain and keep warm, covered in foil, in a low oven.

**2.** Meanwhile, in a medium skillet over medium heat, cook the bacon until crispy; transfer with a slotted spoon to paper towels to drain. Add the red onion to the bacon grease and cook until lightly brown, 5 to 7 minutes. Just before the onion is done, add the garlic and cook until lightly brown. Remove from the heat.

**3.** In a large bowl, combine the butter, ½ cup of the cheese, half of the bacon, half of the green onion, the onion-garlic mixture, cayenne, paprika, sour cream, and salt and pepper to taste. Mix together thoroughly.

**4.** Add the potatoes to the bowl; let stand for a few minutes, until the cheese starts to melt. Fold everything together, taking care not to break up the potatoes. Check the seasonings and adjust to taste. Top with the remaining cheese, bacon, and green onion.

# McAlister Potatoes

## ⇨ SERVES 6 TO 8 ⇦

1 cup sour cream

½ cup chopped drained Peppadew peppers

¼ cup white wine

3 pounds baby Yukon gold potatoes

2 tablespoons kosher salt, plus more for seasoning

¾ pound bacon, diced

2 yellow onions, diced

1 tablespoon minced garlic

1 teaspoon freshly ground black pepper

4 tablespoons olive oil

3 tablespoons grated Parmesan cheese

*It may seem as if I have a lot going on, but I'm pretty consistent in my style and habits. For example, I never go to somebody's house without bringing something, and I've always got to be cooking—I take over people's kitchens about 90 percent of the time. So of course when I went over to my culinary director Korina McAlister's house one night before she worked with me,* **I came rolling in with this potato dish.** *Korina, her husband, "Jimmy Mac," and their kids, Dixie and Mason (Jimmy's from Tennessee),* **loved them so much that they made them themselves the next night!** *So when I got ready to do the recipe on the show, I put them out there as McAlister Potatoes. It's all about tribute!*

**1.** In a small mixing bowl, combine the sour cream, peppadews, and wine. Mix thoroughly and refrigerate for 1 hour.

**2.** In a large stockpot, combine the potatoes, 2 tablespoons salt, and water to cover. Turn the heat to high, bring to a boil, and cook until fork-tender.

**3.** Meanwhile, in a large skillet over medium heat, cook the bacon and onion until the onion browned. Add the garlic and cook 1 or 2 minutes. Transfer the mixture with a slotted spoon to paper towels to drain, leaving the fat in the pan. Sprinkle the bacon and onion mixture on a serving platter and keep warm.

**4.** Drain the potatoes and spread them on a baking sheet. Using a clean kitchen towel over your hand, smash the hot potatoes to approximately ⅓--inch thick. Season them with salt and pepper.

**5.** Reheat the fat in the skillet over medium heat and add 2 tablespoons of the olive oil. Working in batches and adding more oil as needed, brown the potatoes on both sides until crispy, 5 to 7 minutes, then transfer them to the platter with the bacon mixture.

**6.** Top the potatoes with Parmesan and then with the sour cream mixture.

Jimmy ate off the serving spoon . . . I just know it.

# Double-Fried French Fries

Four 4- to 5-inch-long russet potatoes (about 2 pounds)

2 quarts canola oil

1 tablespoon fine sea salt

1 teaspoon freshly ground black pepper (optional)

**Special Equipment:**
Deep-fry thermometer, skimmer

*Fries—when they're good they're really good, and when they're bad . . . well, yep, you'll still eat 'em. But **when they're off da hook—well, they're probably double fried.** Trust me on this one.*

**1.** Peel potatoes, then cut into ⅓-inch slices and then into ⅓-inch sticks. Place the potatoes in a large bowl filled with water as you cut them to keep them from discoloring.

**2.** Soak the potatoes for at least 30 minutes and up to 24 hours in the refrigerator. This will remove the excess starch from the potatoes.

**3.** Fit a heavy stockpot with a deep-fry thermometer. Heat the oil over medium-high heat to 275° to 300°F. Have ready a rack set over a baking sheet.

**4.** Drain the potatoes and pat dry. Add 2 handfuls of potatoes to the hot oil. There should be at least 1 inch of oil above the potatoes. Cook until the potatoes are light brown, 5 to 7 minutes. Use a skimmer to remove the potatoes, gently shaking off excess oil, and put them on the rack to drain. Repeat with the rest of the potatoes. Let all the potatoes cool.

**5.** Increase the heat of the oil to 350°F.

**6.** Cook the potatoes again, 2 handfuls at a time, until golden brown, about 2 minutes. Remove, shake off the excess oil, place in a bowl, and season lightly with salt and pepper. Repeat with the rest of the potatoes and serve immediately.

# The Bomb Bakers

5 cups water

1¼ cups kosher salt

6 medium russet potatoes (about 3 pounds 6 ounces), washed well

2 tablespoons garlic salt

2 tablespoons seasoned salt (I recommend Lawry's)

1 teaspoon freshly ground black pepper

¼ cup canola oil

*These really are the "bomb" bakers. They seal up when cooking and the **internal steam has been known to cause a few blowups**—literally—so be careful, and get ready for some of the most tender and moist baked potatoes you've ever had.*

**1.** In a large bowl, combine the water and 1 cup of the salt. Stir until the salt dissolves. Add the potatoes; make sure all the potatoes are submerged. Brine them for 2 to 8 hours at room temperature.

**2.** Set a rack in the center of the oven and preheat the oven to 400°F.

**3.** Drain the potatoes and pat them dry with paper towels. In a large bowl, combine the remaining ¼ cup salt, the garlic salt, seasoned salt, and pepper. Liberally rub the potatoes with oil and coat them with the spice mixture.

**4.** Place the potatoes on a wire rack placed over a baking sheet. Bake the potatoes for 45 minutes to 1 hour. Do not puncture the potato skins with tongs, a fork, or toothpicks; the potatoes will be soft to the touch when done.

**5.** Let the potatoes rest 5 minutes before cutting.

# The "Big Dunkee"
## Pepper Jack and Horseradish Double-Baked Potatoes

*Big Dunkee is my vice president of production, Mark Dissin. Mark is Burgess Meredith to my Rocky—one of the most influential people in my career. The dude knows food as well as any chef I know. One day we were talking about the Grand Canyon, and he asked me if I'd been and if I'd taken a "duhn-kee" ride. I ask, "What's a duhn-kee?" And he says, how do you say it, the mules, the dunkees? And* **he mocked me for pronouncing it "donkey," insisting it's a dunkee**. *So I brought several people into his office, and we couldn't find one other person who pronounced it dunkee. Later, while brainstorming for Guy's Big Bite with Mark, he described some big stuffed baked potato that he'd had. So I did my monster stuffed potato for the show, and since it was inspired by Mark, I called it the Big Dunkee. A musician writes a song about somebody, I name a dish after them. So there you go, he's the Big Dunkee, a great guy, friend, and mentor.*

**1.** Preheat the oven to 350°F.

**2.** Scrub the potatoes well to remove all the dirt. Dry them and rub with the canola oil, then sprinkle them with kosher salt, and bake on a wire rack on a baking sheet for 1 hour. Let the potatoes cool to a workable temperature. Leave the oven on at 350°F.

**3.** Meanwhile, in a medium skillet over medium heat, cook the bacon until crisp. Drain it on paper towels.

8 extra large russet potatoes

¼ cup canola oil

¼ cup kosher salt, plus more for seasoning

½ pound applewood-smoked bacon, cut into ¼-inch dice

1 cup chopped yellow onion

4 teaspoons diced jalapeño

¼ cup diced garlic

¼ pound (1 stick) butter, at room temperature

4 teaspoons freshly cracked black pepper

¼ cup prepared horseradish

½ cup sour cream

2 cups shredded pepper Jack cheese (about 8 ounces)

1 Hass avocado, pitted, peeled, and diced

**4.** Remove all but 2 tablespoons bacon grease from the pan and heat over medium-high heat. Add the onion and cook for 4 minutes. Add the garlic and lightly cook for 1 minute. Set aside to cool to room temperature.

**5.** Split the cooled potatoes in half and spoon out the insides into a large bowl. Choose the nicest-looking 8 skin halves and place them on a baking sheet. Discard the others.

**6.** Mix in the butter, add the pepper, and then salt to taste. Gently fold in the onion mixture.

**7.** In a small bowl, combine the horseradish, sour cream, 1 cup of the pepper Jack, and the bacon. Fold it into the potato insides. Gently fold in the avocado.

**8.** Mound the potato mixture in the skins. Top with the remaining cheese. Bake for 20 minutes or until the cheese is melted and bubbly and the potatoes are getting crisp around the edges.

**9.** Time to get funkee with "the Big Dunkee."

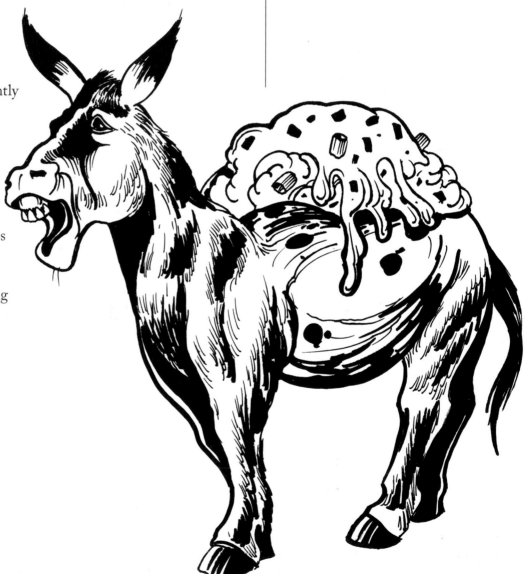

# Mambo Rice

2 cups water

1½ cups Chicken Stock (page 362 or low-sodium store-bought)

2 cups jasmine rice (brown organic if you can)

1 cup chopped flat-leaf parsley

½ cup chopped cilantro

¼ cup minced garlic

¼ cup fresh lime juice

2 tablespoons extra virgin olive oil

2½ tablespoons kosher salt

2 teaspoons freshly ground black pepper

**Special Equipment:**
Rice cooker

*This rice has flair, some spice, and **really dances in your mouth.** Just the reason I called it mambo. Lyyyyyeeea . . . Iyyyeaaaaaah! (Inspirational cheer!)*

**1.** Combine the water, chicken stock, and rice in a rice cooker. Cook according to the directions until al dente.

**2.** Combine the parsley, cilantro, garlic, lime juice, oil, salt, and pepper in a bowl.

**3.** Place the rice in a large bowl and toss, separating the grains with a fork. Slowly stir in the herb-garlic mixture. Serve hot or cold.

> I'm a huge fan of rice cookers. We use them all the time at home, Johnny Garlic's, and Tex Wasabi's. Get one if you don't have one—they make totally consistent rice and are worth the money.

# Rice a Munee

*When something is so cool, so over the top, I usually declare that **it's "money"**! But 'cause I think I'm funny I like to spell it "munee." (Add then Lori says, you're ridiculous—spell it correctly.)*

**1.** In a large saucepan or skillet with a lid, heat the oil and butter over medium-high heat. Add the vermicelli and rice and cook, stirring, until lightly browned, 4 to 5 minutes.

**2.** Add the prosciutto and cook 2 minutes more. Stir in the onion and red pepper and cook for 2 minutes. Add the garlic and cook for 1 minute. Add the wine and scrape up any browned bits on the bottom of the pan.

**3.** Pour in the chicken stock, bring to a simmer, cover, and cook for 16 to 18 minutes, until the liquid is absorbed and the rice is cooked. Gently stir in the peas. Cover and let sit for 5 minutes.

**4.** Season with salt and pepper, if needed. Transfer to a serving bowl and serve immediately.

1 tablespoon olive oil

2 tablespoons unsalted butter

1 cup broken vermicelli

2 cups basmati rice

3 ounces prosciutto, diced

1 cup diced yellow onion

1 red bell pepper, diced

2 tablespoons minced garlic

½ cup white wine

3½ cups Chicken Stock (page 362 or low-sodium store-bought)

¾ cup frozen peas

Salt and freshly cracked black pepper

# Black-Eyed Basmati Salad

4 cups water

2 teaspoons kosher salt

½ cup dried black-eyed peas, rinsed

½ cup basmati rice (I dig brown basmati)

1 teaspoon minced garlic

3 tablespoons whole-grain Dijon mustard

¼ cup apple cider vinegar

1 tablespoon honey

1 tablespoon minced shallot

1 tablespoon finely chopped cilantro

1 teaspoon freshly ground black pepper

¼ cup diced red onion

½ cup diced red bell pepper

⅓ cup Spanish olives, sliced

*Just when you thought beans and rice combos were all served up hot, I unload this super-duper-tasty side dish.* **This one rocks like the band!**

**1.** In a small saucepan with a lid, combine 3 cups water, ½ teaspoon of the salt, and the black-eyed peas. Bring to a boil and cook for 4 minutes. Remove from the heat, cover, and let sit 1 hour.

**2.** Drain the peas, add fresh water to cover, bring to a simmer, and cook until just al dente, about 5 to 8 minutes. Let cool in the cooking liquid.

**3.** In a separate saucepan, combine the rice, 1 cup water, and the garlic. Bring to a simmer, cover, and cook for 16 minutes or until the water is absorbed and the rice is al dente. Let cool. Fluff with a fork.

**4. To make the dressing,** in a glass or other nonreactive bowl, whisk the mustard, vinegar, honey, shallot, cilantro, pepper, and ½ teaspoon salt. Adjust the seasoning if necessary. Set aside until you are ready to assemble the salad.

**5. To serve,** drain the black-eyed peas and place them in a large bowl. Stir in the rice, onion, red bell pepper, and olives. Mix in the dressing. Refrigerate if not using immediately. The dish can be made up to 2 hours ahead.

# Coconut-Cilantro Rice with Peas and Cashews

### ✎ SERVES 6 TO 8 ✎

*If you put the rice with the coconut and you cook it all up. . . . You put the rice with the coconut and you cook it all up. . . .* **Come on, you know the words!** *. . . You put the rice with the coconut . . .*

**1.** In a dry large saucepan over medium-high heat, lightly toast the coconut for 4 to 5 minutes, stirring frequently. Transfer to a small bowl and set aside to cool.

**2.** In the same pot, heat the oil over medium-high heat. Add the rice and cook, stirring, until the rice just starts to brown, 6 to 8 minutes. Add the stock and the coconut milk and stir to combine. Bring to a simmer, reduce the heat to low, cover, and cook for 12 minutes or until liquid is absorbed.

**3.** Remove from the heat and stir in the cilantro, cashews, and peas. Season with salt and transfer to a serving bowl. Garnish with the toasted coconut and serve.

½ cup unsweetened shredded coconut

1 tablespoon canola oil

2 cups jasmine rice

3 cups Chicken Stock (page 362 or low-sodium store-bought)

One 13.5-ounce can coconut milk

¼ cup chopped cilantro

⅓ cup roughly chopped cashews

1 cup frozen peas, thawed and drained

1 teaspoon fine sea salt

# Kale with Roasted Beets and Bacon

2 beets (about 14 ounces total)

1 tablespoon olive oil

Kosher salt and freshly ground black pepper

6 thick-cut applewood-smoked bacon slices (8 ounces), diced

1 large kale head (about 1½ pounds), washed and cut into 1-inch pieces (about 8 cups)

⅓ cup Chicken Stock (page 362 or low-sodium store-bought)

4 tablespoons apple cider vinegar

***Kale, beets, and bacon sounds like a cool band*** *playing in the Flavortown Civic Auditorium. This is a simple tune that will rock your taste buds.*

**1.** Preheat the oven to 425°F.

**2.** Wash and trim the beets, removing both ends. Place them on a 12-inch square sheet of heavy-duty aluminum foil. Drizzle with the olive oil and season generously with salt and pepper. Seal up the foil packet and roast for 1 hour or until the beets are fork-tender.

**3.** In a large skillet over medium heat, cook the bacon until medium-crisp (or however you prefer your bacon). Transfer the bacon to a paper-towel-lined plate. Increase the heat to high and add the kale, stirring to coat in the rendered bacon grease. Cover and cook for a few minutes, and then add the chicken stock and 2 tablespoons of the vinegar. Stir to combine, cover, and allow to wilt for 6 to 8 minutes.

**4.** Peel and cut the beets into ¼-inch sticks, then cut the sticks in half and add them to the kale. Add the bacon, stir to combine, and season with salt and pepper to taste. Stir in the remaining 2 tablespoons of vinegar and serve immediately.

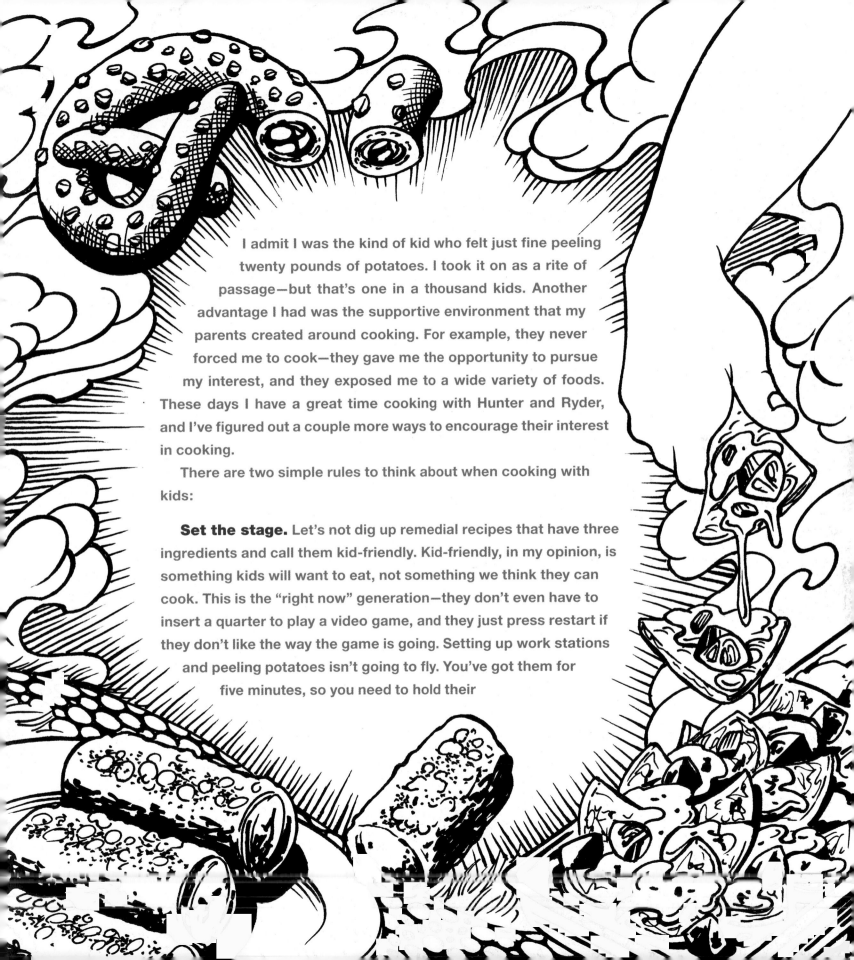

I admit I was the kind of kid who felt just fine peeling twenty pounds of potatoes. I took it on as a rite of passage—but that's one in a thousand kids. Another advantage I had was the supportive environment that my parents created around cooking. For example, they never forced me to cook—they gave me the opportunity to pursue my interest, and they exposed me to a wide variety of foods. These days I have a great time cooking with Hunter and Ryder, and I've figured out a couple more ways to encourage their interest in cooking.

There are two simple rules to think about when cooking with kids:

**Set the stage.** Let's not dig up remedial recipes that have three ingredients and call them kid-friendly. Kid-friendly, in my opinion, is something kids will want to eat, not something we think they can cook. This is the "right now" generation—they don't even have to insert a quarter to play a video game, and they just press restart if they don't like the way the game is going. Setting up work stations and peeling potatoes isn't going to fly. You've got them for five minutes, so you need to hold their attention from the start. Most kids respond to throwing the glory shots, like sautéing the ground beef, hitting the dish with tomatoes, and adding the spices. So cook something they already know they like, and bring them in to help at exciting moments.

**Stoke the fire.** Once they've experienced several instant successes and rewards through helping in small ways, it's time to lead them down the path to the bigger picture. They'll start to understand the components of the meal and begin to ask leading questions like "How do you shuck corn?" Show them how, but don't make them shuck all the ears then and there or you'll lose them—just have them tackle one or two to start. These days when Hunter and I prepare to cook together, we figure out what we want to eat, unload the cupboards, get stations set up for each of the steps, and do mise en place. We map out how it will all roll out so that the whole meal comes together with the right timing. I got Hunter to this stage by figuring out what he liked, not by choosing simple recipes. Please look at the majority of the recipes in this book as potential recipes to cook with kids. Cook something yourself the first time to see if the kids like it, then next time you cook it, prepare the recipe up to the glory moment, bring the kids in to run to the finish line, and then train them later for the marathon.

**One caveat:** I'm not suggesting you do any deep-frying with your aspiring young chef. Yes, kids like taquitos, but you can't have that hot oil around a seven-year-old; he might slip off the stool, or the oil might pop out onto him—not a good idea. (So for the deep frying portion of any recipe, keep the kids at a safe distance!)

Who's that dude with the black hair? (That's Hunter and his cousins Tommy and Matthew.)

At three years old, at the Cloverdale Citrus Fair.

# Hunter, My Favorite Young Chef

**Hunter Fieri:** I've been interested in cooking ever since I heard the story about how my dad cooked his first meal, steak and pasta, when he was young, and his dad said it was the best he had ever had. I decided I wanted to follow in his footsteps and started cooking when I was only six or seven. Today, one of my most favorite dishes to make is chicken parmesan because it was one of the first dishes I ever made, and everyone still loves it.

Early on my dad began including me in his public cooking demos. Once when I was about eight we went to the Sonoma County Fair and cooked together in a big gym. There I was, up there with my dad cooking in front of a bunch of people. At home, I would show off my eight- or nine-year-old culinary skills by cooking a great dinner for him and his friends.

These days Dad is always impressed with my knife chopping skills, and he's also impressed by how I can control a smoking hot pan while he talks to his buddies. My dad and I have a rule at our house—if you cook you don't have to do the dishes, but if you don't cook, you're on dish duty. Sometimes I still do dishes even after I cook just to help out the family. And often when my dad and I cook he lets me taste the food to make sure it tastes all right.

I really love cooking. It's one of my favorite things to do, not because my dad loves it—but it comforts me when I'm upset, and when something really great happens I'm tempted to cook something because of the good mood I'm in. Plus, cooking is a great way to impress a girl or your family with some fantastic food. Next thing you know you're wanted at people's houses and other places to cook for them.

Who knows, maybe someday I'll have a career like my dad's and my own show on the Food Network. But in the meantime I'll keep cookin'!

Catch it, Ryder!

Hunter ridin' solo.

Hangin' in the backyard kitchen, doing one of our favorite family events—making pizza.

Ya see, kids? Dad gets the first slice.

Try on this pizza hat! My favorite moments—cookin' with my family.

# Birth of the Awesome Pretzel Cart

I have a lot of stories about growing up in beautiful Ferndale, California, but there's one story that marks the beginning of my entrepreneurial and culinary career in a big way. It all began with a soft pretzel. . . .

In 1978, I was in fifth grade on a ski trip in Tahoe with my family, and I had lunch money in my pocket. Right across from the ice cream shop I spotted a small pretzel cart. I bought a pretzel and tasted its soft, doughy center and chewy exterior with some salt and mustard on top. It blew my mind. These puppies were steamed, and I thought all pretzels were hard until this encounter. So I bought another, and another, until I spent my entire wad. I had no problem eating ten that day.

After my pretzel-eating marathon I went to meet my parents, who were hanging out in the lounge with their friends. My dad said, "You had pretzels for lunch, that's it!?! You've got to be kidding me! If you love them so much, why don't you start your own pretzel business?" *Yeah, right Dad.* "Yeah! Go ask the pretzel guy where he gets his pretzels from." My dad was always very matter-of-fact. He'd say *we're going to do this,* and that's it, that's what was going to go down. So I cruised down there to see my buddy the pretzel guy, who had even given me a free pretzel that day, already dreaming of my new company. I asked him where he got the pretzels from and he responded, "I'm not going to tell you. You might go open a pretzel cart and try to put me out of business." I looked at the dude in disbelief, thinking, *I'm in* fifth grade. *I'm a kid, and he doesn't want me to put him out of business?* Upset and heartbroken, I told my dad what happened. He advised, "Go down there and wait. When the guy throws out his pretzel box, get that box and bring it to me." I spent the rest of the afternoon sitting down there. He finally threw the box in the Dumpster and I dove in, then brought it back to my dad like a proud bird dog. He pulled off the tag and we went back to Ferndale on a mission to create a pretzel business.

The first task was the cart creation. Dad had me draw up the design and choose the color (yellow, of course). He made me weld, cut the lumber, and paint it. He'd help me along, but I had to actually do the work with him. We'd go over to the shop of Tim Ford, a local cabinetmaker. I worked on this cart a little bit every day into my sixth-grade year. I painted the cart yellow and called it The Awesome Pretzel.

Now, mind you, this is not my first business in the little town of Ferndale. I'd sold my toys, paper bags with faces on them—even Kool-Aid, but my dad shut me down when he caught me with a purple arm, having lost the stirrer. So anyway, with the cart ready, we realized the pretzels needed to be stored frozen to keep fresh, so our friend Gary Edgmon offered room in his meat locker at Ferndale Meat Company to freeze them. I painted a plywood sign in yellow and red, set up a propane tank, and I was in business . . . almost.

**New edition 2010.**

**The original Awesome Pretzel Cart, 1983.**

My goal was to sell them at the Humboldt County Fair. We knew Chuck Townsend, who managed the fairgrounds, so I rode my bike over to ask Chuck if I could sell pretzels. He asked, "Where's your booth?" So I went home and grabbed the cart, which was built on the back of my three-wheeled bike at the time, and rode my pretzel booth down to the fairgrounds. He couldn't believe it. "Where's your health permit?" he asked. Joe Koches was the health department guy, so I took it over to him and he gave my cart a clean bill of health. Next I needed to open a bank account, so Henry Weller at the Bank of Loleta helped me open a Guy The Awesome Pretzel checking account. Then, of course, I needed pretzel inventory. So I got a loan for $500. (I think my dad may have cosigned on the back of the deal.)

Next thing I knew, from 10:00 AM to 10:00 PM for ten days straight, I'm selling pretzels at the fair. This was 1980, I was about twelve years old, and most people in Northern California had never seen a soft pretzel. Here I was at the county fair selling them for fifty cents . . . and I made $1,100. Remember, the pretzels cost fifty cents each, so that translates to 2,200 pretzels sold—out of a *cart!* My parents took pictures of me falling asleep while counting $300 in quarters. A bunch of buddies, including Scott Kristic, Mike Christie, and Rod Wagner, worked for me—and the Awesome Pretzel world was blown up. People wondered, how the hell is this kid selling pretzels? It was the beginning of the Guy empire.

**Friends Jason Mays, Rod Wagner, and Jason Evans.**

I loved the money, and more important, the power. This was familiar ground, as I'd worked from fifth grade at the fair, at the balloon booth, or anywhere I could get a job. But through my cart I met everybody, because everyone from the carnies to the jockeys would come by for pretzels. So I'd trade pretzels for ride tickets with the carnies and bet on the ponies. Dad would stop by, not see me at the cart, and get mad and ask, "Where's Guy!?" They'd say, "I think he's over at the Zipper"—which I'd have ridden fifteen times in a row. Dad would always drag me back to the cart explaining at great length the responsibility I had, and that I needed to stick to it.

There I was rockin' and rollin' the pretzel booth at fairs and rodeos, all the way until I was sixteen. I was known as the pretzel kid. I saved most of my money from doing the pretzels and used a bunch of it to go to France as an exchange student. Eventually, I sold the biz to my sister—actually never was a real sale, never did get money for it (my dad brokered the deal . . . and said he was never paid by me . . . so consider it a wash. Ha ha—that's the family biz). Then she sold it to some girls in Ferndale, and sadly, someone subsequently stole the cart. So if anybody knows where it is, please tell me (seriously).

The other day I stopped at a lemonade stand that some girls were running on the corner near my house in Santa Rosa. I didn't even have any lemonade, but I gave them five bucks anyway because they had the entrepreneurial spirit. To see this spirit in kids these days is rare, and it taught me so many useful lessons. So through the Guy Fieri Foundation I've decided to bring The Awesome Pretzel Cart back to life. The plan is to give the updated cart to nonprofit children's organizations to enable them to raise money for programs while teaching the kids basic culinary, service, and the principles of entrepreneurial business. The goal is to team up with people around the country who share our vision of giving the kids a practical foundation for the future.

I decided that the first carts should go to the eighth-grade class of Ferndale Elementary, for that grade to keep perpetually. At basketball games, the county fair, and more, they can serve organic turkey dogs and other healthy food, along with pretzels, to raise money for the trip that's taken by every eighth-grade class at Ferndale Elementary. The second cart was presented to a fantastic restaurant and tuition-free culinary apprentice program in Santa Rosa called WOW (Worth Our Weight) in

2010, exactly thirty years after the birth of the first Awesome Pretzel cart. My foundation has sponsored the building of the first new carts, but if you'd like to sponsor one or more for your kids or grandkids, let us know and we'll build them. We're in it to win it for the kids, so give the foundation a call and together we'll get to work!

## The Awesome Pretzel Cart Makes History

In eighth grade, my teacher, Miss Moriarty (Mrs. Fisher now), told me about a contest up at Humboldt State College for National History Day. With her encouragement, I did a paper on the history of the pretzel. Mind you, this was before computers, so I had to look it all up in encyclopedias and write the Lutz Pretzel Company in Hanover, Pennsylvania. I researched the theories of how the pretzel came about—shaped like the arms of a praying monk, the whole thing. And I won first place at the competition. My prize was the opportunity to go to the University of Maryland and compete on National History Day itself. My dad and I disassembled the cart and put it back together with wing nuts so I could reassemble it on the other side. I flew by myself to Maryland, (missing eighth grade graduation), and Aunt Pattie picked me up at the airport. I stayed in the dorms that night, woke up, and put my cart together in the morning, then brought out my frozen pretzels. I was open for business! But I didn't win, and I was so disappointed, because I felt no kid had the attachment to their topic that I did. But I got over it quickly and got back to business—and I have a memory that will last forever.

# Pepper Jack Pretzels

## ～ MAKES 20 PRETZELS ～

*You can find some great frozen pretzels that are tasty to steam. But if you're down for cookin' them up fresh, **you're gonna be so stoked** you did.*

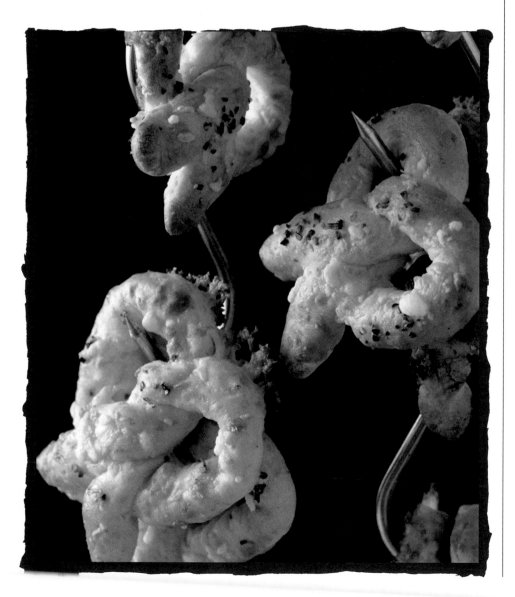

1 ½ cups warm water (110°F)

1 ½ tablespoons active dry yeast (2 packets)

4 cups unbleached all-purpose flour, plus ½ cup for rolling out

1 teaspoon fine sea salt

1 tablespoon sugar

¼ teaspoon cayenne pepper

½ teaspoon granulated garlic

¾ cup grated dry Jack cheese (or Manchego)

2 large eggs

3 cups grated pepper Jack cheese

2 tablespoons milk

2 teaspoons dehydrated onion flakes

2 teaspoons kosher salt

*Special Equipment:*
2 silicone baking mats, pizza stone (optional)

**Ingredients.**

**Turn the dough out onto a lightly floured cutting board and knead 10 to 12 times, adding more flour if sticky.**

**Cut the dough in half and set half aside.**

**Roll 1 dough ball into a 12- by 17-inch rectangle about ⅛-inch thick.**

**Sprinkle ¾ cup of the pepper Jack cheese in a strip down the middle.**

**Fold one-third of the dough over the cheese and sprinkle with the remaining ¾ cup of the pepper Jack.**

**Fold the last third over and pinch the edges of the dough closed.**

**Roll the dough into an 11- by 15-inch rectangle.**

**Cut the dough into ten 1½- by 15-inch strips.**

**Pinch the cut edges of the strips together.**

**Roll each strip into a cigar shape 18 inches in length.**

**Form each strip into a pretzel shape.**

**Pretzel perfection!**

**1.** Preheat the oven to 425°F. Cover 2 large baking sheets with silicone baking mats or parchment paper. If you have a pizza stone, preheat it in the oven.

**2.** In a 2-cup glass measuring cup, combine the warm water and yeast. Stir and let sit 10 minutes, until it foams.

**3.** In a food processor fitted with the plastic dough blade, pulse the flour, sea salt, sugar, cayenne, granulated garlic, and ½ cup of the dry Jack cheese for three 5-second intervals. Add 1 egg and the yeast mixture. Pulse for three 10-second intervals, or until the dough comes together.

**4.** Turn the dough out onto lightly floured cutting board. Knead 10 to 12 times, adding more flour if sticky. Cut the dough in half and set half aside.

**5.** Use a rolling pin to roll out 1 dough ball into a 12- by 17-inch rectangle, about ⅛-inch thick. Sprinkle ¾ cup of the pepper Jack in a strip down the middle (the short way). Fold one-third of the dough over the cheese and sprinkle with another ¾ cup of the pepper Jack. Fold the last third over and pinch the edges of the dough closed. Roll the dough into an 11- by 15-inch rectangle. Cut the dough into ten 1½- by 15-inch strips.

**6.** Pinch the cut edges of the strips together. Roll each strip into a cigar shape, 18 inches in length. Form each strip into a pretzel shape and place the pretzels 3 inches apart on a prepared baking sheet.

**7.** Repeat with the second ball of dough.

**8.** Beat the remaining egg with the milk. Brush the formed pretzels with the egg wash and then sprinkle evenly with the remaining ¼ cup dry Jack, the onion flakes, and the kosher salt.

**9.** Bake for 16 to 18 minutes, until nicely browned. You'll get the best results by putting the baking sheets on a preheated pizza stone, but it isn't necessary.

**10.** Let cool and serve warm or room temperature. Store at room temperature, tightly covered.

# Guy-talian Nachos

### ➤ SERVES 8 ➤

## ITALIAN SALSA

**8 Peppadew peppers, seeded and diced**

**2 tablespoons Peppadew pepper juice**

**4 Roma tomatoes, seeded and cut into small dice**

**⅓ cup minced red onion**

**¼ cup chopped flat-leaf parsley leaves**

**2 tablespoons capers (1 tablespoon roughly chopped, 1 tablespoon whole)**

**¼ cup sliced black olives**

**1 tablespoon minced garlic**

**1 tablespoon extra virgin olive oil**

**1 teaspoon freshly cracked black pepper**

**Pinch kosher salt**

## FILLING

**1 tablespoon extra virgin olive oil**

**½ pound ground beef (80% lean)**

**½ pound Italian turkey sausage, casings removed**

**¼ yellow onion, cut into small dice (about ¼ cup)**

**1 tablespoon minced garlic**

*(cont.)*

*When we opened our Johnny Garlic's in Petaluma, California, I spent a lot of time developing and testing recipes. One time I took wonton skins and thought,* **Well, these are technically pasta**, *so by frying them and then serving them with mozzarella cheese, sausage, and pepperoni,* **they become Italian nachos**. *People loved them, but as the menu evolved naturally they were rotated off the menu. But there were these three vivacious, crazy girls who would come in on Wednesday afternoons to hang out and have some cocktails and appetizers. This was their getaway day. Even after Italian Nachos were pulled from the menu, they'd request them, and since Wednesday was my day to be there, I'd go get the wonton skins, fry them up, and make them their nachos.*

*Fast-forward eight years. We'd sold the Petaluma location and were opening Tex Wasabi's, and as I'm cruising along I meet* **a friend of a friend who ends up being one of the girls** *that would sit at the bar ordering the nachos . . . and that girl is* **the incredible Korina McAlister,** *who became my culinary director. Crazy!! (See page 32 for a word from Korina.)*

**1. To make the salsa,** combine all the ingredients in a nonreactive bowl. Set aside at room temperature to allow the flavors to marry.

**2. To make the filling,** heat 1½ teaspoons of the oil in a medium skillet over medium-high heat. Add the beef and sausage and cook, breaking them up with a spoon or spatula, until cooked through and lightly browned. Using a slotted spoon, transfer to a plate. Discard the fat.

**3.** Add the remaining 1½ teaspoons olive oil and the onion to the pan and cook until the onion turns translucent, 4 to 5 minutes. Stir in the garlic and cook for 2 minutes, taking care that the garlic doesn't burn.

**4.** Return the meat to the pan. Combine the ingredients well and set aside in the pan.

**5.** Combine the ricotta and sour cream in a small food processor or blender and pour into a small resealable plastic bag.

**6. To make the wonton chips,** line a baking sheet with paper towels. Heat the oil to 350°F in a heavy skillet, over medium heat. Working in batches, carefully lower the wonton wrappers into the oil. As soon as they puff up, flip them over—they cook extremely fast. Once they start to brown, transfer them to the paper towels and sprinkle them with salt.

**7. To compose the nachos,** preheat the oven to a low broil and position a rack approximately 9 inches below the burner. Reheat the filling, if necessary.

**8.** In a large baking dish, arrange a layer of half the chips, a layer of half the meat mixture, and a sprinkle of half the mozzarella. Repeat the layers with the second half of the ingredients. Put the dish under the broiler until the cheese has melted, 1 to 3 minutes (keep a close eye on it). Remove from the oven and top with the salami, basil, parsley, and salsa. Cut a small hole in the corner of the ricotta–sour cream bag and drizzle the sauce over the nachos. Sprinkle with the green onions and the pepperoncini, if using, and serve immediately.

**TOPPINGS**

¼ cup ricotta cheese

¼ cup sour cream

2 cups grated mozzarella (about 8 ounces)

2 ounces hard salami, cut in matchsticks

1 tablespoon shredded basil leaves

1 tablespoon chopped flat-leaf parsley

4 green onions, thinly sliced

2 tablespoons sliced drained pepperoncini, optional

**CHIPS**

3 cups canola oil

30 wonton wrappers, cut into 2 triangles each

Kosher salt

# "I've Got the Need, the Need for Fried Cheese!"

### ❧ MAKES 8 ROLLS, TO SERVE 4 ❧

1 quart canola oil

2 eggs

¼ cup milk

¾ cup panko bread crumbs

¾ cup Italian bread crumbs

8 egg roll or spring roll wrappers

16 thin salami slices, 2½ inches in diameter

Eight 1-ounce individually wrapped string cheese sticks

Marinara Sauce (page 363)

2 tablespoons grated Parmesan cheese

2 tablespoons chopped parsley

*I said it once and I'll say it a million times . . . If you're gonna eat something that's not supposed to be good for you (like fried cheese), then eat the **over-the-top, super-duper** (yep, I said it, "super-duper") version of it. In this case, handmade fried cheese!*

**1.** In a medium saucepan, heat the oil to 325°F. Line a plate with paper towels.

**2.** In a shallow bowl, whisk the eggs and milk thoroughly. In another shallow bowl combine the panko and Italian bread crumbs.

**3.** Dredge one side of an egg roll wrapper in the egg wash. Place the wrapper egg wash side up on a work surface and put 2 salami slices in the center of the wrapper, toward the edge closest to you. Place 1 cheese stick on top of the salami. Roll the wrapper edge closest to you over the filling. Tuck in the ends and continue to roll until you have an egg roll shape. (Check out the egg roll demo on page 87.)

**4.** Dredge the rolled wrapper in the egg wash again and thoroughly coat in the bread crumb mixture. (Rolls can be frozen for future use at this point.)

**5.** Add 1 or 2 rolls to oil at a time and cook 2 to 3 minutes, until golden brown. Be careful not to overcook them or cook them on too high a temperature, as the wraps may explode. Transfer the fried cheese rolls to the paper-towel-lined plate and serve immediately with marinara sauce. Garnish with Parmesan and parsley.

# Malty Strawnana

## ~ SERVES 4 ~

*For an adult version*, add ½ cup dark rum.

**1.** Combine all the ingredients in a blender, and blend until smooth. Add a splash more milk if needed.

1 pint best-quality vanilla ice cream

2 tablespoons milk, plus more as needed

5 tablespoons malt powder

1 ½ cups strawberries, hulled

1 small or ¾ large ripe banana

3 tablespoons plain yogurt

# Hot Wieners, Rhode Island Style

#### ~ MAKES 16 HOT DOGS ~

**4 tablespoons (½ stick) margarine**

**2 yellow onions, minced**

**2 tablespoons chili powder**

**2 tablespoons paprika**

**½ teaspoon ground allspice**

**½ teaspoon curry powder**

**1 teaspoon dry mustard**

**1 teaspoon ground cinnamon**

**1 pound ground beef (80% lean)**

**Fine sea salt**

**1¼ cups water**

**16 hot dogs**

**16 hot dog buns**

**Yellow prepared mustard**

**2 tablespoons celery salt**

*While my dad is the number one greatest man in my life, my wife* **Lori's dad, Bob,** *played in the top three. When I first went back to visit her family in Rhode Island, he turned to me and asked with his thick Rhode Island accent, "What do you like to eat? We've got hot grindahs, we can go get gaggahs?" I said, "What's a gaggah?" And he said,* **"A hot weenah. You never had a gaggah before?"** *I was confused and worried but he said it was a Providence specialty. So we drove down to Olneyville New York System, and the dude was making "gaggahs" (hot wieners) up his arm. He was popping in chili meat, minced onion, mustard, and celery salt. This guy banged out ten up his arm. I ended up eating six of these phenomenal creations, and every time we return to the state, I go back for more hot weenahs washed down with coffee milk, just like the locals. This is my best run at it—but watch out; it's easy to get addicked!*

**Every state has a state bird and state flower. This is the state "dog" of Flavortown!**

**1.** In a large skillet over medium heat, melt the margarine. Add half of the minced onion and cook until just translucent, 4 to 5 minutes—do not brown. Add the chili powder, paprika, allspice, curry powder, dry mustard, and cinnamon and stir to combine. Add the beef, stir thoroughly, and cook for 5 minutes or until browned. Season to taste, add the water, and simmer over medium-low heat for 30 to 45 minutes.

**2.** In a large saucepan, boil the hot dogs with 1 teaspoon salt in water to cover until heated through. While boiling, place a wire rack over the top of the pot and steam the buns for 15 to 20 seconds.

**3. To create the hot wiener,** put hot dogs in the warm buns and top with the meat mixture and the remaining minced onion. Top with yellow mustard and a sprinkle of celery salt.

*Note: If you're making fewer hot dogs, the meat sauce freezes well for future use—or you can send it to me!*

# Blazy's Pepperoni-Studded Lasagna

## ⁓ SERVES 8 TO 10 ⁓

6 quarts water

1 tablespoon kosher salt

1 pound dried lasagna sheets

2 cups hand-cut ⅛-inch-thick slices pepperoni

5½ cups Marinara Sauce (page 363)

1 pound ricotta cheese

1 pound shredded mozzarella (about 4 cups)

2 pounds bulk sweet Italian sausage, crumbled, cooked, and drained

¾ cup grated Parmesan cheese

*My buddy Blazy is one of the wildest morning show DJs* *I've ever known, and on top of that he's an incredible philanthropist, a community guy, and a great dad. During* **The Next Food Network Star** *competition, he led the way getting people to vote for me. I call him Blaze Master Blaze. Once when were talking about the contest I told him about a lasagna I was making with pepperoni. I used the rendered pepperoni fat to cook the vegetables that were layered in with the pasta and pepperoni. He was like,* **"Oh my God, I love pepperoni and I love lasagna!"** *He said he just couldn't believe how it was humanly possible (with lots of expletives) that anyone could comprehend how to make such an incredibly good thing. So I had to name it after Blazy. Here's to you, Blazemaster Blaze.*

**1.** Preheat the oven to 375°F. Fill a large bowl with water and ice.

**2.** In a large stockpot, bring the water to a boil. Add a tablespoon of salt and cook the pasta until al dente. Drain the pasta and plunge it into the ice water to stop the cooking. Drain again and set aside.

**3.** In medium saucepan over medium heat, cook the pepperoni until crispy. Drain on a paper towel.

**4.** Pour 1 cup of the marinara sauce into a 10- by 14 by 3-inch baking dish and spread it around the bottom and up the sides. Layer a few lasagna sheets across the bottom of the pan, overlapping by ½ inch. Top with one-third of the ricotta, one-third of the mozzarella, and one-third of the sausage, then sprinkle with ¼ cup of the Parmesan. Top with 1½ cups of the remaining marinara sauce and ¼ cup of the pepperoni. Repeat the layering of ingredients, starting and ending with pasta.

**5.** On the very top sheet, spread the remaining ricotta, marinara sauce, mozzarella, and pepperoni and dust with Parmesan.

**6.** Cover with foil and bake for 40 to 45 minutes, until the lasagna is bubbling. Remove foil and cook for 15 minutes or until crisp and browned on top. Let the lasagna sit for 15 minutes. Cut and serve immediately.

# Hunter's Hero

## ~ SERVES 4 ~

2 tablespoons extra virgin olive oil

1 red onion, diced (about 1 cup)

½ red bell pepper, minced (about ½ cup)

2 tablespoons minced garlic

1 teaspoon kosher salt

1 cup 2% milk

2 slices sourdough bread, crust removed, cut into ½-inch pieces (about 1 cup)

1 pound ground beef (80% lean)

1 pound ground pork

2 tablespoons minced basil

2 tablespoons minced oregano

2 tablespoons minced flat-leaf parsley

1 tablespoon freshly ground black pepper

1½ teaspoons red chili flakes

½ cup finely grated Parmesan cheese plus 2 tablespoons shredded, for garnish

1 egg, beaten

4 hoagie or hero rolls

1 cup Marinara Sauce (page 363)

1 pound mozzarella, cut into 12 slices

*Hunter likes his meatballs, so it was fitting that they were one of the first items we cooked together. They worked well because the process of mixing, rolling, and cooking the meatballs really helps a kid feel the experience, start to finish, and see the return on the investment. We even cooked this together on Guy's Big Bite.*

**1.** In a large skillet over medium heat, heat 1 tablespoon of the oil. Add the onion, red bell pepper, and garlic and cook for 2 minutes. Add the salt and cook until the onion and peppers are tender, 5 to 6 minutes. Transfer the vegetables to a plate to cool. (Set the pan aside to use again.)

**2.** In a medium bowl, pour the milk over the bread and let soak for 5 minutes. Squeeze the excess milk from the bread, until the bread is moist but not soggy, and place the bread in a large bowl.

**3.** To the bread, add the beef, sausage, cooled vegetables, basil, oregano, parsley, pepper, chili flakes, grated Parmesan, and egg. Blend well but gently, then carefully roll the mixture into twenty-four 2-inch balls.

**4.** In same large skillet used for the vegetables, heat the remaining 1 tablespoon oil over medium heat. Cook the meatballs, browning them completely until the temperature registers 165°F on an instant-read thermometer in the middle of a meatball.

**5.** Preheat the broiler.

**6.** Meanwhile, split the rolls, leaving the halves attached. Scoop some of the bread from the insides of the rolls.

**7.** To assemble the heroes, fill the rolls with 6 meatballs each. Drizzle with ¼ cup marinara sauce and top with 3 slices of mozzarella and some shredded Parmesan. Place the heroes, cheese side up, on a baking sheet under the broiler until the cheese melts and turns golden brown.

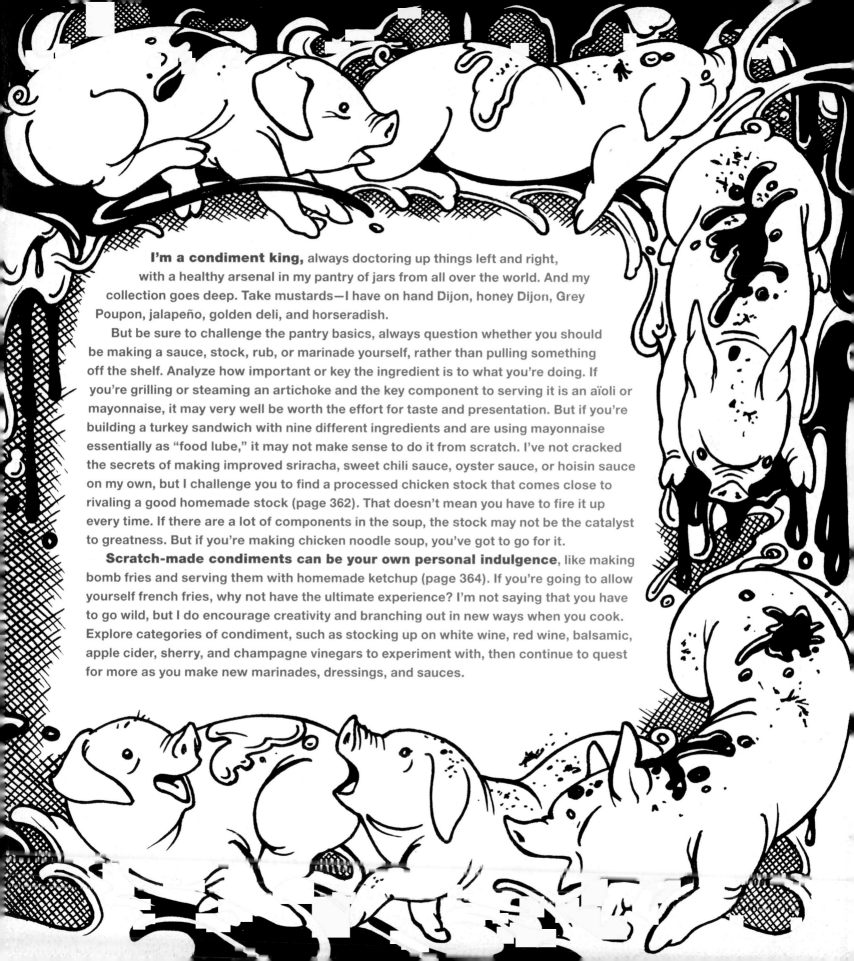

**I'm a condiment king,** always doctoring up things left and right, with a healthy arsenal in my pantry of jars from all over the world. And my collection goes deep. Take mustards—I have on hand Dijon, honey Dijon, Grey Poupon, jalapeño, golden deli, and horseradish.

But be sure to challenge the pantry basics, always question whether you should be making a sauce, stock, rub, or marinade yourself, rather than pulling something off the shelf. Analyze how important or key the ingredient is to what you're doing. If you're grilling or steaming an artichoke and the key component to serving it is an aïoli or mayonnaise, it may very well be worth the effort for taste and presentation. But if you're building a turkey sandwich with nine different ingredients and are using mayonnaise essentially as "food lube," it may not make sense to do it from scratch. I've not cracked the secrets of making improved sriracha, sweet chili sauce, oyster sauce, or hoisin sauce on my own, but I challenge you to find a processed chicken stock that comes close to rivaling a good homemade stock (page 362). That doesn't mean you have to fire it up every time. If there are a lot of components in the soup, the stock may not be the catalyst to greatness. But if you're making chicken noodle soup, you've got to go for it.

**Scratch-made condiments can be your own personal indulgence**, like making bomb fries and serving them with homemade ketchup (page 364). If you're going to allow yourself french fries, why not have the ultimate experience? I'm not saying that you have to go wild, but I do encourage creativity and branching out in new ways when you cook. Explore categories of condiment, such as stocking up on white wine, red wine, balsamic, apple cider, sherry, and champagne vinegars to experiment with, then continue to quest for more as you make new marinades, dressings, and sauces.

# Chicken Stock

¼ cup olive oil

2 carrots, cut into chunks

2 celery stalks, cut into chunks

2 onions, halved

6 garlic cloves, smashed

1 teaspoon red chili flakes

3 pounds chicken backs and necks, cracked

1 tablespoon kosher salt

1 tablespoon freshly ground black pepper

1 gallon water

¼ teaspoon black peppercorns

1 bouquet garni depending on final use (see Note), optional

*You'll find this basic essential in my soups like Cheddar Trans-Porter (page 101), Grilled Chicken Tortellini (page 103), and Ginger Carrot (page 111). And I **use good homemade chicken stock as a base for my sauces** as in Lamb Chops with Marsala-Blackberry Sauce (page 259) or Pork-Outlet (page 218) as well as to simmer flavor into my Mambo Rice and Coconut-Cilantro Rice (pages 330 and 333).*

**1.** In a large stockpot over medium-high heat, heat the olive oil. Add the carrots, celery, and onion and cook until nicely browned, 6 to 8 minutes. Lower the heat to medium, add the garlic and chili flakes, and cook for 2 minutes more.

**2.** Season the chicken pieces with salt and pepper. Add the chicken pieces and cook until they get some nice color, 6 to 8 minutes, stirring as needed.

**3.** Add the water, peppercorns, and bouquet garni, if using. Bring to a boil, then turn the heat to medium-low. Simmer for 1 hour 30 minutes, skimming the foam off the surface as needed. Strain the stock and adjust the seasoning. Use immediately or cool, portion, and freeze for future use.

**4.** If you have a large enough pot, it's good to make a double batch of stock, so that you can have frozen homemade stock ready at any time. It's a wonderful thing! Make sure to date the containers and use within 3 months.

*Note: for different flavors, try these:*
*Italian: sprigs of fresh thyme, oregano, flat-leaf parsley, and marjoram*
*Mexican: sprigs of fresh cilantro, whole cumin seeds, and crushed ancho (dried poblano) chile*

# Marinara Sauce

*Use in Hunter's Hero (page 358), Fieri Spaghetti and Meatballs (page 166), and I've Got the Need, the Need for Fried Cheese (page 352).*

**3 tablespoons extra virgin olive oil**

**1 ½ cups diced yellow onion**

**8 medium garlic cloves, crushed**

**Three 28-ounce cans fire-roasted diced tomatoes (I recommend Muir Glen)**

**¼ cup shredded basil**

**1 tablespoon chopped oregano**

**Salt and freshly ground black pepper**

**1.** In a medium saucepan, heat the olive oil over medium-low heat. Add the onion and cook until translucent, about 4 minutes. Add the garlic and cook until the garlic is almost brown, another 2 minutes. Add the tomatoes. Simmer for 30 minutes.

**2.** Add the basil and oregano, and simmer for 30 minutes more to thoroughly marry the flavors.

**3.** Puree the mixture with a stick blender, food mill, or food processor. Add salt and pepper to taste. Freeze the extra sauce for the future.

# Grilled Ketchup

### ⟿ MAKES 1½ CUPS ⟿

1¼ pounds Roma tomatoes (about 8), cut in half vertically and seeds removed

¼ red bell pepper

¼ small red onion

1 teaspoon olive oil

½ teaspoon kosher salt

½ teaspoon freshly cracked black pepper

1 tablespoon apple cider vinegar

2 tablespoons agave nectar

1½ teaspoons dry mustard

½ teaspoon granulated garlic

*If you're going to jump off the calorie bridge of french fries*, then at least land in the delicious river of homemade ketchup. Use with my fries (page 324) and the Fire-Roasted Shrimp Cocktail (page 66). Just be sure to make more than you think you'll need; this stuff keeps well in the refrigerator.

Me: Sorry! You: Sorry for what? Me: Oh, **sorry for turning you on to this. . . .** It's gonna have you on the quest for gourmet ketchup. (You'll thank me later!)

**1.** Preheat a grill to high. Place the tomatoes skin side up on a baking sheet. Add the red pepper and onion. Brush the vegetables very lightly with the olive oil. Sprinkle with the salt and ½ teaspoon of the black pepper. Turn the tomatoes skin side down and grill all the vegetables until lightly browned, 5 to 8 minutes. Set aside to cool slightly.

**2.** Combine the vegetables, vinegar, agave nectar, mustard, and granulated garlic in a blender or food processor and process until smooth. Taste for seasoning.

**3.** Let the ketchup sit at room temperature until ready to use. You can make it ahead and refrigerate it for up to 1 week.

# Pico de Gallo

### ⤳ MAKES 2 CUPS ⤶

*Serve with Koi Fish Tacos (page 282) and Nor Cal Carnitas (page 228).*

**1.** In a bowl, mix tomatoes, cilantro, onion, garlic, jalapeño, and lime. Season with salt and pepper and refrigerate for 1 hour, to allow the flavors to meld.

**4 Roma tomatoes, seeded and diced**

**2 tablespoons chopped cilantro leaves**

**½ red onion, minced**

**1 teaspoon minced garlic**

**1 jalapeño, seeded and minced**

**Juice of 1 lime**

**Kosher salt and freshly cracked black pepper**

# Teriyaki Sauce

## MAKES 1 CUP

1 tablespoon canola oil

2 tablespoons minced garlic

2 tablespoons minced ginger

½ teaspoon red chili flakes

¾ cup green onions, thinly sliced

½ cup mirin

½ cup soy sauce

2 tablespoons dark brown sugar

2 teaspoons cornstarch

2 teaspoons water

*This was my first real love in Asian foods. It's **sweet, strong, sticky, and gives everything it touches that "glaze."** Of course, I had to make my own.*

*Teriyaki sauce brushed on chicken thighs is a match made in heaven. It's a sauce that actually improves with time, and when it's cooked it glazes, coats, and accentuates the flavor of whatever you've lacquered it onto.*

**1.** In a small saucepan over medium-high heat, heat the canola oil. Add the garlic, ginger, and chili flakes. Stir constantly for 1 minute. Add the green onions and stir in the mirin. Cook to reduce the liquid for 2 to 3 minutes, stirring to scrape up any bits from the bottom of the pan.

**2.** Stir in the soy and brown sugar. Bring to a simmer over medium heat and cook for 5 minutes, stirring occasionally.

**3.** In a small bowl, combine the cornstarch and water. Slowly whisk this mixture into the sauce and cook for 3 minutes, stirring occasionally. Remove from the heat and strain out the solids. Cool the teriyaki sauce and refrigerate for up to 1 week.

A family portrait of flavor!

# Chili Sauce

5 large Roma tomatoes, quartered

1 onion, coarsely chopped

1 jalapeño, seeded and chopped

½ cup apple cider vinegar

2 tablespoons sugar

¼ teaspoon salt

½ teaspoon red chili flakes

*Introducing **Grilled Ketchup's (page 364) wild cousin, Chili Sauce**. A little strong by itself but this guy plays well with others. (Sounds to me like Chili Sauce's report card.)*

*Use this sauce in "Bring It On" Beef Brisket (page 240) and the Texas Hold'em sandwich (page 136).*

**1.** In a medium saucepan over medium-high heat, combine all the ingredients and bring to a boil. Reduce the heat to medium to keep the liquid at a strong simmer and cook for 25 to 30 minutes, until thickened and broken down, stirring occasionally.

**2.** Puree the mixture in a blender. Return the sauce to the saucepan and simmer for 25 to 30 minutes more, stirring occasionally.

**3.** Cool, refrigerate, and use for dressings, BBQ sauces, and so on. The sauce will keep in the refrigerator for 3 weeks.

# Caesar Aïoli

### ⤙ MAKES 1¼ CUPS ⤚

*Mayo is boring "food lube,"* as I call it. Aïoli gets more interesting if you really make it from scratch, but Caesar aïoli packs in the big flavor for anything from dips to salad dressing.

When I Caesar-ize aïoli, I'm taking a combination I love (garlic and mayonnaise) and intensifying it by adding mustard, more garlic, and Worcestershire sauce. You can use it to coat grilled chicken, slather it on grilled shrimp, or serve it as a dip for artichokes or asparagus.

**1.** In a mini food processor or blender, combine all of the ingredients except the olive oil. Pulse and scrape down several times until the ingredients are well combined.

**2.** In a slow, steady stream, add the olive oil. Be extremely diligent about adding it slowly, especially at the beginning; be prepared to allow up to 5 minutes for this step.

**3.** Adjust the seasoning with additional salt and pepper if needed. Refrigerate for 1 hour before using. Keeps in the refrigerator for 1 week.

1 extra large organic egg yolk

2 tablespoons distilled white vinegar

1 tablespoon finely grated Parmesan cheese

1 teaspoon prepared English mustard (I recommend Colman's)

1 teaspoon drained capers

1 teaspoon anchovy paste

1 teaspoon minced garlic

1 tablespoon chopped flat-leaf parsley

½ teaspoon fine sea salt

½ teaspoon freshly cracked black pepper

3 to 4 drops hot sauce (I recommend Tabasco)

3 to 4 drops Worcestershire sauce

1 cup extra light olive oil

# Herbes de Sonoma

1 tablespoon dried savory

1 tablespoon dried tarragon

1 tablespoon dried rosemary

1 tablespoon dried basil

1 tablespoon dried oregano

1 teaspoon dried spearmint

1 teaspoon dried fennel seed, crushed

1 teaspoon dried lavender

*I grow a lot of fantastic organic herbs in my garden. When everything is at its prime, I pick it, dry it, and make this herb blend.*

*I use it in my Petaluma Paté (page 58), but feel free to use the mixture as you would herbes de Provence to fortify dips, marinades, salad dressings, and dry rubs.*

**1.** Combine the herbs and store in an airtight container in a cool dark place for up to 6 months.

# Blackening Spice Rub

### ⤙ MAKES ABOUT ⅓ CUP ⤚

*Find someone who loves to BBQ (smokin' low and slow) and I guarantee they make their own rub. Here's one of mine! Make sure the spices are fresh.*

*This is famously great in my Cajun Chicken Alfredo (page 178), but **try using it on anything that you'd like to Cajun-ate**. Give it a shot when roasting or grilling proteins; use it lightly on green beans, Brussels sprouts, or anything you want to add the "Ooooh . . . Yeahhh . . ." to.*

2 tablespoons salt

1 tablespoon granulated garlic

1 tablespoon freshly cracked black pepper

2 teaspoons ground white pepper

2 teaspoons onion powder

2 teaspoons ground cumin

1 teaspoon cayenne

3 tablespoons paprika

**1.** Combine all the ingredients and store in tightly sealed container in a cool place until needed, for up to 6 months.

I used to believe all the good cocktails had already been invented, and the goofy new concoctions I saw at bars didn't make much sense to me. Not that I was blind or naïve to their popularity—I just figured, how many more juices and extracts can you put into a drink? It turned out that I just hadn't had the proper exposure to the process. My eyes were opened to the true potential of cocktails when I met two incredibly inventive guys. The first was Michael Perea, an effervescent mixologist who worked with me when we opened Tex Wasabi's in Santa Rosa. I could throw Michael any style I was thinking about, using layman's descriptions like "a simple, crazy party punch" or "something fruity but not a mai tai, blended," and he'd pull it all together, translating what I needed in the most amazing ways every time. Michael works in Vegas now, but he's since been a big influence on *Guy's Big Bite*.

The second guy was Manny Hinojosa, also a big contributor on *GBB*, whom I met on a trip to

CODE RED

SILVER SANGRIA

JR'S 50/50

THE GRAPE APE BOWLA

SHARK ATTACK

France for Grey Goose vodka. I sat there and listened to him talking about making his own bitters, and then I started to really observe the development of simple syrups. We got to talking about flavors and dishes and cocktails to go along with them. The diversity of possible ingredients was so rich that I realized I'd been missing out on a big window of opportunity for expression.

These days, I enjoy all types of infused alcohols, but I don't like to drink three specialty cocktails in one evening, because they're usually too distinct or unique to drink in succession. At home and at my restaurants, it's become a real passion of mine to extend the dining experience with a premium cocktail. Always have the standards ready to roll, good wine and spirits, but you'll find that serving one of these cocktails adds another dimension to your entertaining.

SANGRIA PEREA

ROASTED MARY
WITH SPICY
PICKLED
GREEN BEANS

THE SEA DONKEY

FISH BOWL

# Mai Tai Sorbet

2½ cups pineapple juice

2½ cups mango nectar

2½ cups guava nectar

1¾ cups gold rum

⅓ cup grenadine syrup

¼ cup fresh lime juice

⅓ cup agave nectar

**Special Equipment:**
**Ice-cream maker**

*Serve carefully!* **This stuff is dangerous.**

**1.** If your ice-cream maker requires freezing, be sure to freeze the bowl for 24 hours in advance.

**2.** In a large metal or glass bowl, combine all the ingredients, stirring until the sugar has dissolved completely. Pour the mixture into the ice-cream machine's prefrozen bowl and freeze for 1 hour.

**3.** Remove from the freezer and process the mixture according to the manufacturer's instructions.

**4.** Return the sorbet to the freezer for at least 2 hours before serving.

# The Grape Ape Bowla

## MAKES 1 LARGE FISH BOWL, TO SERVE 6

*Hahahaa. I love this one.* **It's like being the suitcase in the Samsonite commercials.** *That's how the Grape Ape has treated a few people, like . . . (shhhhh . . . Michael Perea).*

**1.** In large bowl or (clean!) fish bowl, pour the alcohol, grape juice, and soda over the ice. Stir and garnish with grapes and lime wedges. Serve with long straws.

No letting the ape drive after drinking this one!

- ⅓ cup vodka
- ⅓ cup light (white) rum
- ⅓ cup gin
- ¼ cup triple sec
- 1½ cups purple grape juice
- 1½ cups lemon-lime soda (such as 7Up)
- 3 cups ice cubes
- 1 cup red seedless grapes
- 4 lime wedges

# Roasted Mary with Spicy Pickled Green Beans

### ⇒ SERVES 6 ⇐

6 pounds tomatoes, heirloom preferred

4 garlic cloves

¼ cup chopped onion

1 jalapeño, seeded

1 tablespoon olive oil

¾ teaspoon kosher salt

¾ teaspoon freshly ground black pepper

3 tablespoons extra hot prepared horseradish

4 teaspoons celery salt

2 teaspoons dry mustard

1 teaspoon ground white pepper

2 teaspoons Worcestershire sauce

4 teaspoons pickled vegetable juice (from Spicy Pickled Green Beans, recipe follows)

Spicy Pickled Green Beans, for garnish (recipe follows)

Ice, for serving

12 ounces vodka

*Nothin' beats a tasty, well-made, full-flavored Mary in the morning.* **Call me Dr. Fieri, and I recommend X2. Repeat as needed.** *Paging Dr. Fieri . . . Dr. Fieri to Sauté . . . Stat!*

**1.** Preheat the oven to 350°F.

**2.** Rinse and dry the tomatoes. Remove the stems. Place the tomatoes, garlic, onion, and jalapeño in a 9 by 13-inch glass baking dish. Drizzle the vegetables with the olive oil and sprinkle with the salt and black pepper. Roast for 15 to 25 minutes, until the vegetables are lightly browned.

**3.** Transfer the vegetables to a blender and puree until smooth. Refrigerate the juice in a large pitcher.

**4.** When cool, add the horseradish, celery salt, mustard, white pepper, Worcestershire, and pickled vegetable juice and stir well.

**5.** To serve, place a pickled green bean or two in each glass, fill with ice, add 2 ounces vodka, and then fill with Mary mix. Stir and serve immediately.

# Spicy Pickled Green Beans

**MAKES 2 PINTS**

**1.** In a small saucepan over high heat, bring the water to a boil. Turn off the heat, add 1 teaspoon of the salt and the agave, and stir until dissolved. Set aside to cool.

**2.** In a medium glass bowl, combine the vinegar, lime juice, lime slices, peppercorns, chile, and whole and minced garlic. Add the cooled agave mixture.

**3.** Fill a large bowl with ice and water. Bring a large pot of water to a boil over high heat and add the remaining 1 teaspoon salt. Add the beans and cook for 3 to 4 minutes, until they begin to turn bright green and are just tender. Drain the beans and rinse immediately with cold water. Plunge them in the ice water for 10 minutes to stop the cooking. Drain well.

**4.** Place the beans and vinegar-chile brine in sterilized jars and refrigerate. Just keep the beans under refrigeration and eat them within 1 month.

**5.** Allow the beans to marinate in the liquid for at least 48 hours before eating.

*Note: A red chile is a ripe jalapeño. (If you cannot find a red chile, substitute ½ jalapeño.) Seeds in = hot; seeds out = medium hot.*

1½ cups water

2 teaspoons fine sea salt

1 tablespoon agave nectar

2 cups apple cider vinegar

1 tablespoon fresh lime juice

1 lime, very thinly sliced

2 teaspoons black peppercorns

1 red chile, sliced in 8 long strips (see Note)

6 garlic cloves

2 tablespoons minced garlic

1½ pounds green beans, washed and trimmed

*Special equipment:*
**2 sterilized sealable pint jars**

# Shark Attack

2 cups ice cubes

½ lemon, sliced thin

¼ cup fresh pineapple chunks

¼ cup tequila

¼ cup triple sec

½ cup orange juice

¼ cup pineapple juice

¼ cup high proof rum (I recommended Bacardi 151)

Splash grenadine

¼ cup maraschino cherries, plus more for garnish

*Just when you thought it was safe to go back in the drink.*

**1.** In a large pitcher, combine all the ingredients and stir to mix. Pour into rocks glasses and garnish with additional maraschino cherries if desired.

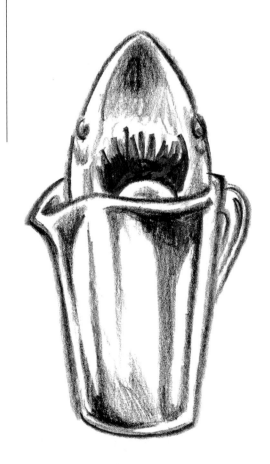

**380** ............ GUY FIERI FOOD

# Sangria Perea

## SERVES 6

*Michael Perea was one of the first true flair bartender mixologists I ever met. He was a big help to me, and his influence and creativity has made its mark on Guy's Big Bite. When we opened Tex Wasabi's and started talking sangria, **I told him I didn't want anything typical.** I wanted our sangria to have an extra twist or two to it, and he most definitely succeeded. Here's to you, Michael.*

½ lemon, sliced thin

½ lime, sliced thin

¼ orange, sliced thin

¼ cup fresh pineapple chunks

¼ cup seedless red grapes

2 cups fruity red wine, such as Merlot

½ cup peach brandy

1 cup orange juice

1 cup lemon-lime soda (such as 7Up)

3 cups ice cubes

**1.** In a pitcher, combine all the ingredients, except ice, and stir to mix. Ideally, wait about 1 hour for the fruit and the wine to infuse each other, and add ice right before serving. But you can drink it right away if desired. Serve in rocks glasses.

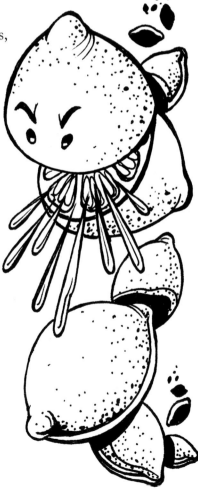

# Code Red

### ～ SERVES 2 ～

4 ounces vodka

3 ounces peach schnapps

3 ounces amaretto

Splash cranberry juice

Splash orange juice

Orange slices, for garnish

Cherries, for garnish

*Please wear the appropriate attire, leave the emergency contact numbers, and* **have the bail money at the ready**—*just as a precaution.*

**1.** Fill a big bowl with ice. Add the vodka, schnapps, amaretto, and cranberry and orange juices, stir, and garnish with orange slices and cherries. Add straws and drink up.

"put on helmet and pads" —... G

# Fish Bowl

## ➤ SERVES 4 ➤

**"Here, fishy,** fishy, fishy . . ."
  *Shhhhh! Do not get in the bowl, please!*

**1.** Combine all the ingredients except the fruit slices in a large bowl or pitcher. Stir and serve in glasses over more ice, garnished with the lemon and lime slices.

Ice

3 ounces coconut rum

3 ounces blue curaçao

3 ounces vodka

Big splash pineapple juice
(fresh if you can)

½ cup sweet-and-sour mix

Big splash lemon-lime soda
(such as 7Up)

Lemon and lime slices,
for garnish

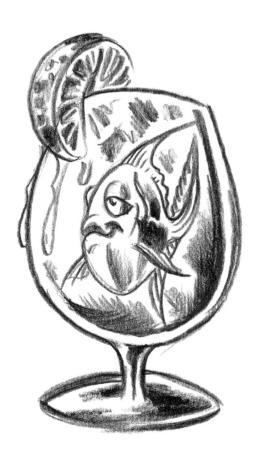

# Silver Sangria

### SERVES 8 TO 12

6 cups ice

6 ounces light rum

One 750 ml bottle sauvignon blanc (don't use chardonnay)

3 ounces peach schnapps

3 ounces sour apple liqueur

¾ cup fresh lime juice

½ cup fresh lemon juice

½ cup sugar

¾ cup lemon-lime soda (such as 7Up)

¾ cup soda water

1 green apple, peeled, cored, and cut into small chunks

1 red apple, peeled, cored, and cut into small chunks

1 peach, peeled, pitted, and cut into small chunks

8 to 12 lemon slices, for garnish

8 to 12 lime slices, for garnish

*This is **for those who don't want red wine** in their drink. . . . Fine, then how's about white? Bottoms up—this is on point.*

**1.** In a large pitcher, thoroughly combine all the ingredients except the lemon and lime slices. Serve over ice, garnished with lemon and lime slices.

# The Sea Donkey

## ⤙ SERVES 1 ⤚

Tex Wasabi's has a big bar with big energy and lots of great stuff going on. We've had a variety of characters as bartenders, and Damon McGovern was one of them. He's a great guy, and for some reason I've called him Sea Donkey for the last ten years. So when we were all sitting around making up cocktails for Guy's Big Bite, I decided to dedicate this one to Sea Donkey. **Eeeehhh—Haw . . . Eeeee . . . hawww!!!**

**3 ounces sweet-and-sour mix**

**1 ounce blanco tequila (I recommend Cabo Wabo blanco)**

**1 ounce orange-flavored vodka**

**¼ ounce blue curaçao**

**¼ ounce melon liqueur (I recommend Midori)**

**Lemon or lime slices, for garnish**

**1.** Combine all the ingredients with ice in a shaker and shake until blended. Strain into a glass over ice. Serve immediately, garnished with the lemon or lime slices . . . and oats and seaweed, if you're a sea donkey.

# JR's 50/50

2 cups ice

3 cups vanilla ice cream

¼ cup frozen orange juice concentrate

½ cup vodka

½ cup sparkling wine

Whipped cream, for garnish

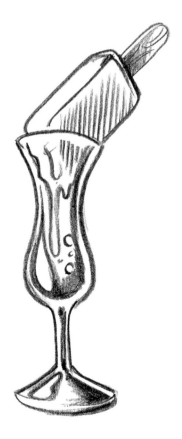

*Back to naming things after my friends . . . What frequently happens inside the Krew is one of them will call me and ask if I can reproduce something they've tasted in the past. So my friend Jen Rota (Dustin's wife and the mother of my godson Landon) called one day and told me about this drink she'd had that tasted like a 50/50 (Creamsicle) bar.* **This brought back memories of Ferndale Elementary,** *where there'd been an ice cream machine in the basement of the school selling 50/50 bars and Fudgsicles. So I pulled a drink together and named it the JR 50/50 (after Jen Rota).*

*About a week later, my bro Mario Lopez called me from* Extra. *The movie* Hangover *had just come out, and he wanted to know what a good hangover cocktail would be. So Mario and I went on and did a competition to see who could make the best JR 50/50. That was a funny gig, but the drink really is* **refreshing and fantastic.** *It's a childhood favorite with a buzz.*

**1.** In a blender, combine the ice, ice cream, orange juice concentrate, vodka, and sparkling wine. Blend until smooth. Pour into decorative glasses and top with whipped cream.

# Agua de Palapa Joe's

## SERVES 4

This recipe is in honor of Palapa Joe's, a funny little joint in a little town down near Colima, Mexico, that we visit every year (www.palapajoes.net). A charismatic dude named Willy owns it; he's a former computer biz guy from Nor Cal, and now **he's my brother by the beach!** He runs the place with his team of Latina chefs—all women. **It's a gringo haven where they serve some great scratch-made food** under a thatched palm roof. One of my favorite things is their outstanding agua fresca *made with rice*. I went back into the kitchen and made it with the girls, throwing my spin on it. In honor of the great team at Palapa Joe's, here it is.

For the last three years my dad, Hunter, Ryder, and I have taken a day off from the beach to throw a charity dinner to benefit the local elementary school. We take over the kitchen at Palapa Joe's and prepare a fixed menu. One year we did Italian, another Asian—we mix it up and raise about $1,000 for the cause each year.

**1.** In a small bowl, soak the rice and cinnamon in 2 cups of the water for 2 hours. Transfer the mixture to a blender and liquefy for 3 to 5 minutes, until the solids are gone. (If your blender does not completely pulverize the cinnamon, pass the mixture through a fine mesh sieve and discard the solids.)

**2.** In a large pitcher, mix the blended rice, 4 cups water, the vanilla, sugar, and condensed milk. Stir and serve over ice.

**1 cup raw white rice**

**½ cinnamon stick**

**6 cups water**

**½ teaspoon pure vanilla extract**

**½ cup sugar**

**¼ cup sweetened condensed milk**

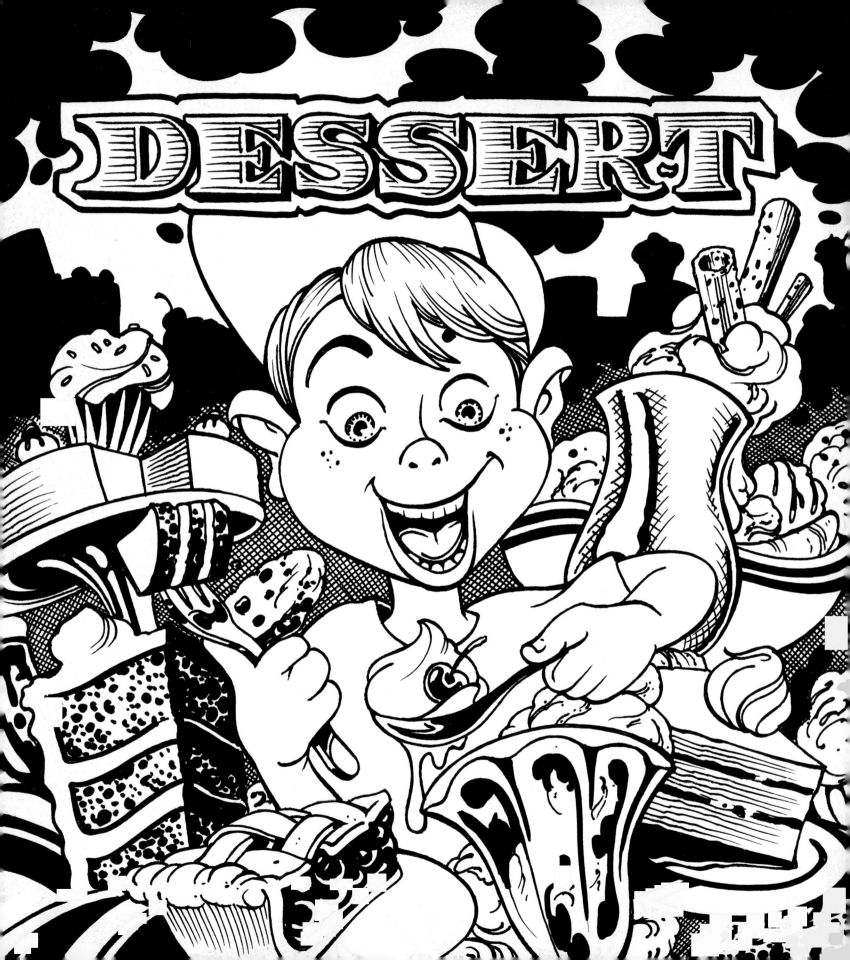

**There's dessert in the book 'cause I have to (JK).**
I'm not a big fan of dessert, not because I dislike it, but because at the end of the meal if I have any room to eat dessert it means that I didn't do well enough on the dinner. I don't want you to save room for dessert—I want you to be so happy with my cooking that you can't take another bite!

Of course, I'm joking a bit, but truth is that I don't make or eat a lot of desserts because when it comes down to it, to me, **dessert is like classical music.** It's calming and soothing, but it needs to be done right, and you don't always feel like listening to it (or eating it). But when you do, you really appreciate it—and **there's no doubt that dessert's a great way to wrap up a really nice dinner.**

The desserts I've got for you here pair well with the big, full-flavored dishes in *Guy Fieri Food*. Can't follow up a Cajun Chicken Alfredo with peach melba ice cream. You dig?

# Irish Dream Cheesecake

### ⟿ SERVES 12 ⟾

## CRUST

**One 9-ounce package chocolate wafer cookies (I recommend Famous Chocolate Wafers)**

**⅛ teaspoon fine sea salt**

**7 tablespoons unsalted butter, melted**

## FILLING

**2 pounds cream cheese, at room temperature**

**1 cup granulated sugar**

**5 large eggs, at room temperature**

**1 teaspoon pure vanilla extract**

**¾ cup Irish cream liqueur**

**¼ cup heavy cream**

**¾ cup chopped semisweet chocolate, melted**

**Boiling water**

## TOPPING

**1½ teaspoons instant coffee powder**

**1 teaspoon hot water**

**1½ cups heavy cream**

*(cont.)*

*This is not your boring "top it with some strawberry preserves" cheesecake. With booze, chocolate, and cream cheese,* **this one will rock ya!**

**1.** Preheat the oven to 350°F.

**2. To make the crust,** crush the cookies in a heavy-duty resealable plastic bag or pulse in a food processor fitted with a steel blade until you have fine crumbs. Add the salt. Brush the bottom and sides of a 10-inch springform pan with a little of the melted butter. Combine the rest of the butter with the cookie crumbs. Reserve ¾ cup of the crumb mixture and press the remaining mixture evenly into the bottom of the pan. Bake for 6 minutes. Remove from the oven and let cool.

**3. To make the filling,** using an electric mixer with a paddle, whip the cream cheese on medium speed for 2 to 3 minutes. Add the sugar and mix for 2 minutes. Reduce the speed to medium-low and add the eggs one at a time, scraping down the sides of the bowl after 3 eggs and again after the last egg. Add the vanilla, liqueur, and heavy cream and increase the speed to medium. Let the machine run for 4 minutes, scraping down the sides after 2 minutes.

**4.** Pour the batter into the prepared crust. Pour the melted chocolate in a spiral pattern over the batter. With a butter knife, swirl the chocolate into the batter, taking care not to touch the bottom crust. Wrap the pan in a double layer of heavy-duty aluminum foil and put it into a large baking pan. Place in the oven and pour boiling water into the larger pan about halfway up the side of the springform to make a water bath. Bake for 25 minutes, then reduce the heat to 225°F and bake for 1 hour 45 minutes to 2 hours, until the middle is no longer shiny and the cheesecake is firm.

**5.** Remove the pan from the oven and the water bath. Run a small, thin knife around the inside edge of the pan and let cool to room temperature. When cool, loosely cover and refrigerate at least 6 hours or overnight.

**6. To make the topping,** dissolve the coffee in the hot water and set aside to cool. In a cold metal bowl with a hand mixer or an electric mixer, beat the cream on medium-high speed for 45 seconds. Add the granulated sugar and the cooled coffee and continue to beat until peaks form, about 3 minutes.

**7.** To serve, remove the cheesecake from the pan and place on a serving platter. Sprinkle the reserved cookie crumbs in a circle around the outside top edge, drizzle the cake with the melted chocolate, dust with the powdered sugar, and serve with the whipped cream.

1 ½ tablespoons granulated sugar

¾ cup chopped semisweet chocolate, melted

¼ cup powdered sugar, for garnish

*Special Equipment:* **10-inch springform pan, heavy-duty aluminum foil**

# Baklava Cigars

### ⟐ MAKES 12 CIGARS ⟐

## SYRUP

2 cups dark brown sugar, firmly packed

1½ cups water

1 tablespoon fresh lime juice

2 to 3 tablespoons honey

3 cinnamon sticks

5 whole cloves

¾ teaspoon red chili flakes

## FILLING

3 large egg whites, at room temperature

2¼ cups shelled walnuts

2¼ cups shelled pecans

⅓ cup dark brown sugar, firmly packed

⅛ teaspoon ground cloves

24 sheets frozen phyllo pastry, thawed

½ pound (2 sticks) unsalted butter, melted

¼ cup slivered almonds, toasted

¼ cup powdered sugar

*Just when my crew thinks the dinner is over, I open up this **humidor of flavor**. It's not time for* Romeo & Juliet; *it's time for Guido's Baklava Cigar.*

**1. To make the syrup,** in a medium saucepan over medium heat, combine all the ingredients and bring to a boil. Reduce the heat and simmer for 20 to 30 minutes, until thickened to a syrup consistency. Set aside to cool, then strain into a medium bowl.

**2.** Preheat the oven to 300°F. Line a baking sheet with parchment paper.

**3. To make the filling,** put the egg whites in a clean bowl and beat with an electric mixer on high until thick, 5 to 6 minutes. Combine the walnuts, pecans, brown sugar, and cloves in a food processor and pulse several times until the nuts are medium-chopped. Gently fold the nut mixture into the egg whites, then drizzle in ¼ cup of the syrup. Stir gently to combine.

**4. To assemble a baklava cigar,** remove the phyllo from the package, taking care to keep it covered and cool. Stack 2 sheets on a work surface. Gently brush with butter and fold the phyllo dough in half lengthwise. Add about ¼ cup of the filling across the bottom half of the pastry. Roll up the phyllo dough, tucking in the ends as you go, to create a cigar shape. Set on the prepared baking sheet and brush with butter. Repeat until all the cigars are assembled. Bake for 25 to 35 minutes, until nicely browned and crispy, keeping an eye on them so they don't brown too quickly.

**5.** Set the baklava cigars aside to cool for 2 minutes. On a clean work surface, cut the baklava in half on the diagonal and transfer to a serving tray or platter. Drizzle with remaining 1¼ cups syrup, sprinkle with the slivered almonds, and dust with powdered sugar. The baklava cigars can be served warm or at room temperature.

# Coffee Bananas Foster

### ~ SERVES 4 ~

*Okay, this is **probably my all-time favorite**. Not just the great flavor and style, but the best memories of being a flambé captain at the Red Lion Inn (see page 244).*

**1.** In a medium skillet over medium-high heat, melt the butter. Add the bananas and cook for 1 minute on each side. Remove them from the pan.

**2.** To the same pan, add the sugar, banana liqueur, rum, and coffee liqueur. Simmer for 2 minutes. If you have experience with flambéing, prop the pan to the side to ignite the alcohol; otherwise, remove the pan from the heat and ignite it with a long kitchen match. When the flame is out, add the orange juice, cinnamon, and nutmeg. Simmer for 3 to 5 minutes, until the desired consistency is achieved.

**3.** Add the bananas back to the pan and ladle the sauce over the bananas for 1 minute to coat.

**4.** To serve, place 1 banana half in each of 4 long bowls with scoops of vanilla ice cream. Spoon the sauce evenly on top.

3 tablespoons unsalted butter

2 bananas, not quite ripe, cut in half lengthwise

⅓ cup dark brown sugar, firmly packed

3 tablespoons banana liqueur

2 tablespoons dark rum (I recommend Myers's Dark Rum)

2 tablespoons coffee liqueur

¼ cup fresh orange juice

¼ teaspoon ground cinnamon

¼ teaspoon ground nutmeg

1 quart vanilla ice cream

# Tequila Lime Tart

### ~ SERVES 8 ~

## CRUST

**10 ounces vanilla wafers**

**⅓ cup pine nuts**

**¼ pound (1 stick) unsalted butter, melted**

## FILLING

**2 large egg whites**

**1 tablespoon sugar**

**¼ cup white tequila**

**½ cup fresh lime juice**

**4 large egg yolks**

**One 14-ounce can sweetened condensed milk**

**Fresh whipped cream, for serving**

*Special Equipment:*
**10-inch removable-bottom tart pan**

*Come on now—tequila, Nilla wafers, and whipped cream. It's like a dessert margarita in a pie shell. One tequila, two tequila, three tequila, floor.*

**1.** Preheat the oven to 350°F.

**2.** Combine the wafers and pine nuts in a food processor and pulse until ground fine. Reserve ¼ cup of the crumbs as a garnish. Pour the remaining crumbs into a large bowl and add the melted butter. Mix with a wooden spoon and press into the bottom of a 10-inch tart pan.

**3.** Bake for 8 minutes or until dry in appearance and just starting to color. Set aside but leave the oven on at 350°F.

**4. For the filling,** in a clean bowl, beat the egg whites until frothy, about 1 minute. Add the sugar and beat until you have soft peaks, about 4 minutes.

**5.** In another bowl, combine the tequila, lime juice, egg yolks, and condensed milk and mix thoroughly. Fold in the egg whites. Pour the mixture into the tart shell and bake for 20 to 25 minutes, until the middle is set.

**6.** Sprinkle with the reserved crumbs and let cool before cutting. Serve with fresh whipped cream.

# Red Lion Flambé Cherries Jubilee

## ⟿ SERVES 2 TO 4 ⟿

*Now to cook this one really off-the-hook you gotta put on some* **brown polyester!!! (Check it out on page 244.)**

**1.** In a large skillet over medium-high heat, combine the butter, sugar, and honey and cook until the sugar dissolves. Add the cherries and their syrup, the orange juice, Kirsch, triple sec, and cinnamon and bring to a simmer. If you have experience with flambéing, prop the pan to the side to ignite the liqueur; otherwise, remove the pan from the heat and ignite it with a long kitchen match. Return to the heat after the flames have died down and continue simmering for 4 to 5 minutes, until slightly thickened.

**2.** In a small bowl, whisk the cornstarch with the water. Stir this slurry into the cherry mixture and cook until the sauce thickens to the desired consistency.

**3.** Serve warm over vanilla ice cream.

3 tablespoons unsalted butter

¼ cup dark brown sugar, firmly packed

1 tablespoon honey

One 15-ounce can pitted Bing cherries in syrup

¼ cup fresh orange juice

3 tablespoons Kirsch

2 tablespoons triple sec

¼ teaspoon ground cinnamon

1 tablespoon cornstarch

¼ cup water

1 pint vanilla ice cream, for serving

# Cherry Cobbler Pizza

## ⇜ SERVES 8 TO 12 ⇝

1 cup quick rolled oats

2 tablespoons dark brown sugar, firmly packed

2 tablespoons unsalted butter, at room temperature

Fine sea salt

¼ teaspoon ground cinnamon

¼ cup sliced almonds

One 10-ounce ball Whole-Wheat Pizza Dough (½ recipe, page 157)

One 21-ounce can cherry pie filling or 1½ cups best-quality cherry preserves

½ cup mascarpone cheese, at room temperature

**Special Equipment:**
**Pizza peel and pizza stone (or pizza pan)**

*You're making pizza . . . so why not bust out some extra dough, leave the oven on high, and blow your crew away with this **pizza payday**?!!?!*

**1.** Place a pizza stone in the center of the oven and preheat the oven to 500°F.

**2.** In a medium bowl, combine the oats, brown sugar, butter, two pinches salt, and the cinnamon and mix with your fingers until well combined. Add the almonds and gently mix.

**3.** Stretch half the dough into a ½-inch-thick 11-inch round. Place on a floured peel or pizza pan. Spread half of the cherry pie filling or preserves over the crust. Top with half of the oat mixture.

**4.** Bake according to the directions on page 157 for 12 minutes or until the crust is golden brown and the cherries are bubbling.

**5.** Garnish the pizza with dollops of half of the mascarpone cheese, cut it into wedges with a pizza cutter, and serve. Repeat with remaining dough to make a second pizza, 'cuz you know you want it!

# Peach and Blueberry Pizza

## ☙ SERVES 8 TO 12 ❧

*Hunter and Ryder are pizza-eating machines. We're cooking pizza in the outdoor wood-fired oven at least once, if not twice, a week. This is how we do it, **dessert-style.***

**1.** Place a pizza stone in the center of the oven and preheat the oven to 500°F.

**2.** In a medium bowl, combine the cream cheese, condensed milk, Grand Marnier, cinnamon, nutmeg, and sea salt and combine well.

**3.** Stretch half the dough into a ½-inch-thick 11-inch round. Place on a floured peel or pizza pan and spread with half of the cream cheese mixture. Arrange half the peach slices in the middle in a fan pattern. Scatter half the blueberries on top and sprinkle with half the pistachios.

**4.** Bake according to the directions on page 157 for 12 minutes or until the crust is golden brown. Set aside to cool for a few minutes, dust with powdered sugar, and use a pizza cutter to cut it into wedges. Repeat with remaining dough to make a second pizza.

¾ cup plain whipped cream cheese

3 tablespoons sweetened condensed milk

2 teaspoons Grand Marnier

½ teaspoon ground cinnamon

Pinch freshly grated nutmeg

Pinch fine sea salt

One 10-ounce ball Whole-Wheat Pizza Dough (½ recipe, page 157)

1-pound bag frozen sliced peaches, thawed

1 cup fresh blueberries

¼ cup chopped pistachios

1 tablespoon powdered sugar

*Special Equipment:*
**Pizza peel and pizza stone (or pizza pan)**

# S'more Pizza

2 store-bought 1-pound pizza dough balls

¼ cup slivered almonds

3 tablespoons unsalted butter

1 sleeve graham crackers, crushed (about 1 ¼ cups crumbs)

½ teaspoon chili powder

¼ teaspoon cayenne pepper

¼ teaspoon fine sea salt

½ cup all-purpose flour

¼ cup fine cornmeal

3 cups mini marshmallows

Two 4-ounce dark chocolate bars, broken into ¼-inch chunks

*Special Equipment:* pizza peel and pizza stone (or pizza pan)

*I say it on Triple D all the time—everything has a "kicker." It's what it takes to make the dish outta bounds.* **The kicker here is chili and cayenne***. . . . Ooooh yeahhhhhh!*

**1.** Preheat the oven to 400°F.

**2.** Form the pizza dough into two 12- to 14-inch rounds, ¼ inch thick. Bake, preferably on a pizza stone, for 4 to 6 minutes, until just beginning to brown. (See page 157 for more help on shaping and baking pizza crusts.) Leave the oven on at 400°F.

**3.** While the pizza crust is baking, toast the almonds in a dry medium skillet over medium-high heat. Transfer the almonds to a plate to cool.

**4.** Melt the butter in the skillet. Add the graham cracker crumbs, chili powder, cayenne, and salt. Cook for 2 to 3 minutes, until the crumbs are well-coated. Remove from the heat and set aside.

**5.** For each pizza, top the crust with half of the marshmallows and scatter half of the chocolate over the marshmallows. Return to the oven for 3 to 5 minutes, until the marshmallows are puffed and lightly browned. Sprinkle the pizza with half of the graham cracker mixture and top with half of the almonds. Let rest 3 to 4 minutes, slice, and serve. Repeat to make the second pizza.

# ACKNOWLEDGMENTS

*My family:* Lori, Hunter, and Ryder Fieri. Jim and Penny Ferry. Morgan, Jules, and Annie. The Price, Langermeier, Barrett, Bowers, Apel, Nelson, Ramsay, and Stansbury families. Donna, Jason, Shauntel, Brandon, and Jordan Brisson.

*Knuckle Sandwich:* Korina McAlister, Tom Nelson, Reid "Kattywompus" Strathearn, Ron "Turtle" Wargo, Tom "The Numbers" Howard.

*The Krew:* Kevin "Kleetus" and Alisa Cox, Paul "Dirty P" and Lisa Thompson, Dustin and Jen Rota, Ariel "The Spanyard" and Nicole Ramirez, Jesse "Possum" and Brandi Smith, "Gorilla" Rich Bacchi, Paul "5-0" Messerschmitt, Carl "Cuban" Ruiz, Glen "GPP" Houde, Daniel "Millie" Millich, Justin "Jenkie" Kunkle, Jimmy McAlister, Matt Pintor, "Cowboy" Mike and Cam Barrer, Milt "Uncle Milt" Close, Brian "Bags" Baglietto, Brian Daly, "Big Jon Snyder," Mike "Part Time" Burwell, "Stretch," "Hodad," Gary and Kelly Maggetti, Christian and Biggi Vaughan, Eric "Reno" Schweikl, Jack Levar, Chris and Amy Lands, Joe and Misty Magelitz, "Panini" Pete Bloehme, Johnny "Sizzleshanks" Quinlan.

*Writing:* Ann Volkwein

*Art and illustration:* Joe Leonard of Monkey Wrench Tattoo.

*Photography:* Ben Fink, John Lee, Alan M. Poulin, and David Clancy.

*Johnny Garlic's and Tex Wasabi's:* Steve Gruber, Amy Solus, Brett Hutchison, Michael Osterman, JC Adams, Bobby Sandoval, Art Robinson and all of the team members.

*WME:* Jason Hodes, Jeff Googel, Bethany Dick, Michele Bernstein, Jon Rosen, Deb Shuwarger, and Dorian Karchmar.

*Brooks Group:* Rebecca Brooks, Erika Martineau, Brianne Carmody-Perea, Amanda Santoro, and Courtney Henderson.

*William Morrow:* Cassie Jones, Jessica Deputato, Liate Stehlik, Lynn Grady, Tavia Kowalchuk, Brianne Halverson, Shawn Nicholls, Joyce Wong, Leah Carlson-Stanisic, Kris Tobiassen, and Karen Lumley.

*Food Network:* Brooke Johnson, Bob Tuschman, Bruce Seidel, Allison Page, Mark "Big Dunkee" Dissin, Jordan Harmon, Geoff Campbell, Susie Fogelson, Brian Lando, Pat Guy, Jenna Zimmerman, Bill Calamita, Robert Madden Jr., Susan Stockton, Miriam Garron, Jill Novatt, Danielle de la Rosa, Liz Tarpy.

*Diners, Drive-ins and Dives:* Mike "Father Time" Morris, Stephanie "Lamb Chop" Halleen, Anthony "Chico" Rodriguez, Matt "Beaver" Giovinetti, David "Big Bunny" and Kate "Ask Kate" Canada, Jeff "Butterbean" Assell, Ron "Fraggle" Gabaldon, Neil "Boy Band" Martin, Ryan "Donnie" Larson, Wade "Jack Panther" Barry, Kat "Mandu" Higgins, Maria "Panda" Carrera, Liz "Erd" Pollock, Drew Sondeland, Margaret Elkins, Kathleen Brown.

*Guy's Big Bite:* See pages 18 to 25.

*Special mention to the rest of the supporting characters in Guy's Food Quest:* The Motley Que: Matt "Mustard" and Melissa Sproules, Mikey Z, Riley, and Unyawn. Mike Lucas of North Coast Fisheries. Marc Summers. Pacific Market. PBR. Jeff Arnett and Jack Daniel's. Seghesio Winery. Rob Meyers and Myers Restaurant Supply. Marcee Katz and Chefworks. Brandt Hoekenga. Gatorz Sunglasses. Sherwood and Globe Shoes. Oakland Raiders. Steve and Sean at Chevy. Serket Watches. Room 101 Jewelry. Fender Guitars. Teddy "Castro" the driver. Ergo Chef. Gia Brands. Fox Run. Golden West/Completely Fresh Foods. Fred Carl and Viking Range Company. Kraft. Ritz Crackers. Sammy Hagar. Matthew McConaughey. Emeril and Alden Lagasse. Mario Batali. Bill Nolan. Tom Rowan. Ray Lampe. The City of Santa Rosa. Jeff Blazy. Chris Smith of the *Press Democrat.* Coach at KJ. DLC Jewelry. California Restaurant Association. DK Embroidery. DJ Cobra. Mike Perea. Manny "Papi" Hinojosa. Fred and Cowboy Mouth. Steve and Landyn Hutchinson. Lisa Krueger. Neal Reagan. Lee Schrager and South Beach Wine & Food Festival. Robert Irvine. Randall Williams. Anne Burrell. Bo Dietl. Kenny and Pom Pom Stabler. Craig, Tom, Nicole, and the *Minute To Win It* team. Eric Lindell. JetSuite. Brent Farris and KZST. Rob and Jocelyn and KFGY. Marcy Smothers. Nico and Sikey. Pete Howe. Young's Market. Roger and Kicker. Ron Little. National Pork Board. Steve from Smash Mouth. Vidalia Grill. Pat Williams. Andrea at Mugnaini. Spitjack. Breville. Kristina De Jorge. All my friends and family in Sonoma County and Ferndale and the great US of A.

# INDEX